M000300786

NORTH AMERICAN AIRLINES HANDBOOK

THIRD EDITION

by Tom Norwood & John Wegg

With thanks to:
Glen Etchells (Canada)
Jorge Seguí Martin (México)
& Joe Wolf (Caribbean & Central America)

COVER: Southwest Airlines epitomizes the success
of the low-fare, no-frills formula.
This is one of its fleet of Boeing 737-700s.
(*Southwest Airlines*)

© Airways International Inc 2002

Art Director: Greg Smith

Printed in Singapore

Published by
Airways International Inc
PO Box 1109, 120 McGhee Road, Sandpoint, ID 83864-0872, USA

First edition 1997
Second edition 1999
Third edition 2002

ISBN 0-9653993-8-9

NORTH AMERICAN AIRLINES HANDBOOK

INTRODUCTION

Welcome to third edition of the *Airways* guide to the airlines of North America. Since the last edition, we have seen merger mania in the US and Canada, terrorist action in the USA, and the increase in public demand for low-fare airlines. There have been many other significant and minor changes, and all the content has been checked and completely revised. Almost all of the photos have been changed to show the latest color schemes and equipment.

Our coverage includes all 50 states of the United States of America—plus the commonwealth of Puerto Rico, the territory of the Virgin Islands, and (for the first time) American Samoa and the Federated States of Micronesia. In addition, Canada, Greenland (part of the Danish realm), Saint-Pierre et Miquelon (a French *collectivite territoriale*, or territorial collectivity, situated off the coast of eastern Canada), the island nations of the Caribbean, México, and Central America are incorporated. With some exceptions, airlines operating regularly scheduled passenger services using turbine-powered aircraft with 19 seats or more, and charter passenger and all-cargo operators of heavy turbine/pure-jet equipment receive a one-page entry, including a color photograph depicting a current type and color scheme.

Other airlines that operate scheduled passenger and/or cargo services, plus selected charter operators, are recorded in the relevant addenda. Indices list all airlines (including alternative names), IATA/ICAO designators, radio call-signs, and aircraft types, and there is a three-letter city decode.

Because of the speed of development and changes in the air transport industry, inevitably some of the information recorded will be out of date by the time this book is printed. All route network and detailed fleet changes, plus other airline news items, are recorded weekly by *Airways News Online* at www.airwaysnews.com. Feature articles about North American airlines appear every month in *Airways* magazine, along with a selection of news photos.

Any corrections, updates, suggestions, and photographs will be welcomed by the compilers for inclusion in future editions.

Airways International Inc
PO Box 1109
Sandpoint ID 83864-0872
USA

Tel: + 1 208 263 2098
Fax: + 1 208 263 5906
Email: airways@airwaysmag.com
Internet: www.airwaysmag.com

EXPLANATION OF ENTRIES & ABBREVIATIONS

(in order of appearance)

IATA Two-letter designator ('airline code') assigned by the International Air Transport Association and used for ticketing and other purposes.

ICAO Three-letter designator ('airline code') assigned by the International Civil Aviation Organization and used for air traffic control and other purposes.

IATA/ARC Three-digit code assigned by IATA or the Airlines Reporting Corp (USA) for accounting purposes.

RADIO Radio call-sign assigned by ICAO.

CONTACTS Admin = Administrative, Info = Information, PR = Public/Press/Media Relations, Res = Reservations.

OPERATION It has been assumed that many primarily scheduled carriers also operate charters and primarily passenger airlines also carry cargo.

Cities/airports served on a scheduled or regular charter basis are listed alphabetically by IATA three-letter codes (*see City and Airport Decode*) and, if the territory served includes areas outside of the airline's home section, then separate entries are made for Canada, Caribbean, México, Central America, South America, Europe, Asia, and Oceania.

ACMI refers to an Aircraft/Crew/Maintenance/Insurance form of lease.

FFP Frequent Flyer Program.

HISTORY/STRUCTURE CEO = Chief Executive Officer, COO = Chief Operating Officer, GM = General Manager; MD = Managing Director.

OWNERSHIP Publicly traded companies stock market abbreviations: AMEX = American Stock Exchange, CDNX = Canadian Venture Echange, IPC = Indice de Precios y Cotizaciones, NASDAQ = National Association of Securities Dealers Automated Quotations, NYSE = New York Stock Exchange, TSE = Toronto Stock Exchange, VSE = Vancouver Stock Exchange.

FLEET Listed in order of size of aircraft.

Seating configurations: C = Business Class (J is often used as an alternative designator), F = First Class, Y = Economy Class (Coach); EMS = Emergency Medical Service; FRTR = Freighter.

Engine Manufacturers: AE = Allison Rolls-Royce, ALF = AlliedSignal, AN = Allison, ASh = Shvetsov, BR = BMW Rolls-Royce, CFM = CFM International (SNECMA/General Electric), CO = Teledyne Continental, GA = Garrett (AlliedSignal), GE = General Electric, IAE = International Aero Engines (Rolls-Royce/Pratt & Whitney/Japanese Aero Engines/FIAT), IV = Ivchyenko Progress, KL = Klimov, LY = Textron Lycoming, NK = NK Engines, PW = Pratt & Whitney, PWC = Pratt & Whitney Canada, RM = Rybinsk Motors (Perm), RR = Rolls-Royce, TU = Turboméca, WA = Walter, WR = Wright.

ADDENDA Information for companies is listed in the sequence: name/alternative name or dba (doing business as), IATA/ICAO/ARC/*Radio*, mail address, telephone, fax, email, Internet address, name of CEO/president, type of operation, fleet information.

BOEING 767-200 *(Joe G Walker)*

ABX AIR (dba Airborne Express)

IATA: GB   **ICAO:** ABX   **IATA/ARC:** 382   **RADIO:** *Abex*

CONTACTS

Mail
145 Hunter Drive
Wilmington, OH 45177

Internet: www.abxair.com

Telephone/Fax
Admin: +1 937 382 5591
Fax: +1 937 382 2452
Info: 1 800 247 2676

OPERATION

Type: Supplemental cargo
Cities served: US: ABE ABQ ALB ANC ATL ATW AUS BDL BFI BHM BIL BMI
BNA BOI BOS BTV BUF BWI CAE CHA CID CLE CLT CNW COS COU CWF
DAL DEN DFW DSM DTW ELP EWR FAR FAT FLL FNT FSD GEG GRR GSO
GSP HRL HSV IAD IAH ICT ILN JAN JAX JFK LAS LAX LBB LGB LIT MCI
MCO MDT MDW MEM MHR MHT MIA MKE MLI MSN MSP MSY OAK OKC
OMA ONT ORD ORF PDX PHL PHX PIE PIT PNS PVD PWM RDU RFD RIC
RNO ROA ROC RST RSW SAN SAT SAV SBN SGF SHV SJC SLC STL SWF
SYR TPA TRI TUL TUS TYS **Canada:** YYZ **Caribbean:** SJU
Other markets served by contract carriers

HISTORY/STRUCTURE

Founded: 1979 (as Airborne Express Inc)
Start date: April 17, 1980
President/CEO: Joseph C Hete
Ownership: Airborne Inc (NYSE: ABF)

FLEET

Type	No	Engines
DC-9-15	2	PW JT8D-7A/-7B
DC-9-30	43	PW JT8D-7A/-7B/-9/-9A/-11
DC-9-40	29	PW JT8D-11/-15
DC-8-61F	8	PW JT3D-3B
DC-8-63F	17	PW JT3D-7
Boeing 767-200	20	GE CF6A-80
Ordered		
Boeing 767-200	10	

RAYTHEON BEECH 1900D *(Ian Bowley)*

AIR MIDWEST

IATA: ZV   **ICAO:** AMW   **IATA/ARC:** 471   **RADIO:** *Air Midwest*

CONTACTS

Mail
2230 Air Cargo Road
Wichita, KS 67209

Telephone/Fax
Admin: +1 316 942 8137
Fax: +1 316 945 0947

Internet: www.mesa-air.com

OPERATION

Type: Domestic passenger/cargo
Cities served: Mesa Airlines: ABQ ALM CNM COS CVN GUP HOB ROW SVC
America West Express: FHU FMN HII IGM PHX PRC **US Airways Express:**
ACY APF ART BFD BNA BWI CID CKB DDC DSM DUJ EYW FKL FOE GBD
GCK GON HYS ICT IPT ITH JAX JHW LBE LEB LIT MBS MCI MCO MGW
MHK MSS MSY OGS PBI PFN PHL PIT PKB PNS RDG SGF SHD SHV SLN
TLH TPA VPS XNA
Operates all Beech 1900D service for Mesa Air Group, as America West
Express (HP*6801-6888), US Airways Express (US*5425-5699), Mesa Airlines
(YV*), or Midwest Express (YX*51-801 on MCI flights)
FFP: US Airways Dividend Miles, FlightFund, Midwest Express Frequent Flyer

HISTORY/STRUCTURE

Founded: May 1965 (as Aviation Services)
Start date: April 1967
President: Greg Stephens
Ownership: Mesa Air Group

FLEET

Type	No	Seats	Engines
Beech 1900D	52	Y19	PWC PT6A-67D

BOEING 717-200 *(Dave Campbell)*

AIRTRAN AIRWAYS

IATA: FL   **ICAO:** TRS   **IATA/ARC:** 332   **RADIO:** *Citrus*

CONTACTS

Mail
9955 AirTran Boulevard
Orlando, FL 32827

Internet: www.airtran.com

Telephone/Fax
Admin: +1 407 251 5600
Fax: +1 407 251 5727
Res: 1 800 247 8726

OPERATION

Type: Domestic/Flag passenger/cargo
Cities served: US: ATL BMI BOS BUF BWI CAK DAY DFW FLL FNT GPT GSO HOU IAD JAX LGA MCO MDW MEM MIA MLI MSP MSY MYR PHF PHL PIT PNS RDU RSW SAV TLH TOL TPA **Caribbean:** FPO
FFP: A-Plus Rewards

HISTORY/STRUCTURE

Founded: 1992 (as ValuJet)
Start date: October 26, 1993
Chairman/CEO: Joseph Leonard
President: Robert Fornaro
Ownership: Airtran Holdings Inc (NYSE: AAI)

FLEET

Type	No	Seats	Engines
DC-9-32	33	C12Y94	PW JT8D-7B/-9/-9A
Boeing 717-200	27	C12Y105	BR BR715
Ordered			
Boeing 717-200	26		

DOUGLAS DC-8-62F *(Jonathan W Holmes)*

AIR TRANSPORT INTERNATIONAL (ATI)

IATA: 8C   **ICAO:** ATN   **IATA/ARC:** 346   **RADIO:** *Air Transport*

CONTACTS

Mail
2800 Cantrell Road
Little Rock, AR 72202-2046

Telephone/Fax
Admin: +1 501 615 3500
Fax: +1 501 603 2097

Internet: www.ati-sky.com

OPERATION

Type: Supplemental passenger/cargo
Areas served: Operates contract services, with several aircraft operated for BAX Global

HISTORY/STRUCTURE

Founded: 1978 (as US Airways)
Start date: 1979
CEO: James L Hobson Jr
Ownership: BAX Global

FLEET

Type	No	Seats	Engines
DC-8-62F	5	P10Y32/Combi/Frtr	PW JT3D-3B/-7
DC-8-63F	1	Freighter	PW JT3D-7
DC-8-71F	11	Freighter	PW CFM56-2C1

BRITISH AEROSPACE BAe 146-200A *(Rob Finlayson)*

AIR WISCONSIN AIRLINES

IATA: ZW   **ICAO:** AWI   **IATA/ARC:** none   **RADIO:** *Wisconsin*

CONTACTS

Mail
W6390 Challenger Drive, Suite 203
Appleton, WI 54915-9120

Telephone/Fax
Admin: +1 920 739 5123
Fax: +1 920 739 1325
PR: +1 920 749 4188
Job hotline: 1 888 364 4505

Internet: www.airwis.com

OPERATION

Type: Domestic passenger/cargo
Cities served: ASE ATW AZO BIL BIS BMI BNA BZN CID COS CWA DEN EGE EUG FAR FSD GRB GUC JAC LAX LIT LNK MEM MKE MLI MSN MSO OKC OMA ORD PIA RAP SBA SBN SBS SDF SGF SJC SLC SMF SPI TVC UIN
All service operated as United Express using only UA flight numbers (5500-5899, 7020-7149)
FFP: United Airlines Mileage Plus

HISTORY/STRUCTURE

Founded: 1965
Start date: August 23, 1965
President/CEO: Geoffrey Crowley
Ownership: CJT Holdings

FLEET

Type	No	Seats	Engines
Dornier 328-100	21	Y32	PWC PW119B/C
Bombardier CRJ200LR	15	Y50	GE CF34-3B1
BAe 146-100A	1	Y86	LY ALF502R-5
BAe 146-200A	12	Y88	LY ALF502R-5
BAe 146-300A	5	Y100	LY ALF502R-5
Ordered			
Bombardier CRJ200LR	69		

BOEING 737-900 *(Joe G Walker)*

ALASKA AIRLINES

IATA: AS   **ICAO:** ASA   **IATA/ARC:** 027   **RADIO:** *Alaska*

CONTACTS

Mail
PO Box 68900
Seattle, WA 98168

Internet: www.alaska-air.com

Telephone/Fax
Admin: +1 206 433 3200
Fax: +1 206 433 3366
Res: 1 800 426 0333
PR: +1 206 433 3170/3134

OPERATION

Type: Domestic/Flag passenger/cargo
Cities served: US: ADQ AKN ANC BET BOS BRW BUR CDV DEN DCA DLG
DUT FAI GEG IAD JNU KTN LAS LAX OAK OME ONT ORD OTZ PDX PHX
PSG PSP RNO SAN SCC SEA SFO SIT SJC SMF SNA TUS WRG YAK
(seasonal: GST) **Canada:** YVR **México:** CUN MZT PVR SJD ZIH ZLO
Code-share: American Airlines, American Eagle, Continental Airlines, ERA
Aviation, Horizon Air, Northwest Airlines, PenAir
FFP: Alaska Airlines Mileage Plan

HISTORY/STRUCTURE

Founded: 1932 (as McGee Airways)
Start date: June 6, 1944
Chairman: John F Kelly
President/CEO: Bill Ayer
Ownership: Alaska Air Group (NYSE: ALK)

FLEET

Type	No	Seats	Engines
Boeing 737-200C	9	Y111/Combi	PW JT8D-17/-17A
Boeing 737-700	16	F12Y108	CFMI CFM56-7B24
Boeing 737-400	40	F8Y132	CFMI CFM56-3C1
MD-82	5	F12Y128	PW JT8D-217/-217A
MD-83	27	F12Y128	PW JT8D-219
Boeing 737-900	6	F12Y162	CFMI CFM56-7B24
Ordered			
Boeing 737-900	5		

BOMBARDIER DHC-8-102 DASH 8 *(Ron Peel)*

ALLEGHENY AIRLINES

IATA: none   **ICAO:** ALO   **IATA/ARC:** 395   **RADIO:** *Allegheny*

CONTACTS

Mail
1000 Rosedale Avenue
Middletown, PA 17057

Telephone/Fax
Admin: +1 717 948 5400
Fax: +1 717 948 5406

Internet: www.alleghenyairlines.com

OPERATION

Type: Domestic passenger/cargo
Cities served: US: ABE ALB AVP BDL BGM BOS BTV BUF BWI CHO CRW
DTW ELM ERI GSO HPN HVN ISP ITH LGA MDT MHT ORH PHF PHL PIT
PVD PWM RDG ROA ROC SCE SYR SWF (seasonal: ACK MVY) **Canada:** YYZ
All service operated as US Airways Express using only US (3500-3999) flight
numbers
FFP: US Airways Dividend Miles

HISTORY/STRUCTURE

Founded: 1946 (as Reading Aviation Services)
Start date: August 1957
President: Keith Houk
Ownership: US Airways Group

FLEET

Type	No	Seats	Engines
DHC-8-102	44	Y37	PWC PW120A

DOUGLAS DC-9-21 *(Flemming Løvenvig)*

ALLEGIANT AIR

IATA: G4   **ICAO:** AAY   **IATA/ARC:** none   **RADIO:** *Allegiant*

CONTACTS

Mail
4955 East Anderson, Suite 120
Fresno, CA 93726

Internet: www.allegiantair.com

Telephone/Fax
Admin: +1 559 455 5715
Fax: +1 559 454 7708
Res: 1 877 202 6444

OPERATION

Type: Domestic passenger/cargo
Cities served: FAT LAS

HISTORY/STRUCTURE

Founded: 1997 (as WestJet Express)
Start date: June 1998
Chairman/CEO: Mitchell Allee
Ownership: Closely held

FLEET

Type	No	Seats	Engines
DC-9-21	1	Y89	PW JT8D-11
MD-87	2	Y139	PW JT8D-219

BOEING 737-700 *(Stephen L Griffin)*

ALOHA AIRLINES

IATA: AQ   **ICAO:** AAH   **IATA/ARC:** 327   **RADIO:** *Aloha*

CONTACTS

Mail
PO Box 30028
Honolulu, HI 96820

Internet: www.alohaair.com

Telephone/Fax
Admin: +1 808 836 4101
Fax: +1 808 836 0303
Res: 1 800 367 5250
PR: +1 808 836 5247

OPERATION

Type: Domestic/Flag passenger/cargo
Cities served: US: HNL ITO KOA LAS LIH OAK OGG SNA
Oceania: CXI JON KWA MAJ MDY
Code-share: IslandAir
FFP: AlohaPass

HISTORY/STRUCTURE

Founded: June 1946 (as Trans-Pacific Airlines)
Start date: July 26, 1946
President/CEO: Glenn Zander
Ownership: Aloha Airgroup

FLEET

Type	No	Seats	Engines
Boeing 737-200	11	F10Y97 or F12Y106	PW JT8D-9A/-15
Boeing 737-200QC	6	F10Y96 or F10Y108	PW JT8D-9A/-15
Boeing 737-700	7	F12Y112	CFMI CFM56-7B24

NOTES

Aloha Airgroup and Hawaiian Airlines propose to merge in 2002 under the umbrella of Aloha Holdings; Hawaiian will be the operating name. Aloha Holdings has indicated it will use solely Boeing 717s for inter-island service.

AIIRBUS A320-231 *(Jonathan W Holmes)*

AMERICA WEST AIRLINES

IATA: HP	**ICAO:** AWE	**IATA/ARC:** 401	**RADIO:** *Cactus*

CONTACTS

Mail
4000 East Sky Harbor Boulevard
Phoenix, AZ 85034

Telephone/Fax
Admin: +1 480 693 0800
Fax: +1 480 693 5546
Res: 1 800 235 9292
PR: +1 480 693 5729

Internet: www.americawest.com

OPERATION

Type: Domestic/Flag passenger/cargo
Cities served: US: ABQ ATL AUS BOI BOS BUR BWI CLE CMH DCA DEN DFW DSM DTW ELP EWR FLL GEG IAH IND JFK LAS LAX LGB MCI MCO MDW MIA MKE MSP MSY OAK OMA ONT ORD PDX PHL PHX RNO SAN SAT SEA SFO SJC SLC SMF SNA STL TPA TUS (seasonal: ANC PSP RSW)
Canada: YVR **México:** ACA MEX MZT PVR SJD ZIH (seasonal: ZLO)
Code-share: Big Sky, Chautauqua, Continental, Continental Express, Mesa
FFP: FlightFund

HISTORY/STRUCTURE

Founded: February 1981
Start date: August 1, 1983
Chairman/CEO: W Douglas Parker
Ownership: America West Holding Corp (NYSE: AWA)

FLEET

Type	No	Seats	Engines
Boeing 737-200	12	F8Y105	PW JT8D-15
Boeing 737-300	40	F8Y118/Y120/Y126	CFMI CFM56-3B1/-3B2
Airbus A319-100	31	F12Y112	IAE V2524-A5
Airbus A320-200	46	F12Y138	IAE V2500-A1/V2527-A5
Boeing 757-200	13	F14Y176 or F14Y175	RR RB211-535E4
Ordered			
Airbus A318	15		
Airbus A319	2		
Airbus A320	9		

BOEING 777-200 (ER) *(Gianfranco Beting)*

AMERICAN AIRLINES

IATA: AA   **ICAO:** AAL   **IATA/ARC:** 001   **RADIO:** *American*

CONTACTS

Mail
PO Box 619616
Dallas/Ft Worth Airport, TX 75261

Internet: www.aa.com

Telephone/Fax
Admin: +1 817 963 1234
Fax:　　+1 817 967 4318
Res:　　 1 800 433 7300
PR:　　 +1 817 967 1575

OPERATION

Type: Domestic/Flag passenger/cargo
Hubs: DFW MIA ORD STL
Cities served: US: ABQ ALB ANC ATL AUS BDL BHM BNA BOS BUF BUR BWI CID CLE CLT CMH COS CVG DAY DCA DEN DFW DSM DTW ELP EWR FAT FLL FSD GSO HNL HOU HPN HSV IAD IAH ICT IND JAX JFK KOA LAS LAX LGA LGB LIH LIT LNK MCI MCO MDT MDW MEM MFE MIA MKE MLI MSP MSY OAK OGG OKC OMA ONT ORD ORF PBI PDX PHL PHX PIT PSP PVD RDU RIC RNO ROC RST RSW SAN SAT SDF SEA SFO SGF SJC SLC SMF SNA STL SWF SYR TPA TUL TUS TYS XNA (seasonal: DRO EGE GUC HDN JAC MTJ RSW) **Canada:** YOW YUL YVR YYC YYZ **Caribbean:** ANU AUA BDA BGI CUR GCM KIN LRM MBJ PAP PLS POP POS SDQ SJU STT STX SXM (seasonal: UVF) **México:** BJX CUN GDL MEX MTY PVR SJD (seasonal: ACA) **Central America:** BZE GUA MGA PTY SAL SAP SJO TGU **South America:** ASU BAQ BOG CCS CLO CNF EZE GIG GRU GYE LIM LPB MAR MDE MVD SCL UIO VVI **Europe:** BRU CDG FRA FCO LGW LHR MAD MAN ZRH (seasonal: GLA) **Asia:** KIX NRT
Global alliance: oneworld
Code-share: Aer Lingus, Air Pacific, American Eagle, Asiana, Chautauqua, China Eastern, Corporate Airlines, EVA Air, Finnair, Grupo TACA, Gulf Air, Gulfstream International, Hawaiian, Iberia, Japan Air Lines, LanChile, LOT, Qantas, Sabena, Swissair, TAM Brasil, TAP Air Portugal, Trans States Airlines, Turkish
FFP: AAdvantage

BOEING 737-800 *(Mark Durbin)*

HISTORY/STRUCTURE

Founded: January 25, 1930 (as American Airways)
Start date: May 5, 1934
Chairman/President/CEO: Donald Carty
Ownership: AMR Corp (NYSE: AMR)

FLEET

Type	No	Seats	Engines
Fokker 100	74	F8Y89	RR Tay 650-15
Boeing 717-200	30*	F16Y95	BR BR715
MD-82	267	F14Y115	PW JT8D-217A/-217C
MD-83	95	F14Y115	PW JT8D-219
Boeing 737-800	77	F20Y114	CFMI CFM56-7B27
Boeing 757-200	144	F22Y154	RR RB211-535E4B
Boeing 767-200	8	F14C30Y121	GE CF6-80A
Boeing 767-200ER	21	F9C30Y119	GE CF6-80A2
Boeing 767-300ER	49	F14C24Y156 or F30Y198	GE CF6-80C2B6
Boeing 767-300ER	9	F14C24Y156 or F30Y198	PW4060
Boeing 777-200ER	40	F18C56Y163 or F16C35Y194	RR Trent 892-17
Airbus A300B4-605R	34	F16Y234/Y235	GE CF 6-80C2A5

* to be retired June 2002

Ordered

Boeing 737-800	41		
Boeing 757-200	7		
Boeing 767-300ER	15		
Boeing 777-200	7		

NOTES

EMBRAER EMB-135LR *(Ken Petersen)*

AMERICAN EAGLE AIRLINES

IATA: MQ   **ICAO:** EGF   **IATA/ARC:** none   **RADIO:** *Eagle Flight*

CONTACTS

Mail
PO Box 619616
MD5475
DFW Airport, TX 75261
Internet: www.aa.com

Telephone/Fax
Admin: +1 817 967 1294
Fax: +1 817 967 0977

OPERATION

Type: Domestic/Flag passenger/cargo
Cities served: US: ABI ABQ ACT ALB AMA AZO BDL BGR BMI BNA BOS BTR BWI CID CLE CLL CMH CLT CMI CRP CVG DAY DCA DBQ DFW DLH DRO DSM DTW EWR EVV EYW FAT FLL FSM FWA GGG GRB GRR GSP HOU HPN HSV IAD ICT ILE IND ISP JAN JAX JFK LAW LAX LBB LGA LIT LRD LSE MAF MCO MDT MEM MIA MKE MRY MSN OAK OKC OMA ORD ORF ORH PHL PHX PIA PIT PSP PVD PWM RDU RIC ROC RSW SAN SAV SBA SBP SDF SGF SHV SJC SJT SMF SPS TOL TPA TVC TUL TXK TYR TYS XNA
Canada: YQB YUL YYZ **Caribbean:** FPO GGT MHH NAS **México:** AGU SLW
All service operated using only AA flight numbers (3200-5299)
Code-share: Alaska Airlines, Continental, Delta Air Lines, Northwest
FFP: AAdvantage

HISTORY/STRUCTURE

Founded: 1978
President: Peter Bowler

Start date: July 1978 (as Simmons Airlines)
Ownership: AMR Corporation

FLEET

Type	No	Seats	Engines
SAAB 340B	100	Y34	GE CT7-9B
ATR42-300	14	Y46	PWC PW120
ATR72-200	26	Y64	PWC PW124B/PW127/PW127F
EMBRAER ERJ 135LR	40	Y37	GM AE3007A3
EMBRAER ERJ 140LR	16	Y44	GM AE3007A3
EMBRAER ERJ 145LR	56	Y50	GM AE3007A3
Bombardier CRJ700	4	Y70	GE CF34-8C1
Ordered			
EMBRAER ERJ 140LR	123		
Bombardier CRJ700	21		

BOEING 757-300 *(Justin Cederholm)*

AMERICAN TRANS AIR (dba ATA)

IATA: TZ   **ICAO:** AMT   **IATA/ARC:** 366   **RADIO:** *Amtran*

CONTACTS

Mail
PO Box 51609
Indianapolis, IN 46251

Internet: www.ata.com

Telephone/Fax
Admin:	+1 317 247 4000
Fax:	+1 317 243 4165
Res:	1 800 435 9282
Job hotline:	+1 317 240 7106

OPERATION

Type: Domestic/Flag passenger/cargo
Cities served: US: DCA DEN DFW EWR FLL HNL IND LAS LAX LGA LIH MCO MDW MIA MSP OGG PHL PHX PIE RSW SEA SFO SRQ **Caribbean:** AUA GCM MBJ PUJ SJU **México:** CUN PVR
Code-share: Chicago Express
FFP: none

HISTORY/STRUCTURE

Founded: August 1973 (as Ambassadair) **Start date:** March 1981
President/CEO: John Tague   **Ownership:** Amtran Inc (NASDAQ: AMTR)

FLEET

Type	No	Seats	Engines
Boeing 727-200	10*	Y168	PW JT8D-15/17
Boeing 737-800	18	Y175	CFMI CFM56-7B27
Boeing 757-200	16	Y216	RR RB211-535E4
Boeing 757-300	7	Y247	RR RB211-535E4-C
L-1011 TriStar 50/100	9	Y362	RR RB211-22B
L-1011 TriStar 500	5	Y307	RR RB211-524B4

*to be retired by June 30, 2002
Ordered

Boeing 737-800	24		
Boeing 757-300	5		

BOEING 727-200 (F) *(Patrick Vinot Préfontaine)*

AMERIJET INTERNATIONAL

IATA: M6   **ICAO:** AJT   **IATA/ARC:** 810   **RADIO:** *Amerijet*

CONTACTS

Mail
2800 South Andrews Avenue
Ft Lauderdale, FL 33316

Internet: www.amerijet.com

Telephone/Fax
Admin: +1 954 320 5300
Fax: +1 954 765 3521
Info: 1 800 927 6059

OPERATION

Type: Supplemental cargo
Areas served: US, Caribbean, México, Central/South America

HISTORY/STRUCTURE

Founded: 1974
Start date: 1974
President/CEO: David Bassett
Ownership: HIG Capital (75%), Bassett Enterprises

FLEET

Type	No	Engines
Boeing 727-200F	5	PW JT8D-9A/-15/-17

USA

BOEING 737-200 (F) *(Josh Rawlin)*

AMERISTAR AIR CARGO

IATA: none **ICAO:** AJI **IATA/ARC:** none **RADIO:** *Ameristar*

CONTACTS

Mail
PO Box 700548
Dallas, TX 75370-0548

Telephone/Fax
Admin: +1 972 725 9000
Fax: +1 972 725 9090

Internet: www.ameristarjet.com

OPERATION

Type: Supplemental cargo
Areas served: US, Canada, México

HISTORY/STRUCTURE

Founded: 1999
Start date: September 2000
President: Tom Wachendorfer Jr
Ownership: Privately held

FLEET

Type	No	Engines
Boeing 737-200C	2	PW JT8D-15

BOEING 727-200 (F) *(Capt Stephen L LeaVell)*

ASIA PACIFIC AIRLINES (Aero Micronesia dba)

IATA: none   **ICAO:** MGE   **IATA/ARC:** none   **RADIO:** *Magellan*

CONTACTS

Mail
156 Diablo Road, Suite 203
Danville, CA 94526-3312

Telephone/Fax
Admin: +1 925 362 4430
Fax: +1 925 362 4432

Internet: www.flyapa.com

OPERATION

Type: Supplemental cargo
Cities served: US: HNL **Asia:** HKG KIX MDC MNL NGO TNN **Oceania:** GUM HIR KSA KWA MAJ PNI ROR SPN TKK YAP

HISTORY/STRUCTURE

Founded: 1998
Start date: March 1999
President: Michael Quinn
Ownership: CTSI (Consolidated Transportation Services Inc)

FLEET

Type	No	Engines
Boeing 727-200F	2	PW JT8D-17

BOMBARDIER CRJ200ER (CL-600-2B19) *(Ron Peel)*

ATLANTIC COAST AIRLINES

IATA: DH   **ICAO:** BLR   **IATA/ARC:** 480   **RADIO:** *Blue Ridge*

CONTACTS

Mail
45200 Business Court
Dulles, VA 20166

Internet: www.atlanticcoast.com

Telephone/Fax
Admin: +1 703 650 6000
Fax: +1 703 650 6299
PR: +1 703 650 6019

OPERATION

Type: Domestic passenger/cargo
Cities served: United Express: ABE ALB AVP BDL BGM BHM BNA BOS BUF CAE CAK CHO CHS CLE CLT CMH CRW DAY DSM DTW EWR FAR FSD FWA GSO GSP HPN IAD IND JAX JFK LAN LEX LGA MBS MDT MEM MHT MSN MSY OKC OMA ORD ORF PHL PIA PIT PVD PWM RDU RIC ROA ROC RSW SAV SCE SGF SWF SYR TUL TYS **Delta Connection: US:** ALB BGR BHM BOS BTV CAE CHS CLE CMH CRW CVG DAY DCA EVV EWR GSO GSP IND JFK LGA PHL PWM RDU RIC SAV SBN TOL **Canada:** YHZ YUL
All service operated as United Express or Delta Connection using UA (7150-7899) or DL (6100-6299) flight numbers
FFP: United Mileage Plus, Delta SkyMiles

HISTORY/STRUCTURE

Founded: 1989   **Start date:** December 15, 1989
Chairman/CEO: Kerry Skeen   **President/COO:** Tom Moore
Ownership: Publicly traded company (NASDAQ: ACAI)

FLEET

Type	No	Seats	Engines
BAe Jetstream 41	31	Y29	GA TPE331-14HR-805H
Fairchild Dornier 328JET	28	Y32	PWC PW306B
Bombardier CRJ200ER	56	Y50	GE CF34-3B1
Ordered			
Fairchild Dornier 328JET	35		
Bombardier CRJ200ER	40		

BOMBARDIER CRJ200ER (CL-600-2B19) *(Dave Campbell)*

ATLANTIC SOUTHEAST AIRLINES (ASA)

IATA: EV **ICAO:** CAA **IATA/ARC:** 862 **RADIO:** *Candler*

CONTACTS

Mail
100 Hartsfield Center Parkway, Suite 800
Atlanta, GA 30354-1356

Internet: www.flyasa.com

Telephone/Fax
Admin: +1 404 766 1400
Fax: +1 404 209 0162
Res: 1 800 221 1212

OPERATION

Type: Domestic/Flag passenger/cargo
Cities served: USA: ABE ABY AEX AGS AMA ATL AUS AVL BHM BNA BQK
BTR BWI CAE CAK CHA CHS CLE CLT CRP CRW CSG DAB DAL DFW DHN
DSM DTW ELP EVV FAY FLO FWA GNV GPT GRR GSP GTR HOU HTS HSV
IAH ICT ILE ILM ISP JAN JFK LBB LEX LFT LIT LYH MCN MDT MEI MEM
MGM MKE MLB MLU MOB MYR OKC OMA ORH PFN PHF PIA PIT ROA SAT
SBN SDF SHV SRQ SWF TLH TOL TRI TUL TUS TXK TYS VLD VPS XNA
(seasonal: LWB) **Canada:** YOW YYZ **México:** MTY
All service operated as Delta Connection using only DL (4000-4999) flight
numbers
FFP: Delta SkyMiles

HISTORY/STRUCTURE

Founded: March 1979
President: Skip Barnette

Start date: June 27, 1979
Ownership: Delta Air Lines

FLEET

Type	No	Seats	Engines
EMB-120ER Brasilia	49	Y30	PWC PW118
ATR72-212	19	Y64	PWC PW127
Bombardier CRJ200ER	65	Y50	GE CF34-3B1
Bombardier CRJ700	2	Y70	GE CF34-8C1
Ordered			
Bombardier CRJ200ER	18		
Bombardier CRJ700	28		

BOEING 747-300F *(Bill Hough)*

ATLAS AIR

IATA: 5Y   **ICAO:** GTI   **IATA/ARC:** 369   **RADIO:** *Giant*

CONTACTS

Mail
2000 Westchester Avenue
Purchase, NY 10577-2543

Internet: www.atlasair.com

Telephone/Fax
Admin: +1 914 701 8210
Fax: +1 914 701 8001

OPERATION

Type: Domestic/Flag passenger/cargo
Areas served: Operates worldwide freight services for major airlines on an ACMI basis

HISTORY/STRUCTURE

Founded: April 1992
Start date: February 1993
CEO: Richard Shuyler
President/COO: James Matheny
Ownership: Atlas Air Worldwide Holdings (NYSE: CGO)

FLEET

Type	No	Engines
Boeing 747-200F	22	GE CF6-50E2
Boeing 747-300F	3	GE CF6-50E2
Boeing 747-400F	12	GE CF6-80C2B1F
Ordered		
Boeing 747-400F	4	

FAIRCHILD SA227-AC METRO III *(Josh Rawlin)*

BIG SKY AIRLINES

IATA: GQ   **ICAO:** BSY   **IATA/ARC:** 387   **RADIO:** *Big Sky*

CONTACTS

Mail
1601 Aviation Place
Billings, MT 59105

Internet: www.bigskyair.com

Telephone/Fax
Admin: +1 406 247 3910
Fax: +1 406 259 8750
Res: 1 800 237 7788

OPERATION

Type: Domestic passenger/cargo
Cities served: BIL BIS BWD DEN DFW ELD FCA GDV GEG GGW GTF HLN HOT HRO HVR ISN JBR LWT MLS MSO MWH OLF PNC SDY WDG

HISTORY/STRUCTURE

Founded: 1978
Start date: September 15, 1978
President/CEO: Terry D Marshall
Ownership: Big Sky Transportation

FLEET

Type	No	Seats	Engines
Metro III	10	Y19	GA TPE331-11U-612G
Metro 23	6	Y19	GA TPE331-12U-701G

CASA C-212-CD AVIOCAR 200 *(Tom Sheridan)*

BOSTON-MAINE AIRWAYS (dba Pan Am Services)

IATA: none   **ICAO:** PXS   **IATA/ARC:** none   **RADIO:** *Panam Express*

CONTACTS

Mail
14 Aviation Avenue
Portsmouth, NH 03801

Telephone/Fax
Admin: +1 603 766 2117
Fax: +1 603 766 2225

Internet: www.bmairways.com

OPERATION

Type: Domestic passenger/cargo
Cities served: ACY BWI CBE HGR HPN PSM (Clipper Connection). Also operates freight service between EWB/MVY/ACK; contract passenger service between BWI and ACY for the FAA Technical Center.

HISTORY/STRUCTURE

Founded: March 1999
Start date: June 1999
President: David Fink
Ownership: Guilford Transportation Industries

FLEET

Type	No	Seats	Engines
BAe Jetstream 31	8	Y19	GA TPE331-10UG-513H
CASA 212	2	Frtr	GA TPE331-10R-512/3C
Ordered			
BAe Jetstream 31	8		

BOEING 727-200 (F) *(Gary Jennings)*

CAPITAL CARGO INTERNATIONAL AIRLINES

IATA: PT   **ICAO:** CCI   **IATA/ARC:** none   **RADIO:** *Cappy*

CONTACTS

Mail
6200 Hazletine National Drive, Suite 100
Orlando, FL 32822

Internet: www.capitalcargo.com

Telephone/Fax
Admin: +1 407 855 2004
Fax: +1 407 855 6620
Info: 1 800 593 9119

OPERATION

Type: Supplemental cargo

HISTORY/STRUCTURE

Founded: September 1995
Start date: April 1996
President/CEO: Peter F Fox
Ownership: Privately held

FLEET

Type	No	Engines
Boeing 727-200F	12	PW JT8D-15/-15A/-17/-17R

BOEING 737-200 *(Harald M Helbig)*

CASINO EXPRESS AIRLINES
(TEM Enterprises dba)

IATA: XP   **ICAO:** CXP   **IATA/ARC:** none   **RADIO:** *Casino Express*

CONTACTS
Mail
976 Mountain City Highway
Eko, NV 89801-2728

Telephone/Fax
Admin: +1 775 738 6040
Fax: +1 775 738 1881
Res: 1 800 258 8800

OPERATION
Type: Domestic/Flag passenger/cargo
Areas served: US, Caribbean, México

HISTORY/STRUCTURE
Founded: 1987
Start date: June 1989
General Manager: Arthur Moses
CEO: Norval Nelson
Ownership: TEM Enterprises (Todd E McClasky)

FLEET

Type	No	Seats	Engines
Boeing 737-200	4	Y122	PW JT8D-15/-17A

BRITISH AEROSPACE BAe 3201 JETSTREAM 32EP *(Zach Gollman)*

CCAIR (dba US Airways Express)

IATA: ED **ICAO:** CDL **IATA/ARC:** 354 **RADIO:** *Carolina*

CONTACTS

Mail
PO Box 19929
Charlotte, NC 28219

Telephone/Fax
Admin: +1 704 359 8990
Fax: +1 704 359 0351

Internet: www.ccairinc.com

OPERATION

Type: Domestic passenger/cargo
Cities served: AGS AHN AVL CHS CLT CVG GSP HKY HTS LEX LYH LWB
OAJ ORF PGV RDU SOP TLH
All service operated as US Airways Express using only US (5001-5249) flight
numbers
FFP: US Airways Dividend Miles

HISTORY/STRUCTURE

Founded: 1979 (as Sunbird Airlines)
Start date: November 15, 1979
President/CEO: Tim Coon
Ownership: Mesa Air Group

FLEET

Type	No	Seats	Engines
BAe Jetstream 32EP	9	Y19	GA TPE331-12UAR-704H
DHC-8-102	7	Y37	PWC PW120A

McDONNELL DOUGLAS DC-10-40F *(Steven J Pinnow)*

CENTURION AIR CARGO

IATA: WE   **ICAO:** CWC   **IATA/ARC:** none   **RADIO:** *Challenge Cargo*

CONTACTS

Mail
PO Box 523979
Miami, FL 33152-3979

Telephone/Fax
Admin: +1 305 869 8333
Fax: +1 305 869 8388

OPERATION

Type: Supplemental cargo
Areas served: Worldwide charter/ACMI services

HISTORY/STRUCTURE

Founded: 1978 (as Challenge Air Transport)
Start date: December 1986
President: William F Spohrer
Ownership: Privately held

FLEET

Type	No	Engines
DC-10-40F	3	PW JT9D-59A

GRUMMAN G-73 FRAKES TURBO MALLARD *(Dick Jordan)*

CHALK'S OCEAN AIRWAYS (Flying Boat dba)

IATA: OP   **ICAO:** none   **IATA/ARC:** 370   **RADIO:** none

CONTACTS

Mail
1000 MacArthur Causeway
Miami, FL 33132

Internet: www.chalksoceanairways.com

Telephone/Fax
Admin: +1 305 371 8628
Fax: +1 305 371 7968
Res: 1 800 424 2557

OPERATION

Type: Domestic/Flag passenger/cargo
Cities served: US: FLL MPB **Caribbean:** NSB PID WKR

HISTORY/STRUCTURE

Founded: July 1919 (as Chalk's Flying Service)
Start date: 1919
President: Jim Confalone
Ownership: Privately held

FLEET

Type	No	Seats	Engines
Turbo Mallard	5	Y17	PWC PT6A-34

BOEING 727-200 *(Josh Rawlin)*

CHAMPION AIR (Grand Holdings dba)

IATA: MG   **ICAO:** CCP   **IATA/ARC:** none   **RADIO:** *Champion*

CONTACTS

Mail
8009 34th Avenue South, Suite 700
Bloomington, MN 55425

Telephone/Fax
Admin: +1 952 814 8700
Fax: +1 952 814 8799

Internet: www.championair.com

OPERATION

Type: Supplemental passenger/cargo

HISTORY/STRUCTURE

Founded: 1995
Start date: July 1995
President: Richard Page
Ownership: GHI-CA (Carl Pohlad 60%, NWA 40%)

FLEET

Type	No	Seats	Engines
Boeing 727-200	12	Y173	PW JT8D-17/-17A

EMBRAER EMB-145LR *(John Davies)*

CHAUTAUQUA AIRLINES

IATA: RP　　**ICAO:** CHQ　　**IATA/ARC:** 363　　**RADIO:** *Chautauqua*

CONTACTS

Mail
2500 South High School Road, Suite 160
Indianapolis, IN 46241

Telephone/Fax
Admin: +1 317 484 6000
Fax:　+1 317 484 6060

Internet: www.flychautauqua.com

OPERATION

Type: Domestic passenger/cargo
Cities served: America West Express: US: BDL BOS BWI CMH EWR ORD
Canada: YYZ **American Connection: US:** CHS CID CLE CVG DAY FWA LEX
LNK MKE OMA PIT SDF SHV STL SUX TYS **Canada:** YYZ **US Airways**
Express: US: AOO BOS BUF CAE CHS CVG DAY FWA GSO GSP HGR IAD
IND JST LAN LEX LGA LNS PIT RDU ROA ROC SAV STL **Canada:** YOW
All service operated as America West Express, American Connection, or US
Airways Express using HP (5201-5299), AA (5700-5899), or US (4201-4924)
flight numbers
FFP: AAdvantage, America West FlightFund, US Airways Dividend Miles

HISTORY/STRUCTURE

Founded: May 3, 1973
Start date: August 1, 1974
President/CEO: Bryan Bedford
Ownership: Wexford Management

FLEET

Type	No	Seats	Engines
SAAB 340A	23	Y30	GE CT7-5A2
EMBRAER ERJ 140LR	4	Y40	GM AE3007A1/3
EMBRAER ERJ 145LR	38	Y50	GM AE3007A1/2
Ordered			
EMBRAER ERJ 140LR	13		

SAAB 340B *(Dick Jordan)*

CHICAGO EXPRESS AIRLINES

IATA: C8   **ICAO:** WDY   **IATA/ARC:** 488   **RADIO:** *Windy City*

CONTACTS

Mail
5333 South Laramie Avenue
Chicago, IL 60638

Telephone/Fax
Admin: +1 773 585 0585
Fax: +1 773 585 4877

Internet: www.chicagoexpress.com

OPERATION

Type: Domestic passenger/cargo
Cities served: DAY DSM GRR IND LAN MDW MKE MSN SPI
All service operated as ATA Connection (ATA flight numbers 3101-3299)
FFP: none

HISTORY/STRUCTURE

Founded: 1993
Start date: August 9, 1993
President: Courtney Anderson
Ownership: Amtran Inc

FLEET

Type	No	Seats	Engines
SAAB 340B	11	Y34	GE CT7-9B

SAAB 340B *(Ron Peel)*

COLGAN AIR

IATA: 9L   **ICAO:** CJC   **IATA/ARC:** 426   **RADIO:** *Colgan*

CONTACTS

Mail
110677 Aviation Lane
Manassas, VA 22110

Internet: www.colganair.com

Telephone/Fax
Admin: +1 703 368 8880
Fax: +1 703 331 3116
Res: 1 800 272 5488

OPERATION

Type: Domestic passenger/cargo
Cities served: ACK ALB AUG BHB BGR BKW BLF BOS CHO CMH DAY HTS HYA IAD ISP LEB LGA MVY ORF PIT PQI PVD RKD ROA RUT
All service operated as US Airways Express using only US (5900-5999) flight numbers
FFP: US Airways Dividend Miles

HISTORY/STRUCTURE

Founded: 1991 (as National Capital Airways)
Start date: December 1, 1991
President/CEO: Charles Colgan
Ownership: Michael and Charles Colgan

FLEET

Type	No	Seats	Engines
Beech 1900C-1	7	Y19	PWC PT6A-65B
Beech 1900D	1	Y19	PWC PT6A-67D
SAAB 340B	8	Y34	GE CT7-9B

BOMBARDIER CRJ100ER (CL-600-2B19) *(Thomas Kim)*

COMAIR

IATA: OH	**ICAO:** COM	**IATA/ARC:** 886	**RADIO:** *Comair*

CONTACTS

Mail
PO Box 75021
Cincinnati, OH 45275

Internet: www.comair.com

Telephone/Fax
Admin: +1 859 767 2550
Fax: +1 859 767 2278
Job hotline: +1 859 767 2667

OPERATION

Type: Domestic/Flag passenger/cargo
Cities served: US: ABE ALB ATL ATW AVL AVP AZO BGR BHM BNA BOS BTV BUF BWI CAE CAK CHA CHS CHO CID CKB CLE CLT CMH CRP CRW CVG DAB DAY DSM DTW EVV EWR EYW FLL FNT FWA GRB GRR GSO GSP HOU HPN HSV IAD IAH ICT IND ISP JAN JAX JFK LAN LAS LEX LGA LIT MCI MCO MDT MDW MEM MHT MIA MKE MLB MSN MSP MYR OKC OMA ORD ORF PBI PHL PIT PNS PVD PWM RDU RIC ROA ROC RSW SAT SAV SBN SDF SRQ STL SWF SYR TLH TOL TRI TUL TYS **Canada:** YUL YYZ
Caribbean: NAS
All service operated as Delta Connection using only DL (5000-6099)flight numbers
FFP: Delta SkyMiles

HISTORY/STRUCTURE

Founded: 1976 (as Wings Airways)
Start date: April 1977
President: Randy Rademacher
Ownership: Delta Air Lines

FLEET

Type	No	Seats	Engines
EMB-120RT Brasilia	7	Y30	PWC PW118
Bombardier CRJ100ER	112*	Y50	GE CF34-3A1
*15 leased to SkyWest, 3 leased to ASA			
Ordered			
Bombardier CRJ100ER/CRJ440	41		
Bombardier CRJ700	27		

RAYTHEON BEECH 1900D *(Bill Hough)*

COMMUTAIR (Champlain Enterprises dba)

IATA: C5   **ICAO:** UCA   **IATA/ARC:** none   **RADIO:** *Commutair*

CONTACTS

Mail
518 Rugar Street
Plattsburgh, NY 12901

Telephone/Fax
Admin: +1 518 562 2700
Fax: +1 518 562 8030

Internet: www.commutair.com

OPERATION

Type: Domestic passenger/cargo
Cities served: ALB BOS BTV BUF HPN ISP LGA MDT MHT PLB PVD PWM ROC SLK SYR UCA
All service operated as Continental Connection using only CO (2351-2642) flight numbers
FFP: Continental OnePass

HISTORY/STRUCTURE

Founded: 1989
Start date: August 1, 1989
President: John A Sullivan Jr
CEO: Tony von Elbe
Ownership: Champlain Enterprises

FLEET

Type	No	Seats	Engines
Beech 1900D	15	Y19	PWC PT6A-67D

BOEING 767-400ER *(Gianfranco Beting)*

CONTINENTAL AIRLINES

IATA: CO   **ICAO:** COA   **IATA/ARC:** 005   **RADIO:** *Continental*

CONTACTS

Mail
PO Box 4607
Houston, TX 77002

Internet: www.continental.com

Telephone/Fax
Admin: +1 713 324 5000
Fax: +1 713 324 2087
Res: 1 800 523 3273
PR: +1 713 324 5080

OPERATION

Type: Domestic/Flag passenger/cargo
Hubs: EWR IAH
Cities served: US: ABQ ATL AUS BDL BHM BNA BOS BRO BTR BUF BWI
CHS CLE CLT CMH COS CRP CVG DCA DEN DFW DTW ELP EWR FLL HNL
IAD IAH IND JAX LAS LAX LGA MCI MCO MDW MFE MHT MIA MSP MSY
MYR OAK OKC OMA ONT ORD ORF PBI PDX PHL PHX PIT PNS PVD RDU
RNO RSW SAN SAT SDF SEA SFO SJC SLC SMF SNA SRQ STL TPA TUL
TUS (seasonal: ANC EGE HDN MTJ PSP PWM) **Canada:** YVR YYC YYZ
(seasonal: YHZ) **Caribbean:** ANU AUA BDA BQN GCM KIN MBJ NAS POP
SDQ SJU SXM STT **México:** ACA BJX CUN CZM GDL MEX MID MTY PVR
SJD VER (seasonal: MZT ZIH) **Central America:** BZE GUA MGA PTY SAL SAP
SJO TGU **South America:** BOG CCS GIG GRU GYE LIM UIO Europe: AMS
BHX BRU CDG DUB FCO FRA GLA LGW LIS MAD MAN MXP SNN ZRH
Asia: HKG NRT TLV **Oceania:** GUM
Global alliance: Wings
Code-share: Air Europa, Alaska Airlines, America West, American Eagle,
Amtrak, BMI British Midland, Commutair, Continental Express, Continental
Micronesia, COPA, Emirates, EVA Airways, Express Airlines I, Gulfstream
International, Hawaiian Airlines, Horizon Air, KLM, KLM cityhopper, Mesaba
Airlines, Northwest, Virgin Atlantic Airways
FFP: OnePass

HISTORY/STRUCTURE

Founded: 1934 (as Varney Speed Lines)
Start Date: July 15, 1934 (July 1, 1937 as Continental)
CEO: Gordon M Bethune
President: Larry Kellner
Ownership: Publicly traded company (NYSE: CAL)

BOEING 737-500 *(Jonathan W Holmes)*

FLEET

Type	No	Seats	Engines
Boeing 737-500	66	F10Y94	CFMI CFM56-3C1
Boeing 737-300	65	F12Y112	CFMI CFM56-3B1
Boeing 737-700	36	F12Y112	CFMI CFM56-7B24
Boeing 737-800	73	F14Y141 or F18Y132	CFMI CFM56-7B26
Boeing 737-900	10	F18Y149	CFMI CFM56-7B26
MD-81	3	F14Y127	PW JT8D-217
MD-82	54	F14Y127	PW JT8D-217/-217A/-219
MD-83	2	F14Y127	PW JT8D-219
Boeing 757-200	41	C16Y156 or F24Y159	RR RB211-535E4-B
Boeing 757-300	2	F24Y186	RR RB211-535E4-C
Boeing 767-200ER	10	C25Y149	GE CF6-80C2B4F
Boeing 767-400ER	6	C35Y200	GE CF6-80C2B7F
Boeing 777-200ER	16	C48Y235	GE GE90-92B
Ordered			
Boeing 737-800	20		
Boeing 737-900	4		
Boeing 757-300	13		
Boeing 767-400ER	18		
Boeing 777-200	2		

NOTES
31 Boeing 737s & MD-80s are grounded, some permanently

BOEING 737-800 *(Edward Lai)*

CONTINENTAL MICRONESIA
(dba Continental/Air Micronesia)

IATA: CS　　**ICAO:** CMI　　**IATA/ARC:** 596　　**RADIO:** *Air Mike*

CONTACTS

Mail
PO Box 8778
Tamuning, GU 96931

Telephone/Fax
Admin: +1 671 647 6453
Fax:　+1 671 646 0219
Res:　1 800 523 3273

Internet: www.continental.com

OPERATION

Type: Domestic/Flag passenger/cargo
Cities served: US: HNL **Asia:** CTS DPS FUK HKG KIJ KIX MNL NGO NRT OKJ SDJ TPE **Oceania:** CNS GUM JON KSA KWA MAJ PNI ROR SPN TKK YAP

HISTORY/STRUCTURE

Founded: 1966 (as Air Micronesia)
Start date: May 16, 1968
President/CEO: William Meehan
Ownership: Continental Airlines

FLEET

Type	No	Seats	Engines
Boeing 737-800	9	F14Y141	CFMI CFM56-7B26
Boeing 767-400ER	1	C35Y200	GE CF6-80C2B7F

Aircraft are leased from Continental on a rotating basis

BRITISH AEROSPACE BAe 3201 JETSTREAM 32EP *(Dave Campbell)*

CORPORATE AIRLINES

IATA: 3C   **ICAO:** CEA   **IATA/ARC:** 310   **RADIO:** *Corp-X*

CONTACTS

Mail
693 Fitzhugh Blvd
Smyrna, TN 37167

Telephone/Fax
Admin: +1 615 223 5644
Fax: +1 615 223 8631
Res: 1 800 555 6565

Internet: www.corporateairlines.com

OPERATION

Type: Domestic passenger/cargo
Cities served: Corporate Airlines: ATL BNA **American Connection:** ALO
BNA BRL CGI IRK MKL MWA OWB PAH STL TBN TRI UIN
Flights code-share with American Airlines using flight numbers 5350-5449.
FFP: AAdvantage

HISTORY/STRUCTURE

Founded: 996
Start date: December 16, 1996
President/CEO: Charles R Howell IV
Ownership: Division of Corporate Flight Management/privately held

FLEET

Type	No	Seats	Engines
BAe Jetstream 32EP	17	Y19	GA TPE331-12UAR-704H

BOEING 727-100C *(James Helbock)*

CUSTOM AIR TRANSPORT

IATA: DG   **ICAO:** CTT   **IATA/ARC:** 373   **RADIO:** *Catt*

CONTACTS

Mail
3305 Southwest 9th Avenue, Floor 2
Ft Lauderdale, FL 33315

Telephone/Fax
Admin: +1 954 523 4211
Fax: +1 954 523 6811
Info: 1 800 473 9131

OPERATION

Type: Supplemental cargo

HISTORY/STRUCTURE

Founded: 1995
Start date: December 9, 1995
President/CEO: Richard Wellman
Ownership: Brent Aviation

FLEET

Type	No	Engines
Boeing 727-100C	1	PW JT8D-7B
Boeing 727-200F	3	PW JT8D-9A

NOTES

Some aircraft operated in colors of Charter America, an affiliated company

BOEING 757-200 *(Ian Bowley)*

DELTA AIR LINES

IATA: DL   **ICAO:** DAL   **IATA/ARC:** 006   **RADIO:** *Delta*

CONTACTS

Mail
PO Box 20706
Atlanta, GA 30320

Internet: www.delta.com

Telephone/Fax
Admin: +1 404 715 2600
Fax: +1 404 715 2596
Res: 1 800 221 1212
PR: +1 404 715 5162

OPERATION

Type: Domestic/Flag passenger/cargo
Hubs: ATL CVG SLC
Cities served: US: ABQ ALB ANC ATL AUS BDL BHM BIL BNA BOI BOS BTR
BUF BWI BZN CAE CAK CHS CLE CLT CMH COS CVG DAB DAY DCA DEN
DFW DTW ELP EWR FCA FLL GEG GSO GSP GTF HLN HNL HOU HSV IAD
IAH IND ISP JAN JAX JFK LAS LAX LEX LGA LIT MCI MCO MDT MDW MEM
MHT MIA MKE MLB MLU MOB MSO MSP MSY OAK OGG OKC OMA ONT
ORD ORF PBI PDX PHL PHX PIT PNS PSC PVD PWM RDU RIC ROC RSW
SAN SAT SAV SDF SEA SFO SHV SJC SLC SMF SNA SRQ STL SYR TLH
TPA TUL TUS TYS VPS (seasonal: EGE GUC) **Canada:** YUL YYZ
Caribbean: AUA BDA GCM NAS SJU STT **México:** CUN GDL MEX SJD
Central America: GUA PTY SAL SJO **South America:** BOG CCS EZE GIG
GRU LIM SCL **Europe:** AMS ATH BCN BRU CDG DUB FCO FRA IST LGW
MAD MAN MUC MXP NCE SNN STR SVO VCE ZRH **Africa:** CAI **Asia:** BOM
DXB FUK NGO NRT TLV
Delta Shuttle operates LGA-DCA; Delta Express operates low-fare service in
selected markets
Global alliance: SkyTeam
Code-share: Aerolitoral, AeroMexico, Aeropostal, Air France, Air Jamaica,
American Eagle, ASA (Delta Connection), Atlantic Coast Airlines (Delta
Connection), British European, China Southern, Comair (Delta Connection),
ČSA Czech Airlines, El Al, LAPA, Royal Air Maroc, SkyWest, South African
FFP: SkyMiles

BOEING 737-200 *(Ken Petersen)*

HISTORY/STRUCTURE

Founded: 1924 (as Huff-Daland Dusters)
Start date: June 17, 1929
President/CEO: Leo Mullin
Ownership: Publicly traded company (NYSE: DAL)

FLEET

Type	No	Seats	Engines
Boeing 737-200	54*	F12Y95 or Y119	PW JT8D-15/-15A
Boeing 737-300	26	F8Y120	CFMI CFM56-3B1/-3B2
Boeing 737-800	67	F16Y138 or Y156	CFM56-7B26
MD-88	120**	F14Y128	PW JT8D-219
MD-90-30	16	F12Y138	IAE V2525-D5
Boeing 727-200	56	F12Y137	PW JT8D-15
Boeing 757-200	121	F24Y159	PW2037
Boeing 767-200	15	F18Y186	GE CF6-80A2
Boeing 767-300	28	F24Y228	GE CF6-80A2 or PW4060
Boeing 767-300ER	59	C48Y147	GE CF6-80C2B6F or PW4060
Boeing 767-400ER	18	F36Y251	GE CG6-80C2B7F
MD-11	15	C50Y210 or C50Y219	PW4460
Boeing 777-200ER	7	C52Y225	

*25 parked (Delta Express)
**10 parked

Ordered			
Boeing 737-800	65		
Boeing 767-400ER	3		
Boeing 777-200ER	6		

AIRBUS A300B4-203 (F) *(Josh Rawlin)*

DHL AIRWAYS (dba DHL Worldwide Express)

IATA: ER   **ICAO:** DHL   **IATA/ARC:** 423   **RADIO:** *Dahl*

CONTACTS

Mail
PO Box 66633
Chicago, IL 60666-0633

Telephone/Fax
Admin: +1 847 842 6300
Info: 1 800 225 5345

Internet: www.dhl-usa.com

OPERATION

Type: Domestic/Flag passenger/cargo
Cities served: US: ATL AUS BDL BOS BWI CVG DEN DFW DTW EWR IAH
JFK LAX MCI MCO MIA MSP ORD PHL PHX SEA SFO SLC SMF TPA
Caribbean: SJU **México:** GDL MEX **Europe:** BRU EMA LHR
All service operated as DHL Worldwide Express; additional cities served by
contract carriers

HISTORY/STRUCTURE

Founded: 1969 (as DHL, by Dalsey, Hillblom & Lynn)
Start date: 1982
Chairman/CEO: Joseph O'Gorman
Ownership: DHL Holdings (USA) (DHL International 52%)

FLEET

Type	No	Engines
Bell 206L LongRanger	1	AN 250-C28B
Boeing 727-100F	7	PW JT8D-7B
Boeing 727-200F	16	PW JT8D-7B/-9A/15/-15A/-17R
DC-8-73F	7	CFM56-2C
Airbus A300B4-100/-200F	6	GE CF6-50C2

CONVAIR 580 *(Andreas Rohde)*

ERA AVIATION

IATA: 7H   **ICAO:** ERH   **IATA/ARC:** 808   **RADIO:** *Erah*

CONTACTS

Mail
6160 Carl Brady Drive
Anchorage, AK 99502-1899

Telephone/Fax
Admin: +1 907 266 8394
Fax: +1 907 266 8483
Res: 1 800 866 8394

Internet: www.era-aviation.com

OPERATION

Type: Domestic/Flag passenger/cargo
Cities served: US: ADQ ANC BET CDV CYF EEK ENA GNU HOM HPB KKH KPN KWK KWN MYU NME OOK PTU SCM TNK VAK VDZ WTL WWT
Canada: YXY (seasonal)
Some scheduled service operated as Alaska Airlines Commuter using AS (4800-4899) flight numbers
FFP: Alaska Airlines Mileage Plan

HISTORY/STRUCTURE

Founded: 1948 (as Economy Helicopters)
Start date: 1948
CEO: Charles Johnson
Ownership: Rowan Companies (RDC)

FLEET

Type	No	Seats	Engines
DHC-6-200/-300	8	Y15/Y19	PWC PT6A-20/-27
DC-3	2*	Y21	PW R-1830-90
DHC-8-100	3	Y37	PWC PW120A/PW121
Convair 580	5	Y50	Allison 501-D13H

*operated by Era Classic Airlines
plus 90 helicopters operated as Era Helicopters

BOEING 747-200B (F) *(Gary Jennings)*

EVERGREEN INTERNATIONAL AIRLINES

IATA: EZ   **ICAO:** EIA   **IATA/ARC:** 494   **RADIO:** *Evergreen*

CONTACTS

Mail
3850 Three Mile Lane
McMinnville, OR 97128-9496

Telephone/Fax
Admin: +1 503 472 0011
Fax: +1 503 434 4210

Internet: www.evergreenairlines.com

OPERATION

Type: Supplemental cargo
Hubs: HKG JFK
Areas served: Operates worldwide contract and charter cargo services

HISTORY/STRUCTURE

Founded: 1975
Start date: November 28, 1975
President: Timothy Wahlberg
Ownership: Evergreen International Aviation

FLEET

Type	No	Engines
DC-9-15F	2	PW JT8D-7A/-7B
DC-9-32/33F	5	PW JT8D-9/-9A
Boeing 747-100F	6	PW JT9D-7A
Boeing 747-200F	5	PW JT9D-7J

ATR72-212 *(Carlos Aleman)*

EXECUTIVE AIRLINES (dba American Eagle)

IATA: NA   **ICAO:** EGF   **IATA/ARC:** none   **RADIO:** *Eagle Flight*

CONTACTS

Mail
PO Box 38082
Airport Station
San Juan, PR 00937

Telephone/Fax
Admin: +1 787 253 6400
Fax: +1 787 253 6572

Internet: www.aa.com

OPERATION

Type: Domestic/Flag passenger/cargo
Cities served: ANU AUA AXA BGI BON CIW CUR EIS GND HEX LRM MAZ POP POS PTP PUJ SDQ SJU SKB SLU STI STT STX SXM
All services operated as American Eagle using AA (5450-5699) flight numbers
FFP: AAdvantage

HISTORY/STRUCTURE

Founded: 1979 (as Executive Air Charter)
Start date: November 1979
President: Jacques Vachon
Ownership: AMR Corporation

FLEET

Type	No	Seats	Engines
ATR42-300	15	Y46	PWC PW120
ATR72-200	17	Y64	PWC PW123/PW126

BOMBARDIER CRJ200LR (CL-600-2B19) *(Bombardier)*

EXPRESS AIRLINES I

IATA: 9E   **ICAO:** FLG   **IATA/ARC:** 430   **RADIO:** *Flagship*

CONTACTS

Mail
1689 Nonconnah Boulevard, Suite 111
Memphis, TN 38132

Telephone/Fax
Admin: +1 901 348 4100
Fax: +1 901 348 6896

Internet: nwairlink.com

OPERATION

Type: Domestic passenger/cargo
Cities served: AEX ATW AZO BHM BTR BUF BTV CAK CHA CHS CID CMH
CWA DSM DTW ELM ERI EVV FNT FSM GLH GRB GSP GTR HAR HSV ICT
JAN JAX JLN LAN LEX LNK MEM MGM MLI MLU MOB MSL MSN MSP OKC
PAH PFN PIB PNS SAV SBN SDF SGF SHV SPI SUX TLH TOL TRI TUL TUP
TYS XNA
All service operated as Northwest Airlink using only NW (5600-5999) flight
numbers
FFP: Northwest WorldPerks

HISTORY/STRUCTURE

Founded: February 1985
Start date: June 1986
President/CEO: Philip H Trenary
Ownership: NWA Inc (to become publicly owned and renamed Pinnacle Airlines
in 2002)

FLEET

Type	No	Seats	Engines
SAAB 340A	12*	Y33	GE CT7-5A2
SAAB 340B	11**	Y33	GE CT7-9B
Bombardier CRJ200LR/CRJ440	34	Y50	GE CF34-3B1
*to be retired 2002; **to be transferred to Mesaba Airlines in 2002			

Ordered

Bombardier CRJ200LR	49		

EMBRAER EMB-145LR *(John Davies)*

EXPRESSJET AIRLINES (dba Continental Express)

IATA: none **ICAO:** BTA **IATA/ARC:** none **RADIO:** *Jetlink*

CONTACTS

Mail
PO Box 4601
Houston, TX 77210
Internet: www.continental.com

Telephone/Fax
Admin: +1 713 324 2639
Fax: +1 713 324 4914

OPERATION

Type: Domestic passenger/cargo
Cities served: US: ABE AEX ALB AMA ATL AVL BDL BHM BNA BOS BPT BRO BTR BTV BUF BWI CAE CHS CLE CLL CLT CMH CRP CRW CVG DAL DAY DCA DFW DRO DTW EFD ELP ERI EWR GPT GRR GSO GSP HPN HRL HSV IAD IAH ICT ILE IND ISP JAN JFK LBB LCH LEX LFT LIT LRD MCI MDT MDW MEM MHT MKE MLU MOB MSN MSP MYR OKC OMA ORD ORF PHL PIT PNS PVD PWM RDU RIC ROC SAV SDF SHV STL SYR TYR TYS VCT (seasonal: ACK MBJ MVY) **Canada:** YHZ YOW YQB YUL YYZ **México:** AGU CUU GDL MZT SLP SLW TAM TRC ZCL ZIH (seasonal: VER)
All service operated as Continental Express using CO (2900-4315) flight numbers
FFP: OnePass

HISTORY/STRUCTURE

Founded: 1956 (as Vercoa Air Service)
Start date: 1968 (as commuter, became Britt Airways)
President: Jim Ream **Ownership:** Continental Airlines

FLEET

Type	No	Seats	Engines
EMB-120ER Brasília	19	Y30	PWC PW118
ATR42-320	31	Y46	PWC PW121
EMBRAER ERJ 135ER	30	Y37	GM AE3007A3
EMBRAER ERJ 145ER/LR	106	Y50	GM AE3007A1/2
Ordered			
EMBRAER ERJ 135ER	20		
EMBRAER ERJ 145LR	44		
EMBRAER ERJ 145XR	75		

AIRBUS A300B4-203 (F) *(George W Hamlin)*

EXPRESS.NET AIRLINES

IATA: none   **ICAO:** XNA   **IATA/ARC:** none   **RADIO:** *Expressnet*

CONTACTS

Mail
101 Aviation Dr North
Naples, FL 34104

Telephone/Fax
Admin: +1 941 430 7080

Internet: www.expressnetairlines.com

OPERATION

Type: Supplemental cargo
Areas served: US, South America

HISTORY/STRUCTURE

Founded: 1994 (as Trans Continental Airlines)
Start date: August 1994
President: James Young
Ownership: David M Clark Trustee

FLEET

Type	No	Engines
Boeing 727-100C	2	PW JT8D-7B
Boeing 727-200F	1	PW JT8D-9A
Airbus A300B4-203F	8	GE CF6-50C2

BOEING 727-200 (F) *(Joe G Walker)*

EXPRESS ONE INTERNATIONAL

IATA: EO   **ICAO:** LHN   **IATA/ARC:** none   **RADIO:** *Longhorn*

CONTACTS

Mail
1420 Viceroy Drive
Dallas, TX 75235-2208

Telephone/Fax
Admin: +1 214 902 2500
Fax: +1 214 350 1399

Internet: www.express-one.com

OPERATION

Type: Supplemental cargo

HISTORY/STRUCTURE

Founded: 1975 (as Jet East International Airlines)
Start date: 1975
CEO: Kevin Good
Ownership: Express One Holdings

FLEET

Type	No	Engines
Boeing 727-200F	18	PW JT8D-9/-9A/-15/-17R

BOEING 727-200 *(Steve Kinder)*

FALCON AIR EXPRESS

IATA: F2   **ICAO:** FAO   **IATA/ARC:** none   **RADIO:** *Panther*

CONTACTS

Mail
7270 NW 12th Street, Suite 680
Miami, FL 33126

Telephone/Fax
Admin: +1 305 592 5672
Fax: +1 305 592 7298

Internet: www.falconairexpress.com

OPERATION

Type: Domestic/Flag passenger/cargo

HISTORY/STRUCTURE

Founded: 1995
Start date: March 1996
President/CEO: Emilio Dirube
Ownership: Emilio Dirube

FLEET

Type	No	Seats	Engines
Boeing 727-200	8	Y170	PW JT8D-9A/-15/-17R
Boeing 727-200	1	Y170	PW JT8D-217C/-15
Boeing 727-200F	1	Freighter	PW JT8D-217C/-15

McDONNELL DOUGLAS MD-10-10F *(Jason Knutson)*

FEDEX EXPRESS

IATA: FX   **ICAO:** FDX   **IATA/ARC:** 023   **RADIO:** *Fedex*

CONTACTS

Mail
PO Box 727
Memphis, TN 38194

Internet: www.fedex.com

Telephone/Fax
Admin: +1 901 369 3600
Fax: +1 901 395 4928
Info: 1 800 463 3339
PR: +1 901 395 3460

OPERATION

Type: Supplemental cargo
Cities served: US: ABE ABQ AFW ALB ANC ATL ATW AUS BDL BFM BHM
BOI BOS BTV BUF BUR BWI CAE CHS CID CLE CLT COS CPR CVG DAY
DEN DFW DLH DSM DTW ELP EWR FAT FLL FNT FSD FWA GEG GFK GJT
GRR GSO GSP GTF HNL HRL HSV HTS IAD IAH ICT IND ITO JAX JFK LAS
LAX LBB LCK LGB MCI MCO MDT MEM MHT MIA MKE MSN MSP MSY OAK
OKC OMA ONT ORD ORF PDX PHL PHX PIA PIT PVD PWM RDU RIC RNO
ROA ROC RST RSW SAN SAT SAV SBN SDF SEA SFO SHV SJC SLC SMF
SNA STL SWF SYR TLH TPA TUL TUS TYS **Canada:** YMX YOW YVR YWG
YYC YYZ **Caribbean:** BQN SJU **México:** GDL MTY TLC **Central America:**
PTY **South America:** BOG EZE SCL VCP VLN **Europe:** ADB AMS ARN BRU
BSL CDG CPH FRA MAN MUC MXP STN **Asia:** BKK BOM CEB CGK DXB
HKG ICN KHH KIX KUL MNL NRT PEK PEN PVG SFS SIN SZX TLV TPE
Oceania: NAN SYD
Other cities served by FedEx Feeder contract carriers

HISTORY/STRUCTURE

Founded: 1971 (as Federal Express)
Start date: April 17, 1973
Chairman: Frederick W Smith
President/CEO: David J Bronczek
Ownership: FedEx Corp (NYSE: FDX)

CESSNA 208B CARAVAN I SUPER CARGOMASTER *(John Wegg)*

FLEET

Type	No	Engines
Cessna 208A/B	258	PWC PT6A-114/-114A
Shorts SD3-60 (300)	11	PWC PT6A-67B
Fokker F27 Mk 500/600	32	RR Dart 532-7/552-7R
Boeing 727-100F	46	PW JT8D-7B
Boeing 727-200F	95	PW JT8D-9A/-15/-17/-17A/-217C
Airbus A310-200F	44	PW JT9D-7R4E1 or GE CF6-80A3
Airbus A310-300F	2	PW PW4152
Airbus A300F-600R	37	GE CF6-80C2A5 or PW4158
DC-10-10	12*	GE CF6-6D
DC-10-10F	29	GE CF6-6D/-6D1A
DC-10-10CF	8	GE CF6-6D
MD-10-10F	8	GE CF6-6D
MD-10-30F	3	GE CF6-50C2
DC-10-30F	12	GE CF6-50C2
DC-10-30CF	11	GE CF6-50C2
MD-11F	36	GE CF6-80C2D1F or PW PW4462

*to be converted to DC-10-10F, plus 29 to be scrapped

Cessna 208 Caravan I Super Cargomasters and Fokker F27 Friendships operated as FedEx Feeder under contract by Baron Aviation, Corporate Air (US and Philippines), CSA Air, Empire Airlines, Morningstar Air Express (Canada, which also operates three 727-100Fs), Mountain Air Cargo, WestAir, and Wiggins Airways; Shorts 360s operated in Europe by Express Airways

Ordered

Airbus A310-200F	5	
Airbus A310-300F	2	
Airbus A300-600F	7	
DC-10-10	2	(ex-American/United)
MD-11F	6	(ex-American & others)
Airbus A380-800F	10	

LOCKHEED L-1011-385-1-14 TRISTAR 200 (F) *(Rob Finlayson)*

FINE AIR

IATA: FB   **ICAO:** FBF   **IATA/ARC:** none   **RADIO:** *Fine Air*

CONTACTS

Mail
PO Box 523726
Miami, FL 33152

Telephone/Fax
Admin: +1 305 871 6606
Fax: +1 305 871 4232

Internet: www.fineair.com

OPERATION

Type: Supplemental cargo
Cities served: US: MIA **Caribbean:** BGI POP POS SDQ SJU **Central America:** MGA PTY SAP SJO TGU **South America:** BOG CCS GYE IQT LIM MAR UIO VLN

HISTORY/STRUCTURE

Founded: 1947 (as Arrow Air)
Start date: May 26, 1981
President: Barry Fine
Ownership: Fine Air Services Inc

FLEET

Type	No	Engines
DC-8-61F	2	PW JT3D-3B
DC-8-62F	7	PW JT3D-7
DC-8-63F	2	PW JT3D-7
L-1011 TriStar 200F	4	RR RB211-535B4-02

DOUGLAS DC-8-71F *(Ben Wang)*

FLORIDA WEST INTERNATIONAL AIRWAYS

IATA: RF   **ICAO:** FWL   **IATA/ARC:** 330   **RADIO:** *Florida West*

CONTACTS

Mail
7500 NW 25th Street, Suite 237
Miami, FL 33122-1714

Telephone/Fax
Admin: +1 305 341 9000
Fax: +1 305 341 9100

Internet: www.fwia.com

OPERATION

Type: Supplemental cargo
Cities served: US: ATL IAH MIA **Caribbean:** POS **South America:** EZE IQT
LIM SCL

HISTORY/STRUCTURE

Founded: 1981 (as Florida West Airlines)
Start date: 1983
President/CEO: Richard Haberly
Ownership: Haberly, Fast Air Group (25%)

FLEET

Type	No	Engines
DC-8-71F	1	CFMI CFM56-2C1
Boeing 767-300F	1	GE CF6-80C2B7F

AIRBUS A319-111 *(Josh Rawlin)*

FRONTIER AIRLINES

IATA: F9   **ICAO:** FFT   **IATA/ARC:** 422   **RADIO:** *Frontier Flight*

CONTACTS

Mail
PO Box 39177
Denver, CO 80239

Internet: www.frontierairlines.com

Telephone/Fax
Admin: +1 303 371 7400
Fax: +1 303 371 7007
Res: 1 800 432 1359

OPERATION

Type: Domestic passenger/cargo
Cities served: ABQ ATL AUS BOS BWI DCA DEN DFW ELP IAH LAS LAX
LGA MCI MDW MSP OMA PDX PHX RNO SAN SEA SFO SLC
Code-share: Great Lakes Airlines, Mesa Airlines (operates Frontier JetExpress)
FFP: Continental OnePass

HISTORY/STRUCTURE

Founded: 1994
Start date: July 5, 1994
CEO: Samuel Addoms
President: Jeff Potter
Ownership: Publicly traded company (NASDAQ: FRNT)

FLEET

Type	No	Seats	Engines
Boeing 737-200	5	Y108	PW JT8D-9A/-17
Boeing 737-300	17	Y136/Y138	CFMI CFM56-3B1/-3B2/-3C1
Airbus A319-111	6	Y132	CFMI CFM56-5B5/P
Ordered			
Airbus A318	6		
Airbus A319	20		

RAYTHEON BEECH 1900D *(Andreas Rohde)*

FRONTIER FLYING SERVICE

IATA: 2F   **ICAO:** FTA   **IATA/ARC:** 517   **RADIO:** *Frontier Air*

CONTACTS

Mail
5245 Airport Industrial Road
Fairbanks, AK 99709

Telephone/Fax
Admin: +1 907 474 1739
Fax: +1 907 474 0774
Res: +1 907 474 0014

Internet: www.frontierflying.com

OPERATION

Type: Domestic passenger/cargo
Cities served: AET AIN AKN AKP ANC ANI ATK BET BRW BTI DLG FAI GAL KAL KYU NUI NUL PIZ RBY SCC TAL

HISTORY/STRUCTURE

Founded: 1959
Start date: 1959
President/CEO: John Hajdukovich
Ownership: Privately held

FLEET

Type	No	Seats	Engines
Cessna 207	2	Y5	TCM IO-520-F
Piper Chieftain/T-1020	7	Y9	LY TIO-540-J2B/-J2BD
Beech 1900C-1	4	Y19	PWC PT6A-65B
Beech 1900D	1	Y19	PWC PT6A-67D

McDONNELL DOUGLAS MD-11F *(Josh Rawlin)*

GEMINI AIR CARGO

IATA: GR   **ICAO:** GCO   **IATA/ARC:** 358   **RADIO:** *Gemini*

CONTACTS

Mail
44965 Aviation Drive, Suite 300
Dulles, VA 20166-6254

Telephone/Fax
Admin: +1 703 260 8100
Fax: +1 703 260 8102

Internet: www.gac-cargo.com

OPERATION

Type: Domestic/Flag passenger/cargo
Areas served: Operates aircraft for dedicated freight services on behalf of other carriers

HISTORY/STRUCTURE

Founded: 1995
Start date: October 24, 1996
President: Bill Stockbridge
Ownership: Closely held

FLEET

Type	No	Engines
DC-10-30F	12	GE CF6-50C2
MD-11F	4	GE CF6-80C2D1F

RAYTHEON BEECH 1900D *(Dick Jordan)*

GREAT LAKES AIRLINES

IATA: ZK   **ICAO:** GLA   **IATA/ARC:** 846   **RADIO:** *Lakes Air*

CONTACTS

Mail
1022 Airport Parkway
Cheyenne, WY 82001

Telephone/Fax
Admin: +1 307 432 7000
Fax: +1 307 432 7001

Internet: www.greatlakesav.com

OPERATION

Type: Domestic/Flag passenger/cargo
Cities served: AIA ALO ALS AMA BFF BKX BRL CDR CEZ CNY COD COS
CPR CYS DBQ DDC DEC DEN DIK DVL EAR FMN GCC GCK GRI GUC HDN
HON HYS IMT ISN IWD JMS LAR LBF LBL MBL MCK MKG MSP OFK ORD
OSH PGA PHX PIR PUB RIW RKS SAF SHR SLN TEX VEL WRL
Additional cities served on cargo services for US Postal Service. All passenger
flights use UA flight numbers (6300-6729)(as United partner) and F9 flight
numbers (Frontier code-share)
FFP: United Mileage Plus

HISTORY/STRUCTURE

Founded: April 5, 1977 (as Spirit Lake Airways)
Start date: October 12, 1981
President/CEO: Douglas G Voss
Ownership: Great Lakes Aviation (NASDAQ: GLUX)

FLEET

Type	No	Seats	Engines
Beech 1900C	4	Freighter	PWC PT6A-65B
Beech 1900D	40	Y19	PWC PT6A-67D
EMB-120ER/RT Brasília	8	Y30	PWC PW118/118A

FAIRCHILD DORNIER 328-300 (328JET) *(Dick Jordan)*

GREAT PLAINS AIRLINES (Ozark Air Lines dba)

IATA: ZO   **ICAO:** OZR   **IATA/ARC:** 507   **RADIO:** *Ozark*

CONTACTS

Mail
6501 E Apache St
Tulsa OK 74115

Telephone/Fax
Admin: +1 918 835 3500
Fax: +1 918 835 2353
Res: 1 866 929 8646

Internet: www.gpair.com

OPERATION

Type: Domestic passenger/cargo
Cities served: ABQ BNA COS OKC TUL
Code-share: Rio Grande Air
FFP: The Flying Buffalo Club

HISTORY/STRUCTURE

Founded: 1999 (as Ozark Air Lines)
Start date: April 6, 2001
President/CEO: Jim Swartz
Ownership: Great Plains Airline Holding Co

FLEET

Type	No	Seats	Engines
Fairchild Dornier 328JET	2	Y32	PWC PW306B

BEECH 1900C-1 AIRLINER *(Dick Jordan)*

GULFSTREAM INTERNATIONAL AIRLINES

IATA: 3M   **ICAO:** GFT   **IATA/ARC:** 449   **RADIO:** *Gulf Flight*

CONTACTS

Mail
1815 Griffin Road, Suite 400
Dania, FL 33004

Internet: www.gulfstreamair.com

Telephone/Fax
Admin: +1 954 266 3000
Fax: +1 954 266 3030
Res: 1 800 525 0280

OPERATION

Type: Domestic/Flag passenger/cargo
Cities served: US: EYW FLL MCO MIA PBI RSW TPA **Caribbean:** ELH FPO
MHH NAS TCB
All service operated as Continental Express using CO (9120-9516) flight
numbers. Some flights also use United, Northwest, or COPA Panamá flight
numbers; a Boeing 737-300 is wet-leased from Continental for MIA-HAV charter
service
FFP: Continental OnePass, Northwest WorldPerks, United Mileage Plus

HISTORY/STRUCTURE

Founded: October 1988
Start date: December 1, 1990
President/CEO: Thomas L Cooper
Ownership: G-Air Holdings Corp

FLEET

Type	No	Seats	Engines
Beech 1900C	7	Y19	PWC PT6A-65B
Beech 1900D	25	Y19	PWC PT6A-67D

BOEING 717-200 *(Stephen L Griffin)*

HAWAIIAN AIRLINES

IATA: HA   **ICAO**: HAL   **IATA/ARC:** 173   **RADIO:** *Hawaiian*

CONTACTS

Mail
PO Box 30008
Honolulu, HI 96820

Internet: www.hawaiianair.com

Telephone/Fax
Admin: +1 808 835 3700
Fax: +1 808 835 3690
Res: 1 800 367 5320
PR: +1 808 838 6778

OPERATION

Type: Domestic/Flag passenger/cargo
Cities served: US: HNL ITO KOA LAS LAX LIH LNY MKK OGG PDX SAN SEA SFO **Oceania:** PPG PPT
Code-share: American Eagle
FFP: AAdvantage, HawaiianMiles, Continental OnePass, Northwest WorldPerks

HISTORY/STRUCTURE

Founded: January 30, 1929 (as Inter-Island Airways)
Start date: November 11, 1929
Chairman: John Adams   **President/CEO:** Robert W Zoller Jr
Ownership: public (AMEX: HA)

FLEET

Type	No	Seats	Engines
Boeing 717-200	13	F8Y115	BR BR715
DC-10-10	10	F34Y270	GE CF6-6K
DC-10-30	5	F34Y265	GE CF6-50C2
Boeing 767-300ER	3	F18Y234	PW4000
Ordered			
Boeing 767-300ER	13		

NOTES

Hawaiian Airlines and Aloha Airgroup propose to merge in 2002 under the umbrella of Aloha Holdings; Hawaiian will be the operating name

BOMBARDIER CRJ700 (CL-600-2C10) *(Ben Wang)*

HORIZON AIR

IATA: QX   **ICAO**: QXE   **IATA/ARC**: 481   **RADIO**: *Horizon Air*

CONTACTS

Mail
PO Box 48309
Seattle, WA 98148

Internet: www.horizonair.com

Telephone/Fax
Admin: +1 206 241 6757
Fax: +1 206 431 4696
Res: 1 800 547 9308
PR: +1 206 431 4672

OPERATION

Type: Domestic/Flag passenger/cargo
Cities served: US: ACV ALW BIL BLI BOI BTM BZN CLM DEN EAT EUG FAT FCA GEG GTF HLN IDA LAX LMT LWS MFR MSO MWH OTH PDT PDX PIH PSC PUW RDD RDM SAN SEA SJC SMF SUN TUS YKM (seasonal: PSP)
Canada: YEG YLW YVR YYC YYJ
Operates as an Alaska Airlines Commuter using AS (2001-2599) flight numbers, and partners with American, Canadian, Continental, and Northwest
FFP: AAdvantage, Alaska Airlines Mileage Plan, Continental OnePass, Northwest WorldPerks

HISTORY/STRUCTURE

Founded: May 1981   **Start date:** September 1, 1981
CEO: Jeff Pinneo
Ownership: Horizon Air Industries/Alaska Air Group

FLEET

Type	No	Seats	Engines
DHC-8-102	9	Y37	PWC PW120A
DHC-8-202	28	Y37	PWC PW123D
DHC-8-401	10	Y70	PWC PW150A
Bombardier CRJ700	5	Y68	GE CF34-8C1
Fokker F28 Mk 4000	18	Y69	RR Spey 555-15P
Ordered			
DHC-8-400	5		
Bombardier CRJ700	25		

BOMBARDIER DHC-8-102 DASH 8 *(Stephen L Griffin)*

ISLAND AIR (Aloha Islandair dba)

IATA: WP   **ICAO:** PRI   **IATA/ARC:** 347   **RADIO:** *Princeville*

CONTACTS

Mail
99 Kapalulu Place
Honolulu, HI 96819

Internet: www.islandair.com

Telephone/Fax
Admin: +1 808 833 7108
Fax: +1 808 833 5498
Res: 1 800 323 3345

OPERATION

Type: Domestic passenger/cargo
Cities served: HNL HNM ITO JHM KOA LNY MKK OGG
All service operated for Aloha using only AQ (1100-1699) flight numbers
FFP: AlohaPass

HISTORY/STRUCTURE

Founded: 1980 (as Princeville Airways)
Start date: September 9, 1980
President: Neil M Takekawa
Ownership: Aloha Airgroup

FLEET

Type	No	Seats	Engines
DHC-6-300	2	Y18	PWC PT6A-27
DHC-8-102	4	Y37	PWC PW120A

AIRBUS A320-232 *(Ian Bowley)*

JETBLUE AIRWAYS

IATA: B6   **ICAO**: JBU   **IATA/ARC**: 279   **RADIO**: *JetBlue*

CONTACTS

Mail
80-02 Kew Gardens Road
Kew Gardens, NY 11415-3600

Internet: www.jetblue.com

Telephone/Fax
Admin: +1 718 286 7900
Fax: +1 718 286 4110
Res: 1 800 538 2583
Job hotline: +1 718 286 4130

OPERATION

Type: Domestic passenger/cargo
Cities served: US: BTV BUF DEN FLL IAD LGB MCO MSY JFK OAK ONT PBI ROC RSW SEA SLC SYR TPA **Caribbean:** SJU

HISTORY/STRUCTURE

Founded: February 1999 (as New Air)
Start date: February 11, 2000
CEO: David Neeleman
President: David Barger
Ownership: Closely held

FLEET

Type	No	Seats	Engines
Airbus A320-200	22	Y162	IAE V2527-A5
Ordered			
Airbus A320	62 + 49 options		

BOEING 747-100 (F) *(Gary Tahir)*

KALITTA AIR

IATA: none   **ICAO:** CKS   **IATA/ARC:** none   **RADIO:** *Connie*

CONTACTS

Mail
818 Willow Run Airport
Ypsilanti, MI 48198

Telephone/Fax
Admin: +1 734 484 0088
Fax: +1 734 544 5008

Internet: www.kalittair.com

OPERATION

Type: Supplemental cargo
Areas served: Worldwide ad hoc cargo charters and ACMI services

HISTORY/STRUCTURE

Founded: 2000
Start date: November 2000
President: Doyle Sanderlin
Ownership: Conrad A Kalitta

FLEET

Type	No	Engines
Boeing 727-200F	3	PW JT8D-9A
Boeing 747-100F	2	PW JT9D-7A
Boeing 747-200F	2	PW JT9D-7F/-7J

BOEING 727-200 (F) *(Steven J Pinnow)*

KITTY HAWK AIRCARGO

IATA: KR   **ICAO:** KHA   **IATA/ARC:** none   **RADIO:** *Kitty Hawk*

CONTACTS

Mail
PO Box 612787
Dallas/Ft Worth Airport, TX 75261

Telephone/Fax
Admin: +1 972 456 6000
Fax: +1 972 456 2277

Internet: www.kha.com

OPERATION

Type: Supplemental cargo
Cities served: (Kitty Hawk Aircargo) **US:** ATL AUS BDL BNA BOS BWI CLT
DEN DFW ELP EWR FWA HSV IAH LAX MCI MCO MFE MSP OAK PDX PHL
PHX ROC SEA TUS **Canada:** YYZ **Caribbean:** SJU **México:** GDL
Operates contract charters for several forwarders in the US, such as BAX Global

HISTORY/STRUCTURE

Founded: 1976 (as Kitty Hawk Airways)
Start date: 1985
President/CEO: Tilmon Reeves
Ownership: Kitty Hawk Group (NASDAQ: KTTEQ)

FLEET

Type	No	Engines
Boeing 727-200F	34	PW JT8D-9/-9A/-15/-15A

LOCKHEED 382G (L-100-30) HERCULES *(James Helbock)*

LYNDEN AIR CARGO

IATA: L2   **ICAO:** LYC   **IATA/ARC:** 344   **RADIO:** *Lynden*

CONTACTS

Mail
6441 South Airpark Place
Anchorage, AK 99502

Telephone/Fax
Admin: +1 907 243 0215
Fax: +1 907 245 0213

Internet: www.lac.lynden.com

OPERATION

Type: Supplemental Cargo
Cities served: ANC BET DLG OME OTZ

HISTORY/STRUCTURE

Founded: 1995
Start date: August 31, 1995
President: Mike Hart
Ownership: Lynden Inc

FLEET

Type	No	Engines
L-100-30	5	Allison 501-D13A

EMBRAER EMB-145LR *(George Hamlin)*

MESA AIRLINES

IATA: YV   **ICAO:** ASH   **IATA/ARC:** 533   **RADIO:** *Air Shuttle*

CONTACTS

Mail
410 North 44th Street
Suite 700
Phoenix, AZ 85008

Internet: www.mesa-air.com

Telephone/Fax

Admin:	+1 602 685 4000
Fax:	+1 602 685 4350
Res:	1 800 637 2247 (Mesa)

OPERATION

Type: Domestic passenger/cargo
Cities served: America West Express: US: ASE BFL BOI BUR CLD CMH COS DCA DFW DRO ELP EUG FAT FLG GJT LAX LGA LGB MRY ORD PHX PSP SAT SBA SBP SJC TUS YUM (seasonal: RSW MTJ) **México:** GDL GYM HMO   **Frontier JetExpress:** DEN ONT SJC STL **US Airways Express: US:** ATL BHM BNA BTR BTV CAE CAK CHA CHS CLE CLT CMH CRW CVG DCA ELM GRR GSP HSV IND JAN JAX LEX LIT MGM MOB MSP PHL PWM RIC ROA RDU SBN SDF STL SYR TYS XNA (seasonal: ACK MVY) **Canada:** YUL
FFP: America West FlightFund, US Airways Dividend Miles

HISTORY/STRUCTURE

Founded: 1980
Start date: October 12, 1980
Chairman/CEO: Jonathan Orenstein
Ownership: Mesa Air Group (NASDAQ: MESA)

FLEET

Type	No	Seats	Engines
DHC-8-202	12	Y36	PWC PW123D
EMBRAER ERJ 145LR	23	Y50	GM AE30071/2
Bombardier CRJ200ER	32	Y50	GE CF34-3B1
Ordered			
EMBRAER ERJ 145	13		
Bombardier CRJ700	20		
Bombardier CRJ900	20		

BRITISH AEROSPACE BAe 146-200A (AVRO RJ85) *(Norbert Raith)*

MESABA AIRLINES (Mesaba Aviation dba)

IATA: XJ   **ICAO:** MES   **IATA/ARC:** 582   **RADIO:** *Mesaba*

CONTACTS

Mail
7501 26th Avenue South
Minneapolis, MN 55450

Internet: www.mesaba.com

Telephone/Fax
Admin: +1 612 726 5151
Fax: +1 612 726 1568
PR: +1 612 725 4915

OPERATION

Type: Domestic/Flag passenger/cargo
Cities served: US: ABE ABR ALO APN ATW ATY AZO BEH BGM BHM BIS BJI
BMI BRD BTR BUF CAK CID CIU CLE CLT CMH CMI CMX CRW CVG CWA
DAY DBQ DLH DSM DTW EAU ELM ERI EVV FAR FNT FOD FSD FWA GFK
GPT GPZ GRB HIB HPN HSV INL LAF LAN LEX LNK LSE MBS MCW MDT
MEM MKG MLI MQT MSN MSP OMA PIA PIR PIT PLN PWM RAP RHI ROA
ROC RST SBN SCE SDF STC STL SUX TOL TVC TVF TYS XNA YNG
(seasonal: ASE LYU) **Canada:** YOW YQT YUL YWG YXU (seasonal: YQK)
All service operated as Northwest Airlink and using only NW (2700-3699) flight
numbers. Some flights additionally code-share with Continental
FFP: Northwest WorldPerks

HISTORY/STRUCTURE

Founded: 1944 (as Mesaba Aviation)
Start date: February 4, 1973
President/CEO: Paul Foley
Ownership: Mesaba Holdings (NASDAQ: MAIR)

FLEET

Type	No	Seats	Engines
SAAB 340A	24	Y30	GE CT7-5A2
SAAB 340B	50	Y34	GE CT7-9B
Avro RJ85	36	F16Y53	LY LF507-1F
Ordered			
SAAB 340B	11	(ex-Express Airlines I)	

BOEING 737-800 *(Carlos Aleman)*

MIAMI AIR INTERNATIONAL

IATA: none **ICAO:** BSK **IATA/ARC:** none **RADIO:** *Biscayne*

CONTACTS

Mail
PO Box 660880
Miami, FL 33266-0880

Telephone/Fax
Admin: +1 305 876 3600
Quest Cargo: +1 305 870 1800
Fax: +1 305 871 4222

Email: marketing@miamiair.com
Internet: www.miamiair.com

OPERATION

Type: Domestic/Flag passenger/cargo
Cargo charters operate as Quest Cargo International (QCI)

HISTORY/STRUCTURE

Founded: August 1990
Start date: October 15, 1991
Chairman: Jim Crane
President & CEO: D Ross Fischer
Ownership: Fischer and employees (18%), Eagle Global Logistics consortium

---

FLEET

Type	No	Seats	Engines
Boeing 737-800	2	Y173	CFMI CFM56-7B26
Boeing 727-200	4	Y172	PW JT8D-15
Boeing 727-200F	4	Freighter	PW JT8D-15/-15A
Ordered			
Boeing 737-800	4		

BOEING 737-700 *(Ian Bowley)*

MIDWAY AIRLINES

IATA: JI   **ICAO**: MDW   **IATA/ARC**: 878   **RADIO**: *Midway*

CONTACTS

Mail
2801 Slater Road, Suite 200
Morrisville, NC 27560

Internet: www.midwayair.com

Telephone/Fax
Admin: +1 919 595 6000
Fax: +1 919 595 6480
Res: 1 800 446 4392

OPERATION

Type: Domestic/Flag passenger/cargo
Cities served: BOS DCA EWR FLL JAX LGA MCO RDU TPA
FFP: Midway Airlines FFP

HISTORY/STRUCTURE

Founded: 1993
Start date: November 15, 1993
President: Robert Ferguson
Ownership: public (NASDAQ: MDWYQ)

FLEET

Type	No	Seats	Engines	
Boeing 737-700	5	F8Y118	CFMI CFM56-7B22	

McDONNELL DOUGLAS MD-88 *(Gary Jennings)*

MIDWEST EXPRESS AIRLINES

IATA: YX   **ICAO:** MEP   **IATA/ARC:** 453   **RADIO:** *Midex*

CONTACTS

Mail
6744 South Howell Avenue
Oak Creek, WI 53154-1402

Telephone/Fax
Admin: +1 414 570 4000
Fax: +1 414 570 0199
Res: 1 800 452 2022
PR: +1 414 570 3640

Internet: www.midwestexpress.com

OPERATION

Type: Domestic passenger/cargo
Cities served: US: ATL ATW BDL BOS DCA DEN DFW EWR IAD LAS LAX LGA MCI MCO MKE MSN MSY OMA PHL PHX SAT (seasonal: FLL RSW SFO TPA)
Code-share: Air Midwest, American Eagle, Skyway Airlines
FFP: Midwest Express Frequent Flyer

HISTORY/STRUCTURE

Founded: 1983
Start date: April 29, 1984
President/CEO: Timothy E Hoeksema
Ownership: Midwest Express Holdings (NYSE: MEH)

FLEET

Type	No	Seats	Engines
DC-9-14/15	8	F60	PW JT8D-7B
DC-9-30	16	F84	PW JT8D-7B/-9A
MD-81	8	F116	PW JT8D-209/-217C
MD-82	3	F116	PW JT8D-217C
MD-88	2	F112	PW JT8D-219
Ordered			
Boeing 717-200	20		

BOEING 757-200 *(Gary Jennings)*

NATIONAL AIRLINES

IATA: N7   **ICAO:** ROK   **IATA/ARC:** 007   **RADIO:** *Red Rock*

CONTACTS

Mail
PO Box 26598
Las Vegas, NV 89126-6598

Internet: www.nationalairlines.com

Telephone/Fax
Admin: +1 702 944 2800
Fax: +1 702 944 2947
Res: 1 888 757 5387
PR: +1 702 944 2777

OPERATION

Type: Domestic passenger/cargo
Cities served: DCA DFW EWR JFK LAS LAX MDW MIA ORD PHL SFO

HISTORY/STRUCTURE

Founded: April 1995
Start date: May 27, 1999
President/CEO: Michael J Conway
Ownership: Closely held

FLEET

Type	No	Seats	Engines
Boeing 757-200	15	F22Y153	RR RB211-535E4

NOTES

Filed Chapter 11 bankruptcy protection in December 2000; its planned reorganization for 2002 includes 737-300s

BOEING 757-200 *(Jonathan W Holmes)*

NORTH AMERICAN AIRLINES

IATA: XG   **ICAO: NAO**   **IATA/ARC:** 455   **RADIO:** *North American*

CONTACTS

Mail
Suite 250 Building 75
North Hangar Road
JFK International Airport
Jamaica, NY 11430

Telephone/Fax
Admin: +1 718 656 2650
Fax: +1 718 995 3372

Internet: www.northamair.com

OPERATION

Type: Domestic/Flag passenger/cargo
Areas served: Worldwide charters including US sub-services for El Al.
Scheduled charters to Borinquen, Guyana, and Santo Domingo

HISTORY/STRUCTURE

Founded: 1989
Start date: January 20, 1990
President/CEO: Dan McKinnon
Ownership: Dan McKinnon (75.1%), El Al (24.9%)

FLEET

Type	No	Seats	Engines
Boeing 737-800	2	Y169 or C20Y139	CFMI CFM56-7B26
Boeing 757-200	4	Y215 or C24Y179	RR RB211-535E4

DOUGLAS DC-6A (C-118A) *(Gary Jennings)*

NORTHERN AIR CARGO

IATA: HU   **ICAO:** NAC   **IATA/ARC:** 345   **RADIO:** *Northern Air Cargo*

CONTACTS

Mail
3900 West International Airport
Anchorage, AK 99502

Telephone/Fax
Admin: +1 907 243 3545
Fax: +1 907 249 5190

Internet: www.nacargo.com

OPERATION

Type: Supplemental cargo
Cities served: ADQ ANC ANI BET BRW DLG FAI GAL ILI KSM MCG OME OTZ RDB SCC SNP STG UNK

HISTORY/STRUCTURE

Founded: 1956 (as Sholton & Carlson Inc)
Start date: 1956
CEO: Rita Sholton
President: Marjorie McLaren
Ownership: Sholton family

FLEET

Type	No	Engines
DC-6A/B	6	PW R-2800-CB16
Boeing 727-100F	3	PW JT8D-7B

AIRBUS A320-212 *(John Wegg)*

NORTHWEST AIRLINES

IATA: NW   **ICAO:** NWA   **IATA/ARC:** 012   **RADIO:** *Northwest*

CONTACTS

Mail
5101 Northwest Drive
St Paul, MN 55111-3034

Internet: www.nwa.com

Telephone/Fax	
Admin:	+1 612 726 2111
Fax:	+1 612 726 6599
Res:	1 800 225 2525
PR:	+1 612 726 2331
Job Hot Line:	+1 612 727 7450

OPERATION

Type: Domestic/Flag passenger/cargo
Hubs: AMS DTW MEM MSP NRT
Cities served: US: ABE ABQ ALB ANC ATL AUS AZO BDL BHM BIL BNA BOI BOS BTR BUF BWI BZN CLE CLT CMH COS CVG DAY DCA DEN DFW DLH DSM DTW EWR FAR FCA FLL FNT FSD GEG GFK GPT GRB GRR GSO GSP GTF HNL HPN IAD IAH ICT IND JAX JFK LAN LAS LAX LGA LIT LSE MBS MCI MCO MDT MDW MEM MHT MIA MKE MOT MSN MSO MSP MSY OKC OMA ONT ORD ORF PBI PDX PHL PHX PIT PVD PWM RAP RDU RIC RNO ROC RST RSW SAN SAT SBN SDF SEA SFO SJC SLC SMF SNA STL SYR TPA TUS TVC VPS (seasonal: EGE FAI HDN PSP SRQ) **Canada:** YEG YUL YQR YVR YWG YXE YYC YYZ **Caribbean:** MBJ SJU (seasonal: GCM POP PUJ SXM) **México:** MEX (seasonal: ACA CUN CZM SJD PVR ZIH) **Central America:** (seasonal: LIR) **Europe:** AMS CDG FCO FRA LGW **Asia:** BKK BOM DEL HKG ICN KHH KIX KUL MNL NGO NRT PEK PVG SIN SPN TPE **Oceania:** GUM
Global alliance: 'Wings'
Code-share: Air China, Alaska, America West, American Eagle, Big Sky, Braathens, Continental, Continental Express, Eurowings, Express Airlines I, Gulfstream International, Hawaiian, Horizon, Japan Air System, KLM, KLM exel, KLM uk, MALÉV, Mesaba, Pacific Island Aviation, Swisswings
FFP: WorldPerks

HISTORY/STRUCTURE

Founded: September 1, 1926 (as Northwest Airways)
Start date: October 1, 1926
CEO: Richard H Anderson   **President:** Douglas Steenland
Ownership: Northwest Airlines Corp (NASDAQ: NWAC)

BOEING 747-200B (F) *(Kazuhiko Kimura)*

FLEET

Type	No	Seats	Engines
DC-9-14/15	9	F14Y64	PW JT8D-7B
DC-9-31/32	113	F16Y84	PW JT8D-7B/-9A/-15
DC-9-41	12	F16Y94	PW JT8D-11
DC-9-51	34	F16Y109	PW JT8D-17
Airbus A319-100	33	F16Y108	CFMI CFM56-5A5
Boeing 727-200	25	F12Y137 or F56	PW JT8D-15/-15A/17/-17R
Airbus A320-200	72	F16Y134	CFMI CFM56-5A1/-5A3
Boeing 757-200	53	F22Y158/Y162	PW2037
DC-10-30	24	C26Y247	GE CF6-50C/-50C2/-50C2B
DC-10-40	13	F42Y256 or F34Y247	PW JT9D-20/-20J
Boeing 747-200	18	C63Y292 or C55Y282 or F22Y412 or C18Y400	PW JT9D-7F/-7Q/-7R4G2
Boeing 747-200F	12	Freighter	PW JT9D-7F/-7Q
Boeing 747-400	14	C41Y338	PW4056
Ordered			
Airbus A319-100	41		
Airbus A320-200	10		
Airbus A330-300	24		
Boeing 757-200	3		
Boeing 757-300	16		
Boeing 747-400	2		

McDONNELL DOUGLAS DC-10-10 *(Josh Rawlin)*

OMNI AIR INTERNATIONAL

IATA: X9   **ICAO:** OAE   **IATA/ARC:** none   **RADIO:** *Omni Express*

CONTACTS

Mail
PO Box 582527
Tulsa, OK 74158

Telephone/Fax
Admin: +1 918 836 5393
Fax: +1 918 834 4850

Internet: www.omniairintl.com

OPERATION

Type: Domestic/Flag passenger/cargo
Areas served: Worldwide

HISTORY/STRUCTURE

Founded: 1983 (as Continental Air Transport)
Start date: March 21, 1984
CEO: Sanford P Burnstein
Ownership: Privately held

FLEET

Type	No	Seats	Engines
DC-10-10	2	Y360	GE CF6-6K
DC-10-30	3	Y370	GE CF6-50C2

BOEING 737-200 *(Flemming Løvenvig)*

PACE AIRLINES (Piedmont Aviation Services dba)

IATA: none   **ICAO:** none   **IATA/ARC:** none   **RADIO:** none

CONTACTS

Mail
PO Box 525
Winston-Salem, NC 27105

Telephone/Fax
Admin: +1 336 776 6100
Fax: +1 336 776 6101

Internet: www.flypiedmont.com/pace/pace.html

OPERATION

Type: Supplemental passenger/cargo
Areas served: US, Canada, Caribbean, South America; contract carrier for Atlanta Hawks/Dallas Mavericks/New York Knicks/New York Rangers sports teams; operations for Patriot Air and Vacation Express

HISTORY/STRUCTURE

Founded: 1940 (as Piedmont Aviation)
Start date: January 2, 1996
President/CEO: Jim A Taylor
Ownership: Piedmont Aviation Services

FLEET

Type	No	Seats	Engines
Boeing 737-200	5*	various	PW JT8D-7B/9A/15A
Boeing 737-300	4**	Y137	CFMI CFM56-3B1
Boeing 737-400	1	executive	CFMI CFM56-3C1
Boeing 757-200	1	executive	RR RB211-535E4

*2 operated for Patriot Air
**operated for Vacation Express

BOEING 727-200 *(John van den Berg)*

PAN AMERICAN AIRWAYS

IATA: PN   **ICAO:** PAA   **IATA/ARC:** none   **RADIO:** *Clipper*

CONTACTS

Mail
14 Aviation Avenue
Pease International Tradeport
Portsmouth, NH 03801

Telephone/Fax
Admin: +1 603 766 2000
Fax: +1 603 766 2094
Fax: 1 800 359 7262

Internet: www.flypanam.com

OPERATION

Type: Domestic/Flag passenger/cargo
Cities served: US: ABE BGR BWI GYY ORH PIE PSM SFB **Caribbean:** FPO
SJU

HISTORY/STRUCTURE

Founded: 1996
Start date: September 26, 1996
President/CEO: David Fink
Ownership: Guilford Transportation

FLEET

Type	No	Seats	Engines
Boeing 727-200	7	Y149	PW JT8D-15/-17/-17R

CESSNA 208 CARAVAN I *(Andreas Rohde)*

PENINSULA AIRWAYS (dba PenAir)

IATA: KS   **ICAO**: PEN   **IATA/ARC**: 339   **RADIO**: *Peninsula*

CONTACTS

Mail
6100 Boeing Avanue
Anchorage, AK 99502

Internet: www.penair.com

Telephone/Fax
Admin: +1 907 243 2485
Fax: +1 907 243 6848
Res: 1 800 448 4226

OPERATION

Type: Domestic/Flag passenger/cargo
Cities served: ADQ ADK AKB AKN ANC ANI BIC BSZ CDB CFA CLP DLG DUT EGX EHM IGG IKO KBW KCL KCQ KEK KGK KKU KLL KMO KNW KQA MCG PCA PFA PIP PML PNF PTH SDP SNP STG TOG TWA UGB UNK WKK WSN
Operates as Alaska Airlines Commuter on selected routes using AS (4200-4399) flight numbers
FFP: Alaska Airlines Mileage Plan

HISTORY/STRUCTURE

Founded: 1955
Start date: 1967 (scheduled service)
President: Orin D Seybert
Ownership: Seybert family

FLEET

Type	No	Seats	Engines
PA-32-301	11	Y5	LY IO-540-K1G5
G-21A Goose	3	Y6	PW R-985
PA-31 Chieftain	4	Y9	LY TIO-540-J2BD
Piper T-1040	1	Y9	PWC PT6A-11
Cessna 208	4	Y9	PWC PT6A-114/-114A
Metro III	4	Y19	GA TPE331-11U-612G
Metro 23	2	Y18	GA TPE331-12U-701G
SAAB 340B	3	Y30	GE CT7-9

BOMBARDIER DHC-8-201 DASH 8 *(Zach Gollman)*

PIEDMONT AIRLINES

IATA: PI   **ICAO:** PDT   **IATA/ARC:** 531   **RADIO:** *Piedmont*

CONTACTS

Mail
5443 Airport Terminal Road
Salisbury, MD 21804-1700

Telephone/Fax
Admin: +1 410 742 2996
Fax: +1 410 742 4069

Internet: www.piedmont-airlines.com

OPERATION

Type: Domestic/Flag passenger/cargo
Cities served: US: AVL BGR BWI CAE CHA CHO CHS CLT CMH CRW CSG
DCA EWN EYW FAY FLO GNV GSO GSP HHH HPN HVN ILM JAX LEX MCO
MGM MHT MIA MYR ORF PBI PHF PHL PIT PNS RDU ROA SBY TLH TPA TRI
TYS **Canada:** YOW YUL YYZ **Caribbean:** ELH GHB MHH TCB
All service operated as US Airways Express using only US (3000-3499) flight
numbers
FFP: US Airways Dividend Miles

HISTORY/STRUCTURE

Founded: 1964 (as Henson Airlines)
Start date: October 1, 1964
President/CEO: John F Leonard
Ownership: US Airways Group

FLEET

Type	No	Seats	Engines
DHC-8-102	37	Y37	PWC PW120A
DHC-8-200	18	Y37	PWC PW123C
DHC-8-300	7	Y50	PWC PW123

BOEING 727-200 *(Gerhard Plomitzer)*

PLANET AIRWAYS

IATA: none   **ICAO**: PLZ   **IATA/ARC**: none   **RADIO**: *Planet*

CONTACTS

Mail
7380 Sand Lake Road, Suite 350
Orlando, FL 32819

Telephone/Fax
Admin: +1 407 363 1800
Fax: +1 407 363 4410

Internet: www.planetairways.com

OPERATION

Type: Supplemental passenger/cargo
Cities served: US, Caribbean, South America

HISTORY/STRUCTURE

Founded: 1997 (as Airship Airways)
Start date: January 6, 2000
CEO: Peter V Garrambone
President: Tony DeCamillis
Ownership: Louis J Pearlman

FLEET

Type	No	Seats	Engines
Boeing 727-100	1	Y128	PW JT8D-7B
Boeing 727-200	3	Y173	PW JT8D-15

BOEING 747-400F *(Steven J Pinnow)*

POLAR AIR CARGO

IATA: PO   **ICAO**: PAC   **IATA/ARC**: 403   **RADIO**: *Polar Tiger*

CONTACTS

Mail
100 Gate Ocean, 15th Floor
Long Beach, CA 90802

Telephone/Fax
Admin: +1 562 436 7471
Fax: +1 562 436 9333
PR: +1 562 528 7317

Internet: www.polaraircargo.com

OPERATION

Type: Domestic/Flag passenger/cargo
Cities served: US: ANC ATL HNL JFK LAX MIA ORD **South America:** MAO SCL VCP **Europe:** AMS GOT PIK **Asia:** HKG ICN NRT **Oceania:** AKL NAN SYD

HISTORY/STRUCTURE

Founded: June 1990
Start date: July 1994
CEO: Jim Jenson
Ownership: Atlas Air Worldwide Holdings

FLEET

Type	No	Engines
Boeing 747-100F	4	PW JT9D-7A
Boeing 747-200F	5	PW JT9D-7Q
Boeing 747-400F	4	GE CF6-80C2B1F
Ordered		
Boeing 747-400F	1	

FAIRCHILD DORNIER 328-110 *(Gary Tahir)*

PSA AIRLINES

IATA: none **ICAO:** JIA **IATA/ARC:** none **RADIO:** *Blue Streak*

CONTACTS

Mail
3400 Terminal Drive
Vandalia, OH 45377-1041

Telephone/Fax
Admin: +1 937 454 1116
Fax: +1 937 264 3910

Internet: www.psaairlines.com

OPERATION

Type: Domestic/flag passenger/cargo
Cities served: US: AZO BNA BTV CAE CAK CHA CHS CLE CLT CRW CVG DAY DCA DTW ELM EVV GRR GSP LAN LEX PHL PIT PWM RDU RIC ROA ROC SBN SDF STL TRI TYS **Canada:** YOW YUL YYZ
Alll service operated as US Airways Express using only US (4000-4199) flight numbers
FFP: US Airways Dividend Miles

HISTORY/STRUCTURE

Founded: 1969 (as Vee Neal Airlines)
Start date: May 19, 1980 (renamed Jetstream International December 1, 1983)
President/CEO: Richard Pfenning
Ownership: US Airways Group

FLEET

Type	No	Seats	Engines
Dornier 328-110	25	Y31/32	PWC PW119B

DOUGLAS DC-9-15F *(Winfried Giese)*

RELIANT AIRLINES

IATA: none   **ICAO:** RLT   **IATA/ARC:** none   **RADIO:** *Reliant*

CONTACTS

Mail
827 Willow Run Airport
Ypsilanti, MI 48198-0899

Telephone/Fax
Admin: +1 734 483 3616
Fax: +1 734 484 9808

Internet: www.reliantairlines.com

OPERATION

Type: Supplemental cargo
Areas served: North America, Central America, Caribbean

HISTORY/STRUCTURE

Founded: April 1984
Start date: June 1984
President: Reese Zantop
Ownership: ESOP

FLEET

Type	No	Seats	Engines
Falcon 10	1	F7	GA TFE731-2-1C
Falcon 20	12	Freighter	GE CF700-2D2
DC-9-15F	4	Freighter	PW JT8D-7B

AIRBUS A320-231 *(Steven J Pinnow)*

RYAN INTERNATIONAL AIRLINES

IATA: 1I   **ICAO:** RYN   **IATA/ARC:** none   **RADIO:** *Ryan*

CONTACTS

Mail
266 North Main Street
Wichita, KS 67202-1504

Telephone/Fax
Admin: +1 316 265 7400
Fax: +1 316 293 1449

Internet: www.flyryan.com

OPERATION

Type: Supplemental passenger/cargo
Areas served: 737-200 aircraft operated for Gold Transportation; operates for
Transglobal Vacations during northern winter and JMC Air in summer seasons;
operates for Apple Vacations West; DC-10s operate for SunTrips

HISTORY/STRUCTURE

Founded: 1973
Start date: March 3, 1973
President/CEO: Ronald D Ryan
Ownership: Ryan Aviation Corp

FLEET

Type	No	Seats	Engines
Boeing 737-200	2	Y130	PW JT8D-9A
Boeing 737-400	3	Y156	CFMI CFM56-3B2
Boeing 727-100F	4	Freighter	PW JT8D-7B
Boeing 727-200F	11	Freighter	PW JT8D-7B/-15
Boeing 727-200	1	Y170	PW JT8D-9A
Airbus A320	6*	Y180	CFMI CFM56-5B4/P or IAE V2500-A1
Boeing 757-200	2*	Y235	RR RB211-535E4
DC-10-10	2	Y380	GE CF6-6D

*leased from JMC Air

FOKKER F27 MK 200 FRIENDSHIP *(Ben Wang)*

SCENIC AIRLINES (Eagle Canyon Airlines dba)

IATA: YR   **ICAO**: YRR   **IATA/ARC**: 398   **RADIO**: *Scenic*

CONTACTS

Mail
2705 Airport Drive
North Las Vegas, NV 89032

Telephone/Fax
Admin: +1 702 638 3200
Fax: +1 702 638 3255
Res: 1 800 634 6801

Internet: www.scenic.com

OPERATION

Type: Domestic passenger/cargo
Cities served: ELY GCN LAS MCE

HISTORY/STRUCTURE

Founded: 1967
Start date: June 1967
President: Norman Freeman
Ownership: Eagle Group

FLEET

Type	No	Seats	Engines
Cessna 402	2	Y9	CO TSIO-520-E
Beech 1900C	1*	Y19	PWC PT6A-65B
DHC-6-300	12	Y19	PWC PT6A-27
Fokker F27 Mk 200/600	3*	Y44	RR Dart 532-7R
Fokker F27 Mk 500	2*	Y48	RR Dart 532-7R

* operated by Eagle Jet Charter dba Eagle Air/Air Laughlin Tours/Scenic Airlines

BOMBARDIER DHC-8-102 DASH 8 *(Ron Peel)*

SHUTTLE AMERICA

IATA: S5   **ICAO:** TCF   **IATA/ARC:** none   **RADIO:** *Shuttlecraft*

CONTACTS

Mail
334 Ella Grasso Turnpike
Windsor Locks, CT 06096

Internet: www.shuttleamerica.com

Telephone/Fax
Admin: +1 860 386 4200
Fax: +1 860 386 4266
Res: 1 888 999 3273

OPERATION

Type: Domestic passenger/cargo
Cities served: BED BNA CLE HPM IND IPT LEX LGA LYH MDT PHL PIT ROA SDF TOL TTN
All service operated as US Airways Express using only US flight numbers

HISTORY/STRUCTURE

Founded: 1995
Start date: November 12, 1998
CEO: Scott Hackett
Ownership: Wexford Management

FLEET

Type	No	Seats	Engines
SAAB 340A	3	Y30	GE CT7-5A2
DHC-8-102	3	Y37	PWC PW120A
Ordered			
SAAB 340A	10 from Chautauqua		

BOEING 737-200 *(Joe G Walker)*

SIERRA PACIFIC AIRLINES

IATA: SI   **ICAO:** SPA   **IATA/ARC:** none   **RADIO:** *Sierra Pacific*

CONTACTS

Mail
7700 North Business Park Drive
Tucson, AZ 85743

Telephone/Fax
Admin: +1 520 744 1144
Fax: +1 520 744 0138

OPERATION

Type: Domestic/Flag passenger/cargo; operates for US Forest Service (USFS) &
US Department of Justice Prisoner and Alien Transportation System (JPATS)

HISTORY/STRUCTURE

Founded: 1976 (as Mountainwest Aviation)
Start date: February 1976
President: Gar M Thorsrud
Ownership: Sierra Pacific Corp

FLEET

Type	No	Seats	Engines
Boeing 737-200	2	Y122	PW JT8D-17

FAIRCHILD DORNIER 328-300 (328JET) *(Fairchild Dornier)*

SKYWAY AIRLINES (Astral Aviation dba)

IATA: AL   **ICAO**: SYX   **IATA/ARC**: none   **RADIO**: *Skyway Ex*

CONTACTS

Mail
1190 West Rawson Avenue
Oak Creek, WI 53154

Telephone/Fax
Admin: +1 414 570 2300
Fax: +1 414 570 1441

Internet: www.midwestexpress.com

OPERATION

Type: Domestic passenger/cargo
Cities served: US: ATW BNA BWI CLE CMH CVG CWA DAY DCA DSM ESC FNT GRB GRR IAD IND LAN LSE MLI MKE MKG MSN MSP MQT OMA PIT RDU SDF STL **Canada:** YYZ
All service operated as Midwest Express Connection using only YX (1000-2500) flight numbers
FFP: Midwest Express Frequent Flyer

HISTORY/STRUCTURE

Founded: 1993
Start date: February 3, 1994
President: James Rankin
Ownership: Astral Aviation (subsidiary Midwest Express Holdings)

FLEET

Type	No	Seats	Engines
Beech 1900D	15	Y19	PWC PT6A-67D
Fairchild Dornier 328JET	8	Y32	PWC PW306B
Ordered			
EMBRAER ERJ 140	20		
Fairchild Dornier 328JET	4		

EMBRAER EMB-120ER BRASÍLIA *(Joe G Walker)*

SKYWEST AIRLINES

IATA: OO   **ICAO:** SKW   **IATA/ARC:** 302   **RADIO:** *Skywest*

CONTACTS

Mail
444 South River Road
St George, UT 84790

Telephone/Fax
Admin: +1 435 634 3000
Fax: +1 435 634 3505
PR: +1 435 634 3522

Internet: www.skywest.com

OPERATION

Type: Domestic passenger/cargo
Cities served: Delta Connection: US: ABQ AUS BHM BIL BNA BOI BTM BZN CDC COD COS CPR DSM EKO ELP EUG FAT GEG GJT GSO HLN IAH ICT IDA JAC LAS MCI MOB MSO MSP OAK OKC OMA ONT PHX PIH PSC PSP RAP RNO SGU SJC SLC SMF SNA SUN TLH TUL TUS TWF (seasonal: WYS) **Canada:** YVR YYC **United Express: US:** ACV BFL BOI CEC CIC CLD COS DEN DRO EUG FAT GCT IPL IYK LAX MFR MOD MRY MTJ OAK ONT OXR PDX PHX PSC PSP RAP RDD RDM SAN SBP SEA SFO SJC SMF SMX SNA TUS VIS YUM **Canada:** YVR YYJ
All service operated as Delta Connection using DL (3400-3999) flight numbers or United Express using UA (5400-5499, 6800-7019, 7900-7999) flight numbers
FFP: Delta SkyMiles, United Mileage Plus

HISTORY/STRUCTURE

Founded: 1972
Start date: June 19, 1972
President/CEO: Jerry C Atkin
Ownership: SkyWest Inc (NASDAQ: SKYW)

FLEET

Type	No	Seats	Engines
EMB-120ER Brasília	89	Y30	PWC PW118A
Bombardier CRJ100LR	24*	Y50	GE CF34-3A1
Bombardier CRJ200LR	26	Y50	GE CF34-3B1
*15 leased from Comair			
Ordered			
Bombardier CRJ200LR	69 + 29 conditional		

McDONNELL DOUGLAS DC-9-82 (MD-82) *(Dick Jordan)*

SOUTHEAST AIRLINES
(Sun Jet International dba)

IATA: JX   **ICAO:** SNK   **IATA/ARC:** none   **RADIO:** *Sun King*

CONTACTS

Mail
12552 Belcher Road South
Largo, FL 33773

Telephone/Fax
Admin: +1 727 532 1632
Fax: +1 727 530 1515
Res: 1 800 359 7325

Internet: www.flyseal.com

OPERATION

Type: Supplemental passenger/cargo
Areas served: US, Caribbean, México
Cities served: EWR PIE (scheduled)

HISTORY/STRUCTURE

Founded: 1993 (as Sun Jet International Airlines)
Start date: July 1993
President: P Thomas Kolfenbach
Ownership: Privately held

FLEET

Type	No	Seats	Engines
DC-9-32	6	Y110 or F56	PW JT8D-9A
MD-82	2	Y165	PW JT8D-217
MD-88	2	Y165	PW JT8D-219

BOEING 747-200B (F) *(James Helbock)*

SOUTHERN AIR

IATA: 9S   **ICAO:** SOO   **IATA/ARC:** none   **RADIO:** *Southern Air*

CONTACTS

Mail
PO Box 32485
Columbus, OH 43232

Telephone/Fax
Admin: +1 614 759 5000
Fax: +1 614 759 7011

OPERATION

Type: Supplemental cargo
Areas served: Worldwide ad hoc charter and ACMI contract services

HISTORY/STRUCTURE

Founded: 1999
Start date: December 1999
CEO: Thomas A Gillies
Ownership: Privately held

FLEET

Type	No	Engines
Boeing 747-200F	3	GE CF6-50E2

BOEING 737-700 *(Kevin Cook)*

SOUTHWEST AIRLINES

IATA: WN **ICAO:** SWA **IATA/ARC:** 526 **RADIO:** *Southwest*

CONTACTS

Mail
PO Box 36611
Dallas, TX 75235-1611

Internet: www.southwest.com

Telephone/Fax
Admin: +1 214 904 4000
Fax: +1 214 904 5097
Res: 1 800 435 9792
PR: +1 214 792 4847
Job hotline: +1 214 904 4803

OPERATION

Type: Domestic passenger/cargo
Cities served: ALB ABQ AMA AUS BDL BHM BNA BOI BUF BUR BWI CLE
CMH CRP DAL DTW ELP FLL GEG HOU HRL IAH IND ISP JAN JAX LAS LAX
LBB LIT MAF MCO MDW MCI MHT MSY OAK OKC OMA ONT ORF PBI PDX
PHX PVD RDU RNO SAN SAT SDF SEA SJC SLC SMF SNA STL TPA TUL
TUS
FFP: Rapid Rewards

HISTORY/STRUCTURE

Founded: 1967
CEO: Jim Parker
Ownership: Publicly traded company (NYSE: LUV)

Start date: June 18, 1971
President: Colleen C Barrett

FLEET

Type	No	Seats	Engines
Boeing 737-200	32	Y122	PW JT8D-9A/-15
Boeing 737-500	25	Y122	CFMI CFM56-3B1
Boeing 737-300	194	Y137	CFMI CFM56-3B1
Boeing 737-700	117	Y137	CFMI CFM56-7
Ordered			
Boeing 737-700	119		

McDONNELL DOUGLAS DC-9-82 (MD-82) *(Dave Campbell)*

SPIRIT AIRLINES

IATA: NK   **ICAO:** NKS   **IATA/ARC:** 487   **RADIO:** *Spirit Wings*

CONTACTS

Mail
2800 Executive Way
Miramar, FL 33025

Internet: www.spiritair.com

Telephone/Fax
Admin: +1 954 447 7965
Fax: +1 954 447 7979
Res: 1 800 772 7117

OPERATION

Type: Domestic/Flag passenger/cargo
Cities served: US: ACY DEN DTW FLL LAX LGA MCO MYR OAK ORD RSW
TPA (seasonal: PBI) **Caribbean:** SJU

HISTORY/STRUCTURE

Founded: 1989 (as Charter One)
Start date: September 8, 1990
President/CEO: Jacob Schorr
Ownership: Privately held

FLEET

Type	No	Seats	Engines
DC-9-30	2	Y117	PW JT8D-7B/-9A/-11
DC-9-40	1	Y127	PW JT8D-17
MD-87	1	Y133	PW JT8D-219
MD-81	6	Y164	PW JT8D-217/-217C
MD-82	14	Y164	PW JT8D-217/-217A/-219
MD-83	4	Y164	PW JT8D-219

BOEING 737-800 *(G Plomitzer)*

SUN COUNTRY AIRLINES

IATA: SY   **ICAO:** SCX   **IATA/ARC:** 337   **RADIO:** *Sun Country*

CONTACTS

Mail
2520 Pilot Knob Road, Suite 250
Mendota Heights, MN 55120

Internet: www.suncountry.com

Telephone/Fax
Admin: +1 651 681 3900
Fax: +1 651 681 3970
Res: 1 800 797 2537

OPERATION

Type: Domestic/Flag passenger/cargo
Cities served: DEN IFP LAS MCO MIA MSP PNS RSW SAT SEA SJC

HISTORY/STRUCTURE

Founded: July 1, 1982
Start date: January 20, 1983
President: David Banmiller
Ownership: MN Airlines LLC

FLEET

Type	No	Seats	Engines
Boeing 727-200	2	Y170	PW JT8D-17A/-217C
Boeing 737-800	2	C8Y160	CFMI CFM56-7B26

NOTES

BOEING 727-200 *(Steven J Pinnow)*

SUNWORLD INTERNATIONAL AIRLINES

IATA: SM   **ICAO**: SWI   **IATA/ARC**: none   **RADIO**: *Sunworld*

CONTACTS

Mail
207 Grandview Drive
Fort Mitchell, KY 41017

Internet: www.sunworld-air.com

Telephone/Fax
Admin: +1 859 331 0091
Fax: +1 859 331 6383
Res: 1 800 728 3008

OPERATION

Type: Domestic/Flag passenger/cargo
Cities served: BDL ICT IND MCI PHL (scheduled)

HISTORY/STRUCTURE

Founded: 1995
Start date: July 1996
President: William J Yung
Ownership: William J Yung

FLEET

Type	No	Seats	Engines
Boeing 727-200	2	Y170	PW JT8D-15

AIRBUS A300B4-203 (F) *(Ian Bowley)*

TRADEWINDS AIRLINES

IATA: WI   **ICAO:** TDX   **IATA/ARC:** 490   **RADIO:** *Tradewinds Express*

CONTACTS

Mail
7306 West Market Street
Greensboro, NC 27409-1844

Telephone/Fax
Admin: +1 336 665 7149
Fax: +1 336 668 7145

OPERATION

Type: Supplemental passenger/cargo
Cities served (cargo): US: BDL GSO **Caribbean:** BQN
Also operates ACMI services

HISTORY/STRUCTURE

Founded: 1969 (as Wrangler Aviation)
Start date: 1973
President: Jeff Conry
Ownership: Express One Holdings

FLEET

Type	No	Engines
Airbus A300B4-200F	7	GE CF6-50C2
L-1011 TriStar 1F	1	RR RB211-22B

BOEING 727-200 *(Bill Hough)*

TRANSMERIDIAN AIRLINES

IATA: T9   **ICAO:** TRZ   **IATA/ARC:** none   **RADIO:** *Transmeridian*

CONTACTS

Mail
680 Thornton Way
Lithia Springs, GA 30122

Telephone/Fax
Admin: +1 770 732 6900
Fax: +1 770 732 6956

Internet: www.transmeridian-airlines.com

OPERATION

Type: Supplemental passenger/cargo

HISTORY/STRUCTURE

Founded: 1995
Start date: October 30, 1995
President/CEO: Glen Schaab
Ownership: Privately held

FLEET

Type	No	Seats	Engines
Boeing 727-200	5	Y170	JT8D-15/-17/-217C
Ordered			
Boeing 757-200	2		

BRITISH AEROSPACE BAe 4101 JETSTREAM 41 *(Dick Jordan)*

TRANS STATES AIRLINES

IATA: 9N **ICAO:** LOF **IATA/ARC:** 414 **RADIO:** *Waterski*

CONTACTS

Mail
9275 Genaire Drive
St Louis, MO 63134

Telephone/Fax
Admin: +1 314 895 8700
Fax: +1 314 895 1040

Internet: www.transstates.net

OPERATION

Type: Domestic passenger/cargo
Cities served: American Connection: BMI CID CMI EVV FWA GRR JLN LEX MEM MLI MSN SBN SGF SPI STL SUX XNA **US Airways Express:** BGM BHM BNA BWI DTW ELM ERI EWR GSO GSP ITH LIT MEM MSN PIT RIC ROC SBN STL SWF SYR TOL
All service operated as American Connection or US Airways Express using only AA (5450-5699) & US (5250-5424) flight numbers
FFP: AAdvantage, US Airways Dividend Miles

HISTORY/STRUCTURE

Founded: May 1982 (as Resort Air)
Start date: April 1983
President/CEO: Hulas Kanodia
Ownership: Privately held

FLEET

Type	No	Seats	Engines
BAe Jetstream 41	25	Y30	GA TPE331-14HR-805H
ATR42-300	5	Y48	PWC PW120
EMBRAER ERJ 145ER	12	Y50	AE AE3007A
ATR72-200	3	Y68	PWC PW124B

BOEING 767-300 (ER) *(Jonathan W Holmes)*

UNITED AIRLINES

IATA: UA   **ICAO:** UAL   **IATA/ARC:** 016   **RADIO:** *United*

CONTACTS

Mail
PO Box 66100
Chicago, IL 60666

Internet: www.united.com

Telephone/Fax
Admin: +1 847 700 4000
Fax: +1 847 700 2214
Res: 1 800 241 6522
PR: +1 847 700 5501

OPERATION

Type: Domestic/Flag passenger/cargo
Hubs: DEN IAD ORD LAX SFO
Cities served: US: ABQ ALB ANC ATL AUS BDL BIL BNA BOI BOS BTV BUF BUR BWI CID CLE CLT CMH COS CVG DAY DCA DEN DFW DSM DTW EUG EWR FLL GEG GRR GSO HNL HPN IAD IAH ICT IND JFK KOA LAS LAX LGA LIH MCI MCO MDT MFR MHT MIA MSP MSY OAK OGG OKC ONT ORD PBI PDX PHL PHX PIT PVD RIC RNO ROC RSW SAN SAT SEA SFO SJC SLC SMF SNA STL SYR TPA TUL TUS (seasonal: EGE GUC HDN JAC MTJ PSP) **Canada:** YVR YYC YYZ **Caribbean:** AUA SJU STT **México:** MEX **Central America:** GUA SAL SJO **South America:** CCS EZE GIG GRU MVD SCL **Europe:** AMS BRU CDG DUS FRA LHR MUC MXP **Asia:** BKK HKG ICN KIX NRT PEK PVG SIN TPE **Oceania:** AKL MEL SYD
Global alliance: Star
Code-share: Air Canada, Air Canada Regional, Air New Zealand, All Nippon, Aloha, Ansett Australia, Austrian, BMI British Midland, BWIA, Cayman, Dutch Caribbean Express, Emirates, Great Lakes, Gulfstream International, Lufthansa, Mexicana, SAS, Saudi Arabian, Spanair, Thai Airways International, United Express (Air Wisconsin, Atlantic Coast, SkyWest), VARIG
FFP: Mileage Plus

HISTORY/STRUCTURE

Founded: February 1, 1929 (as United Aircraft & Transport Corp)
Start date: July 1, 1931
Chairman/CEO: John Creighton
President: Rono Dutta
Ownership: UAL Corp (55% employees) (NYSE: UAL)

AIRBUS A320-232 *(Gary Jennings)*

FLEET

Type	No	Seats	Engines
Boeing 737-500	57	F8Y96 or F8Y108	CFM56-3C1
Boeing 737-300	101	F8Y112 or F8Y126	CFM56-3C1
Airbus A319-100	47	F8Y112	IAE V2522-A5
Airbus A320-200	86	F12Y126	IAE V2527-A5
Boeing 757-200	98	F24Y158	PW2037
Boeing 767-200	17	F10C32Y126 or F10C33Y125	PW JT9D-7R4D
Boeing 767-300ER	37	F10C38Y158 or F34Y210	PW4060/PW4052
Boeing 777-200	22	F12C49Y197 or F12C49Y215 or F36Y312	PW4077
Boeing 777-200ER	34	F10C49Y216 or F12C49Y215	PW4090
Boeing 747-400	44	F14C73Y260 or F18C84Y270	PW4056

Ordered

Type	No
Airbus A319-100	32
Airbus A320-200	31
Boeing 777-200ER	5

NOTES

Biz-jet operations are conducted by Avolar, a subsidiary company

AIRBUS A300F4-622R *(Rafal Szczypek)*

UNITED PARCEL SERVICE (UPS)

IATA: 5X   **ICAO:** UPS   **IATA/ARC:** 406   **RADIO:** *UPS*

CONTACTS

Mail
1400 North Hurstbourne Parkway
Louisville, KY 40223

Internet: www.ups.com

Telephone/Fax
Admin: +1 502 329 6500
Fax: +1 502 329 6550
Info: 1 800 743 5877
PR: +1 502 329 6522

OPERATION

Type: Domestic/Flag passenger/cargo
Cities served: US: ABQ ABY ALB ANC ATL AUS BDL BFI BFM BHM BIL BOI
BOS BUF BUR BWI CAE CID CLE CLT DEC DEN DFW DSM DTW EFD ELP
EWR FAT FLL FSD FWA GEG GSO GSP HNL HRL IAD ICT JAN JAX JFK KOA
LAN LAS LAX LCK LFT LGB LIT MCI MCO MDT MEM MHR MHT MIA MKE
MSP MSY OAK OGG OKC OMA ONT ORD ORF PBI PDX PHL PHX PIE PIT
PVD RAP RDU RFD RIC RNO ROA RSW SAN SAT SBN SDF SGF SHV SJC
SLC SNA STL SWF SYR TUL TYS **Canada:** YHM YMX YVR YWG YYC
Caribbean: SDQ SJU **México:** GDL MEX MTY **Central America:** GUA MGA
SAL SAP SJO **South America:** BOG CCS EZE GYE LIM LPB MAO UIO VCP
VVI **Europe:** BCN CDG CGN CIA EMA HHN IST MAD MMX OSL PTY STN TLS
TSF VIE VLC WAW **Asia:** BKK BOM HKG ICN KIX KUL MNL NRT PEK PEN
PVG SGN SHJ SIN TLV TPE **Oceania:** NAN SYD
Other cities served by contract air carriers

HISTORY/STRUCTURE

Founded: 1907
Start Date: February 1, 1988
President: Thomas H Weidemeyer
Ownership: United Parcel Service

BOEING 727-100C (QF) *(Dick Jordan)*

FLEET

Type	No	Engines
Boeing 727-100C (QF)	43	RR Tay 651-54
Boeing 727-200F	8	PW JT8D-15/-17
Boeing 757-200PF	75	PW2040 (35) or RR RB211-535E4
DC-8-71/-73F	49	CFMI CFM56-2
Airbus A300F4-600R	21	PW4158
Boeing 767-300F (ER)	32	GE CF6-80C2B7F
MD-11F	3	PW4460
Boeing 747-100F	12	PW JT9D-7A
Boring 747-200F	9	PW JT9D-7J/7Q

Ordered

Airbus A300F4-600R	69	
MD-11F	10	

AIRBUS A319-112 *(Ian Bowley)*

US AIRWAYS

IATA: US   **ICAO:** USA   **IATA/ARC:** 037   **RADIO:** *USAir*

CONTACTS

Mail
2345 Crystal Drive
Arlington, VA 22227

Internet: www.usairways.com

Telephone/Fax
Admin: +1 703 872 7000
Fax: +1 703 872 5437
Res: 1 800 428 4322
PR: +1 703 872 5100

OPERATION

Type: Domestic/Flag passenger/cargo
Hubs: CLT PHL PIT
Cities served: US: ABE ALB ATL AUS AVL BDL BHM BNA BOS BTV BUF BWI
CAE CHS CLE CLT CMH DAY DCA DEN DFW DTW EWR FLL GSO HPN IAD
IAH ILM IND JAX LAS LAX LGA MCI MCO MDT MEM MHT MIA MKE MSP
MSY MYR ORD ORF PBI PHL PHX PIT PNS PVD PWM RDU RIC ROC RSW
SAN SAV SDF SEA SFO SNA SRQ STL SYR TOL TPA TYS (seasonal: LWB)
Canada: YOW YUL YYZ **Caribbean:** BDA BGI FPO GCM MBJ NAS SJU STT
STX SXM UVF **México:** CUN CZM **Europe:** CDG FCO FRA LGW MAD MAN
MUC
Code-share: Deutsche BA, US Airways Express (Air Midwest, Allegheny,
Chautauqua, Commutair, Mesa, Piedmont, PSA Airlines, Shuttle America, Trans
States)
FFP: US Airways Dividend Miles

HISTORY/STRUCTURE

Founded: March 5, 1937 (as All American Airways)
Start date: August 12, 1940
Chairman/President: Stephen M Wolf
Ownership: US Airways Group (NYSE: U)

AIRBUS A321-211 *(Michael Carter)*

FLEET

Type	No	Seats	Engines
Boeing 737-300	85	F12Y114	CFM56-3B1/-3B2
Boeing 737-400	54	F12Y132	CFM56-3B2
Airbus A319-100	66	F12Y108 or Y132	CFM56-5B6/P
Airbus A320-200	24	F16Y126 or Y150	CFM56-5B4/P
Airbus A321-200	23	F26Y143	CFM56-5B3/P
Boeing 757-200	34	F24Y158	RR RB211-535E4
Boeing 767-200ER	10	C24Y179	GE CF6-80C2B2
Airbus A330-300	9	F6C36Y224	PW PW4168A

35 Fokker 100s and 25 MD-81/82s are grounded

Ordered

Airbus A319	3
Airbus A320	21
Airbus A321	18
Airbus A330-300	1

DOUGLAS DC-9-32F *(Patrick Dean)*

USA JET AIRLINES

IATA: U7   **ICAO:** JUS   **IATA/ARC:** none   **RADIO:** *Jet USA*

CONTACTS

Mail
2064 D Street
Belleville, MI 48111-1278

Internet: www.activeaero.com

Telephone/Fax
Admin: +1 734 483 7833
Fax: +1 734 480 0014
Res: 1 800 872 5387

OPERATION

Type: Supplemental cargo
Areas served: Primarily *ad hoc* charters in US

HISTORY/STRUCTURE

Founded: 1994
Start date: December 1994
President: Robert Phelps
Ownership: Active Aero Group

FLEET

Type	No	Engines
Falcon 20	13	GE CF700-2D2
DC-9-15F	8	PW JT8D-7B
DC-9-32F/-33F	4	PW JT8D-9/-15

AIRBUS A320-214 *(Apple Vacations/Airbus)*

USA 3000 AIRLINES

IATA: none   **ICAO**: GWY   **IATA/ARC**: none   **RADIO**: *Getaway*

CONTACTS

Mail
335 Bishop Hollow Rd #100
Newtown Square PA 19013

Telephone/Fax
Admin: +1 610 325 1280
Fax: +1 610 325 1285

Internet: www.usa3000airlines.com

OPERATION

Type: Domestic/Flag passenger/cargo
Areas served: US, Caribbean, México
Operates on behalf of Apple Vacations

HISTORY/STRUCTURE

Founded: March 20, 2000 (as Brendan Air)
Start date: December 21, 2001
CEO: James B Kenney
Ownership: Brendan Aviation Holdings (John Mullen family)

FLEET

Type	No	Seats	Engines
Airbus A320-200	2	Y174	CFMI CFM56-5B4P
Ordered			
Airbus A320	5		

McDONNELL DOUGLAS DC-9-82 (MD-82) *(Bill Hough)*

VANGUARD AIRLINES

IATA: NJ   **ICAO:** VGD   **IATA/ARC:** 311   **RADIO:** *Vanguard Air*

CONTACTS

Mail
533 Mexico City Avenue
Kansas City, MO 64153

Telephone/Fax
Admin: +1 816 243 2100
Fax: +1 816 243 2178
Res: 1 800 826 4827
PR Fax: +1 816 243 2134

Internet: www.flyvanguard.com

OPERATION

Type: Domestic passenger/cargo
Cities served: ATL AUS BUF COS CVG DEN DFW LAS LAX MCI MDW MSP MSY MYR PIT SFO

HISTORY/STRUCTURE

Founded: 1994
Start date: December 2, 1994
President/CEO: Robert Spane
Ownership: Publicly traded company

FLEET

Type	No	Seats	Engines
Boeing 737-200	8	Y120	PW JT8D-9A/-15/-17
MD-87	1	C12Y100	PW JT8D-217
MD-81	1	C14Y118	PW JT8D-217
MD-82	2	C14Y118	PW JT8D-217
MD-83	1	C14Y118	PW JT8D-219
Ordered			
MD-87	1		
MD-82	2		

McDONNELL DOUGLAS DC-10-30 (Jonathan W Holmes)

WORLD AIRWAYS

IATA: WO   **ICAO**: WOA   **IATA/ARC**: 468   **RADIO**: *World*

CONTACTS

Mail
HLH Building
101 World Drive
Peachtree City, GA 30269

Telephone/Fax
Admin: +1 770 632 8000
Fax: +1 770 632 8075

Internet: www.worldair.com

OPERATION

Type: Supplemental passenger/cargo
Areas served: Worldwide passenger/freight contracts; major USAF-AMC contractor

---

HISTORY/STRUCTURE

Founded: March 29, 1948
Start date: May 1948
Chairman/CEO: Hollis L Harris
President: Gil Morgan
Ownership: Directors/officers/employees (45%), public (NASDAQ: WLDA)

FLEET

Type	No	Seats	Engines
DC-10-30	2	Y380	GE CF6-50C2
DC-10-30F	5	Freighter	GE CF6-50C2
MD-11	5	Y360 or C34Y302 or C90/Y140	PW4462
MD-11CF/F	2	Y360/Freighter	PW4462
MD-11F	1	Freighter	PW4462

LOCKHEED 188A (F) ELECTRA *(John P Stewart)*

ZANTOP INTERNATIONAL AIRLINES

IATA: none   **ICAO:** ZAN   **IATA/ARC:** none   **RADIO:** *Zantop*

CONTACTS

Mail
840 Willow Run Airport
Ypsilanti, MI 48198-0840

Internet: www.flyzantop.com

Telephone/Fax
Admin: +1 734 485 8900
Fax: +1 734 485 4813
Info: 1 800 777 7455

OPERATION

Type: Supplemental cargo

HISTORY/STRUCTURE

Founded: May 1972
Start date: 1972
President: Jim Zantop
Ownership: Zantop family

FLEET

Type	No	Engines
Lockheed Electra	10	AN 501-D13A

US Addenda

AIR CARGO CARRIERS (3U/SNC/*Night Cargo*) 4984 South Howell Avenue, Milwaukee, WI 53207; +1 414 482 1711, Fax +1 414 486 5550, www.aircar.com. James Germek. On-demand passenger/cargo. 18 x Shorts 330, 9 x Shorts 360

AIR CARGO EXPRESS (ACE)(Tatonduk Outfitters dba) (3K/FXG/*Cargo Express*) PO Box 61680, Fairbanks, AK 99706; +1 907 474 3488, Fax +1 907 474 4602, www.aircargoexpressak.com. Robert Everts. Supplemental cargo. 2 x C-46, 8 x DC-6

AIR EXCURSIONS PO Box 16, Gustavus, AK 99826; +1 907 697 2375, Fax +1 907 697 2376, www.airexcursions.com. Michael Loverink. Commuter passenger/cargo. 1 x Cessna 172, 2 x Cessna 185, 3 x Piper Cherokee SIX

AIRNOW (RLR/) 1563 Walloomsac Road Suite 1, Bennington, VT 05201; +1 802 447 2111, Fax +1 802 447 2116, www.airnow.com. David Corey. On-demand passenger/cargo. 2 x Cessna 208, 12 x Bandeirante

AIR ONE EXPRESS (RNR/*Runner*) 701 West National Guard Drive, Sioux Falls, SD 57104; +1 605 373 0303, Fax +1 605 373 9595. Dennis Sherrill. On-demand passenger/cargo. 3 x Metro, 1 x Beech 1900

AIRPAC AIRLINES (APC/*Airpac*) 7277 Perimeter Road South, Seattle, WA 98108; +1 206 762 8006, Fax +1 206 762 6357, www.airpacairlines.com. Gregory Thompson. On-demand cargo. 6 x Seneca, 6 x Chieftain, 3 x Cessna 404, 1 x Beech 99

AIR ST THOMAS (Virgin Air dba) (ZP/STT/315/*Paradise*) PO Box 302788, Cyril King Airport, St Thomas, VI 00803; +1 340 776 2722, Fax +1 340 776 2992, Res 1 800 522 3084, www.airst-thomas.com. Paul Wikander. Commuter passenger/cargo. 3 x Piper Aztec, 1 x Cessna 402

AIR SUNSHINE (YI/RSI/806/*Air Sunshine*) PO Box 37698 Airport Station, San Juan, PR 00937; +1 787 791 8900, Res 1 800 327 8900, www.airsunshine.com. Allen Adili. Commuter passenger/cargo. 7 x Cessna 402, 1 x Bandeirante

AIR TAHOMA (5C/HMA/*Tahoma*) 5469 Kearney Villa Road, Suite 201, San Diego, CA 92123; +1 858 560 4544, Fax +1 858 560 0664. Noel Rude. Supplemental cargo. 4 x Convair 240, 4 x Convair 580

AIR VEGAS (6V/VGA/389/*Air Vegas*) PO Box 11008, Las Vegas, NV 89111; +1 702 736 3599, Fax +1 702 896 2906, Res 1 800 255 7474, www.airvegas.com. James Petty. On-demand passenger/cargo. 9 x Beech 99

ALASKA CENTRAL EXPRESS (KO/AER/*Ace Air*) PO Box 190248, Anchorage, AK 99519; +1 907 245 0231, Fax +1 907 245 0243, www.acepak.com. Mike Bergt. On-demand cargo. 4 x Cessna 207, 6 x Beech 1900C, 1 x Brasília

ALASKA SEAPLANE SERVICE (UI) 1873 Shell Simmons Drive, Juneau, AK 99801; +1 907 789 3331, Fax +1 907 789 3221, Res 1 800 478 3360, www.akseaplanes.com. Craig Loken. Commuter passenger/cargo. 1 x Cessna 180, 2 x Beaver

ALPINE AIR (5A/AIP/*Alpine Air*) 3450 West Mike Jense Parkway, Provo, UT 84601; +1 801 373 1508, Fax: +1 801 373 3781, www.alpineairaviation.com. Bill Distefano. On-demand passenger/cargo. 17 x Beech 99, 8 x Beech 1900C

AMERIFLIGHT (AMF/*Amflight*) 4700 Empire Avenue, Hangar 1, Burbank, CA 91505; +1 818 980 5005, Fax +1 818 980 5018, www.ameriflight.com. Gary Richards. On-demand passenger/cargo. 20 x Piper Lance, 15 x Cessna 402, 41 x Navajo/Chieftain, 1 x King Air 200, 47 x Beech 99, 5 x Lear 35, 11 x Beech 1900C, 40 x Metro III/Expediter, 3 x Brasília

AMERISTAR JET CHARTER (AJI/*Ameristar*) PO Box 700548, Dallas, TX 75307; +1 972 248 2478, Fax +1 972 931 6011, www.ameristarjet.com. Tom Wachendorfer. On-demand passenger/cargo. 1 x King Air, 4 x Super King Air, 18 x Lear 24/25, 13 x Falcon 20

ARCTIC CIRCLE AIR SERVICE (5F/CIR/*Air Arctic*) PO Box 190228, Anchorage, AK 99519; +1 907 243 1380, Fax +1 907 248 0042, www.arctic-circle-air.com. Steve Anderson. Commuter passenger/cargo. 1 x Piper Lance, 1 x Cessna 206, 7 x Cessna 207, 3 x Cessna 402, 1 x Cessna 208, 3 x Skyvan

ARCTIC TRANSPORTATION SERVICES (7S/RCT/*Arctic Transport*) 5701 Silverado Way, Unit L, Anchorage, AK 99516; +1 907 562 2227, Fax +1 907 563 8177, www.atsak.com. John Eckels. Commuter passenger/cargo. 9 x Cessna 207, 1 x Cessna 402, 2 x CASA 212

AUSTIN EXPRESS (7V/TXX/342/*Cowboy*) 9501 Cargo Avenue, Suite 200, Austin, TX 78719; +1 512 530 2320, Fax +1 512 530 2327, www.austinexpress.com. Larry Risley. On-demand passenger/cargo. 3 x Metro III

BAKER AVIATION (8Q/BAJ/*Baker Aviation*) PO Box 708, Kotzebue, AK 99752; +1 907 442 3108, Fax +1 907 442 2745. Marjorie Baker. Commuter passenger/cargo. 1 x Cessna 206, 2 x Cessna 207

BALTIMORE AIR TRANSPORT (CJY/*SeaJay*) 1515 Martin Boulevard, Middle River, MD 21220; +1 410 687 9997. On-demand passenger/cargo. 2 x King Air 200, 12 x Cessna 208, 2 x Metro III

BARON AVIATION SERVICES (BVN/*Show Me*) PO Box 518, Vichy, MO 65580; +1 573 299 4744, Fax +1 573 299 4272. Charles Schmidt. On-demand cargo/operates FedEx Feeder flights in Midwest. 40 x Cessna 208

BASLER AIRLINES (BFC/*Basler*) PO Box 2305, Oshkosh, WI 54903; +1 920 236 7827, Fax +1 920 236 7833, www.baslerflightservice.com. Rod McNeal. On-demand cargo. 2 x DC-3, 1 x DC-3 Turbo Express

BELLAIR (7G) PO Box 60311, Fairbanks, AK 99706; +1 907 457 8396, Fax +1 907 479 2239. Michael Spisak. Commuter passenger/cargo. 4 x Piper Cherokee SIX/Lance, 1 x Chieftain, 2 x Beech 18

BEMIDJI AVIATION SERVICES (dba Bemidji Airlines/Air Direct) (CH/BMJ/872/*Bemidji*) PO Box 624, Bemidji, MN 56619; +1 218 751 1880, Fax +1 218 759 3552, Res 1 800 332 7133, www.bemidjiaviation.com Larry Diffley. Commuter passenger/cargo. 3 x Aztec, 2 x Baron, 18 x Queen Air, 1 x King Air, 7 x Beech 99

BERING AIR (8E/BRG/*Bering Air*) PO Box 1650, Nome, AK 99762; +1 907 443 5422, Fax +1 907 443 5919, Res +1 907 443 5464, www.beringair.com. James Rowe. Commuter passenger/cargo. 2 x Cessna 207, 6 x Navajo Chieftain/T-1020, 5 x Cessna 208B, 2 x CATPASS 250, 1 x CASA 212

BERRY AVIATION (BYA/*Berry*) 1807 Airport Drive, San Marcos, TX 78666; +1 512 353 2379, Fax +1 512 353 2593, www.berryair.com. Harry Berry III. On-demand passenger/cargo. 12 x Merlin IV/Metro II/Metro III

BIGHORN AIRWAYS (BHR/*Bighorn Air*) PO Box 4037, Sheridan, WY 82801; +1 307 672 3421, Fax +1 307 674 4468, www.bighornairways.com. Bob Eisele. On-demand passenger/cargo. 2 x Chieftain, 1 x Cessna 425, 4 x Dornier 228, 2 x CASA 212

BUSINESS AVIATION COURIER (DKT/*Dakota*) 3501 Aviation Avenue, Sioux Falls, SD 57104; +1 605 336-7791, Fax +1 605 336 6810, www.busav.com. Dale Froelich. Passenger/Cargo charter. 4 x Cessna 310, 8 x Cessna 402, 1 x Cessna 404, 1 x Cessna 208B, 6 x Metro III

C&M AIRWAYS (RWG/*Red Wing*)7335 Boeing Drive, El Paso, TX 79925; +1 915 779 3097, Fax +1 915 779 0479. Bradley Cryderman. Part 125 cargo. 6 x Convair 640

CAPE AIR (Key West Express/Nantucket Airlines)(Hyannis Air Service dba) (9K/KAP/306/*Cair*) 660 Barnstable Road, Hyannis, MA 02601; +1 508 790 3122, Fax +1 508 778 1870, Res 1 800 352 0714, www.flycapeair.com. Dan Wolf. Commuter passenger/cargo. 50 x Cessna 402C

CAPE SMYTHE AIR SERVICE (6C/CMY/879/*Cape Smythe Air*) PO Box 549, Barrow, AK 99723; +1 907 852 8333, Fax +1 907 852 8332, www.capesmythe.com. Grant B Thompson. Commuter passenger/cargo. 1 x Cessna 185, 7 x Cessna 207, 3 x Chieftain, 1 x Cheyenne IIXL, 2 x Piper T-1040, 2 x Beech 99

CATALINA FLYING BOATS (CBT/*Catalina Air*) 3215 East Spring Street, Long Beach, CA 90806; +1 562 595 5026, Fax +1 562 490 0777. Steve Franklin. 1 x Chieftain, 5 x Beech 18, 2 x DC-3

CHERRY-AIR (CCY/*Cherry-Air*) 4584 Claire Chennault Road, Dallas, TX 75248, +1 972 248 1707, Fax +1 972 380 2344, www.cherryair.com. Kenneth Donaldson. On-demand passenger/cargo. 9 x Lear 24/25, 7 x Falcon 20

COASTAL AIR TRANSPORT (DQ/CXT/457/*Coastal*) PO Box 3985, Christiansted, St Croix, VI 00822; +1 340 773 6862. Michael W Foster. Commuter passenger/cargo. 1 x Cessna 402

CONTRACT AIR CARGO (TSU/*Trans Auto*) 6860 South Service Drive, Waterford, MI 48327; +1 248 666 9630, Fax +1 248 666 9614. Alan Ross. Part 125 cargo. 8 x Convair 580, 3 x Convair 5800, 1 x 727-100F

CORPORATE AIR (CPT/*Air Spur*) PO Box 30998, Billings, MT 59107; +1 406 248 3131, Fax +1 406 248 3152, www.flybillings.com/corpair.html. Linda Overstreet. Supplemental cargo/operates FedEx Feeder flights in Rocky Mountain area. 2 x Commander 500, 42 x Cessna 208, 6 x Beech 99, 4 x Twin Otter, 2 x Beech 200, 4 x Beech 1900C, 3 x Shorts 330, 2 x Shorts 360, 5 x Brasília

CSA AIR (IRO/*Iron Air*) 260 Riverhills Road, Kingsford, MI 49801; +1 906 774 3101, Fax +1 906 779 1304, www.csaair.com. Robert Norton. On-demand cargo/operates FedEx Feeder flights in Midwest. 28 x Cessna 208

DESERT AIR TRANSPORT 180 North 2400 West, Salt Lake City, UT 84116, +1 801 539 8555, Fax +1 801 539 1923. Dennis Gladwin. On-demand cargo. 3 x DC-3

DISCOVER AIR (DCV/*Discover*) 83 Nilson Way, Orlando, FL 32803; +1 407 894 0708, Fax +1 407 894 8343, www.discoverair.com. Scott Williams. On-demand passenger/cargo. 4 x Jetstream 31/32, 2 x Brasília

EMPIRE AIRLINES (EM/CFS/464/*Empire Air*) 2115 Government Way, Coeur d'Alene, ID 83814; +1 208 667 5400, Fax +1 208 667 8787, www.empirecoe.com. Mel Spelde. Supplemental cargo/operates FedEx Feeder flights in western US. 35 x Cessna 208, 1 x F-27F, 12 x Fokker F27

EXECUTIVE AIRLINES (YL/ORA/*Long Island*) 1300 New Highway, Farmingdale, NY 11735; +1 631 694 0600, Fax +1 631 694 0172, www.executiveairlines.com. Michael Peragrine. On-demand passenger/cargo. 3 x Jetstream 31, 1 x Lear 25

40-MILE AIR (Q5/MLA/519/*Mile Air*) PO Box 539, Tok, AK 99780; +1 907 883 5191, Fax +1 907 883 5194, www.40-mileair.com. Leif Wilson. Commuter passenger/cargo. 5 x Super Cub, 1 x Cessna 185, 3 x Cessna 206, 3 x Cessna 207, 1 x Navajo, 1 x Otter

FOUR STAR AIR CARGO (HK/FSC/861/*Four Star*) One Air Cargo Center, St Thomas, VI 00802; +1 340 776 8847, Fax: +1 340 776 5536, www.fourstaraircargo.com. Curtis White. On-demand cargo. 5 x DC-3

FREEDOM AIR (Aviation Services dba) (FRE/*Freedom*) PO Box 1578, Agana, GU 96932; +1 671 472 8010, Fax +1 671 472 8080. Joaquin Flores. Domestic/Flag passenger/cargo. 2 x Cessna 172, 5 x Cherokee SIX, 1 x Aztec, 1 x Navajo, 1 x Shorts 330

FREIGHT RUNNERS EXPRESS (FRG/*Freight Runners*) 1901 East Layton Avenue, Milwaukee, WI 53207; +1 414 744 5525, Fax +1 414 744 4850. Charles Zens. On-demand passenger/cargo. 2 x Cessna 207, 3 x Cessna 402, 1 x Beech H18, 5 x Beech 99

F S AIR SERVICE (4A/EYE/*Sockeye*) 6121 South Airpark Place, Anchorage, AK 99502; +1 907 248 9595, Fax +1 907 243 1247. Sandra Saltz. On-demand passenger/cargo. 2 x Chieftain, 1 x Merlin III, 2 x Metro III, 1 x Volpar Turboliner, 1 x CASA 212, 1 x Lear 35

GENAVCO AIR CARGO 38 Lagoon Drive, Honolulu, HI 96819, +1 808 836 3467. Harry Clark. On-demand cargo. 2 x DC-3

GRAND AIRE EXPRESS (GAE/*Grand Express*) 11777 West Airport Service Rd, Swanton, OH 43558; +1 419 865 1780, Fax +1 419 865 2965, www.grandaire.com. Tahir Cheema. On-demand passenger/cargo. 2 x Aerostar, 7 x Metro II, 13 x Falcon 20

GRAND CANYON AIRLINES (CVU/*Canyon View*) PO Box 3038, Grand Canyon, AZ 86023; +1 520 638 2463, Fax +1 520 638 9461, www.grandcanyonairlines.com. John Seibold. On-demand passenger/cargo. 4 x DHC-6-300

GRANT AVIATION (GS) PO Box 92200, Anchorage, AK 99509; +1 907 248 7025, Fax +1 907 248 7031, Res 1 800 478 1944, www.flygrant.com. Mark Hiekel. Commuter passenger/cargo. 2 x Cessna 172, 10 x Cessna 207, 4 x Chieftain, 2 x Cessna 208, 1 x King Air 200

GULF AND CARIBBEAN AIR (Gulf and Caribbean Cargo dba) (8G/486) 1100 Lee Wagener Blvd, Suite 317, Fort Lauderdale, FL 33315; +1 954 359 7776, Fax +1 954 359 7656. Frederick Mason. Supplemental passenger/cargo. 1 x Convair 440, 1 x Convair 580

HAGELAND AVIATION SERVICES (H6/HAG/*Hageland*) PO Box 220610, Anchorage, AK 99522; +1 907 245 0119, Fax +1 907 245 5745, Res +1 907 543 3900. Mike Hageland. Commuter passenger/cargo. 1 x Cessna 206, 14 x Cessna 207, 1 x Cessna 402, 4 x Cessna F406, 6 x Cessna 208

HOMER AIR PO Box 302, Homer, AK 99603; +1 907 235 8591, Fax +1 907 235 2301, www.homerair.com. Larry Thompson. On-demand passenger/cargo. 3 x Cessna 206, 2 x Islander

IBC AIRWAYS (II/CSQ/*Chasqui*) 8401 NW 17th Street, Miami, FL 33126; +1 305 591 8080, Fax +1 305 639 6478. Joseph Costigan. On-demand cargo. 1 x Cessna 402, 6 x Metro II/III, 1 x Shorts 360

ILIAMNA AIR TAXI (LS/IAR/*Iliamna Air*) PO Box 109, Iliamna, AK 99606; +1 907 571 1248, Fax +1 907 571 1244. Timothy LaPorte. Commuter passenger/cargo. 1 x Cessna 185, 1 x Bonanza, 2 x Cessna 207, 1 x Baron, 4 x Beaver, 1 x Chieftain, 1 x PC-12

INDIGO CORPORATE JET AIRLINE (Indigo)(Air-Serv dba) (I9/IBU/*Indigo Blue*) 5713 South Central Avenue, Chicago, IL 60638; +1 773 585 5155, Fax +1 773 767 4664, Res 1 877 446 3446, www.flyindigo.com. Matthew G Anderson. On-demand passenger/cargo. 3 x Falcon 20

INLAND AVIATION SERVICES (7N) PO Box 244, Aniak, AK 99557; +1 907 675 4624, Fax +1 907 675 4641, www.inlandaviation.com. Stephen Hill. Commuter passenger/cargo. 1 x Cessna 172, 2 x Cessna 207, 2 x Helio Courier

INTER ISLAND EXPRESS AMF Station, PO Box 810239, Carolina, PR 00981; +1 787 253 1400, Fax +1 787 253 1410, www.interislandexpress.com. Eric Stubbe. 2 x Cessna 208, 1 x PC-12

ISLAND AIRLINES (IS/ISA/*Island*) PO Box 2495, Nantucket, MA 02584; +1 508 228 7575, Fax +1 508 228 6645, Res 1 800 248 7779, www.nantucket.net/trans/islandair. William McGrath. Commuter passenger/cargo. 7 x Cessna 402C, 1 x Beech H18

ISLAND EXPRESS (Safe Air International dba) (2S/SDY/579/*Sandy Isle*) 622 SW 34th Street, Building 2, Ft Lauderdale, FL 33315; +1 954 359 0383, Fax +1 954 359 7944, Res +1 954 359 0380. Ruben Acrich. Commuter passenger/cargo. 1 x Cessna 402

JIM HANKINS AIR SERVICE (HKN/*Hankins*) PO Box 10652, Jackson, MS 39289; +1 601 354 2789, Fax +1 601 352 8984, www.jimhankins.com. James Hankins. On-demand passenger/cargo. 4 x Baron, 2 x King Air, 6 x Beech 18, 2 x DC-3

KENMORE AIR HARBOR (M5) PO Box 82064, Kenmore, WA 98028-0064; +1 425 486 1257, Fax +1 425 486 5471, Res 1 800 543 9595, www.kenmoreair.com. Robert B Munro. Commuter passenger/cargo. 4 x Cessna 180, 10 x Beaver/Turbo Beaver, 6 x Turbo Otter

KEY LIME AIR (LYM/*Key Lime*) 7625 South Peoria, Suite D15, Englewood, CO 80112; +1 303 768 9626, Fax +1 303 768 8144, www.keylimeair.com. On-demand passenger/cargo. 4 x Chieftain, 1 x Cessna 404, 10 x Metro II/III/23, 1 x Lear 24

KITTY HAWK CHARTERS (KFS/*Kalitta*) 843 Willow Run Airport, Ypsilanti, MI 48198; +1 734 484 7376, Fax +1 734 487 6420, www.kittyhawkcharters.com. Toby Skaar. On-demand passenger/cargo. 2 x MU-2, 7 x Volpar Turboliner, 19 x Lear 23/24/25, 2 x Lear 35/36, 1 x Falcon 20

LAB FLYING SERVICE (JF/LAB/510/*Lab*) PO Box 272, Haines, AK 99827; +1 907 766 2222, Fax +1 907 766 2734, Res 1 800 426 0543. Layton A Bennett. Commuter passenger/cargo. 6 x Cherokee, 2 x Helio Courier, 21 x Cherokee SIX/Lance/Saratoga, 4 x Seneca, 1 x Aerostar, 1 x Islander, 3 x Chieftain

LARRY'S FLYING SERVICE (J6) 3822 University Avenue, Fairbanks, AK 99709; +1 907 474 9169, Fax +1 907 474 8815, www.larrysflying.com. Lawrence A Chenaille. Commuter passenger/cargo. 5 x Cherokee SIX/Lance/Saratoga, 2 x Cessna 207, 5 x Chieftain

LYNX AIR INTERNATIONAL (LXF/*Lynxflight*) 255 NW 55th Court, Hangar 24, Ft Lauderdale, FL 33309; +1 954 772 9808, Fax +1 954 772 1141, www.lynxair.com. Linda Tonks. Domestic/Flag passenger/cargo. 3 x Metro III

M&N AVIATION (W4) PO Box 9066566, San Juan, PR 00906; +1 787 722 5980, Fax +1 787 723 0465. Jose Maldonado. On-demand passenger/cargo. 2 x Cessna 402, 4 x Cessna 208, 2 x Citation

MARTINAIRE (MRA/*Martex*) 2550 Midway Road, Suite 190, Carrollton, TX 75006; +1 972 349 5700, Fax +1 972 349 5750, www.martinaire.com. C Edward Acker. On-demand passenger/cargo. 23 x Cessna 208B, 2 x Metro III

MERLIN AIRWAYS (MEI/*Avalon*) 2220 Grant Road, Billings, MT 59102; +1 406 247 3131, Fax +1 406 896 3213. Linda Overstreet. On-demand passenger/cargo. 13 x Metro III/23

METHOW AVIATION (MER/*Methow*) 3311 109th Street SW #221, Everett, WA 98204; +1 425 355 2055, Fax +1 425 742 6868. Blair Estenson. On-demand passenger/cargo. 1 x Aztec, 1 x Baron, 8 x Beech 18/Hamilton Westwind

MIAMI VALLEY AVIATION (OWL/*Night Owl*) 1707 Run Way, Middletown, OH 45042; +1 937 422 5050, Fax +1 937 422 1494, www.flymva.com. Terrence Hogan. On-demand passenger/cargo. 3 x Aztec, 3 x Beech 18, 2 x Lear 25, 1 x Lear 35, 1 King Air 200, 5 x DC-3, 1 x Falcon 20

MID-ATLANTIC FREIGHT (MDC/*Night Ship*) PO Box 35409, Greensboro, NC 24725; +1 336 722 1396, Fax +1 336 668 4434, www.c208.com. Don Godwin. On-demand passenger/cargo. 18 x Cessna 208

MOUNTAIN AIR CARGO (MTN/*Mountain*) PO Box 488, Denver, NC 28037; +1 828 464 8741, Fax +1 828 465 5281, www.mtaircargo.com. Walter Clark. Supplemental cargo/operates FedEx Feeder services in eastern US. 42 x Cessna 208, 2 x Shorts 330, 20 x F27

MURRAY AIR 816 Willow Run Airport, Ypsilanti, MI 48198; +1 734 482 5802, Fax +1 734 482 2923. Mark Murray. Part 125 cargo. 2 x DC-8-63F

MURRAY AVIATION (MUA/*Murray Air*) 835 Willow Run Airport, Ypsilanti, MI 48918; +1 734 484 4800, Fax +1 734 484 4875, www.murray-aviation.com. Preston Murray. On-demand passenger/cargo. 1 x MU-2, 3 x King Air 90, 1 x BAe Jetstream 31, 4 x CASA 212

NEW ENGLAND AIRLINES (dba Block Island Air Line/Air Charter) (EJ/NEA/367/*New England*) 56 Airport Road, Westerly, RI 02891; +1 401 596 2460, Fax +1 401 596 7366, Res 1 800 243-2460, www.block-island.com/nea/. William G Bendokas. Commuter passenger/cargo. 1 x Cherokee, 3 x Cherokee SIX, 2 x Islander

NORTH SOUTH AIRWAYS (SPK/*Sparkle*) 1954 Airport Road, Suite 200, Atlanta, GA 3041; +1 770 445 7575, Fax +1 770 455 7550, www.nsair.com. Richard Hilde. On-demand passenger/cargo. 2 x Seneca, 2 x MU-2, 4 x Brasília

NORTH STAR AIR CARGO (SBX/*Sky Box*) 4984 South Howell Avenue, Milwaukee, WI 53207; +1 414 744 8012, Fax +1 414 744 8033. Baxter Snider. On-demand cargo. 6 x Skyvan

NORTHWEST SEAPLANES (2G) PO Box 1845, Renton, WA 98057; +1 425 277 1590, Fax +1 425 277 8831, Res 1 800 690 0086, www.nwseaplanes.com. Clyde E Carlson. Commuter passenger/cargo. 7 x Beaver, 1 x Cessna 208, 2 x Panther Chieftain

OLSON AIR SERVICE (4B) PO Box 142, Nome, AK 99762; +1 907 443 5599, Fax +1 907 443 5017. Donald Olson. Commuter passenger/cargo. 2 x Cessna 207, 1 x Cessna 402

PACIFIC AIRWAYS (3F) PO Box 5158, Ketchikan, AK 99901; +1 907 225 3500, Fax +1 907 247 3500, www.flypacificairways.com. Mike Rhoads. Commuter passenger/cargo. 5 x Beaver

PACIFIC ISLAND AVIATION (9J/PSA/321/*Pacific Isle*) PPP 318, PO Box 10000, Saipan, MP 96950; +1 670 234 3600, Fax +1 670 234 3604, www.pacificislandaviation.com. Robert F Christian. Domestic/Flag passenger/cargo. 3 x Shorts 360

PACIFIC WINGS (Air Nevada Airlines dba) (LW/NMI/568/*Tsunami*) PO Box 791537, Paia, HI 96779; +1 808 873 0877, Fax +1 808 873 7920, Res 1 888 575 4546, www.pacificwings.com. James Kahlstorf. Commuter passenger/cargo. 2 x Cessna 172, 5 x Cessna 402

PAPILLON GRAND CANYON HELICOPTERS (Papillon Airways dba) (HI/563) PO Box 455, Grand Canyon, AZ 86023; +1 520 638 9330, Fax +1 520 638 9349, www.papillon.com. Elling Halvorson. Commuter passenger/cargo. 18 x Bell JetRanger/LongRanger

PRESIDENTIAL AIRWAYS 1383 General Aviation Drive, Melbourne, FL 32935; +1 321 253 0209, Fax +1 321 253 0039. Richard Pere. On-demand passenger/cargo. 1 x Cessna 208, 1 x King Air, 3 x CASA 212

PROMECH AIR (Seaborne Seaplane Adventures)(Promech dba) (Z3) 1515 Tongass Avenue, Ketchikan, AK 99901; +1 907 225 3845, Fax +1 907 247 3875, Res 1 800 860 3845, www.promechair.com. Kevin Hack. Commuter passenger/cargo. 3 x Cessna 185, 4 x Beaver, 2 x Twin Otter

RHOADES INTERNATIONAL (RDS/*Rhoades Express*) 4770 Ray Boll Boulevard, Columbus, IN 47203; +1 812 372 1819, Fax +1 812 378 2708, www.rhoadesaviation.com. Jack Rhoades. Supplemental cargo. 1 x Cessna 310, 1 x Cessna 402, 1 x Cessna 421, 1 x Lear 25, 4 x DC-3, 2 x Convair 240, 1 x Convair 340, 1 x Convair 440, 3 x Convair 600, 2 x Convair 640

RIO GRANDE AIR (E2/GRN/*Grande*) PO Box 1617, El Prado, NM 87529; +1 505 737 0505, Fax +1 505 737 9791, Res 1 877 435 9742, www.iflyrga.com. Timothy Wooldridge. Commuter passenger/cargo. 1 x Cessna 207, 2 x Cessna 208

ROBLEX AVIATON PO Box 6386, Bayamon, PR 00960; +1 787 723 8827, Fax +1 787 723 8828, www.roblex.com. Roberto Rodriguez. On-demand passenger/cargo. 1 x Islander, 1 x DC-3, 2 x Shorts 360

ROYAL AIR FREIGHT (RAX/*Air Royal*) 2141 Airport Road, Waterford, MI 48327; +1 248 666 3070, Fax +1 248 666 4719. William Kostich. On-demand passenger/cargo. 6 x Cessna 310, 3 x Cessna 402, 3 x MU-2, 5 x Bandeirante, 8 x Lear 23/24/25

SABER CARGO AIRLINES (SBR/854/*Freighter*) 4825 Express Drive, Charlotte, NC 28219; +1 704 359 8456, Fax +1 704 359 8275, www.sabercargo.com. Michael Dockery. On-demand cargo. 1 x Hughes 369, 2 x Bell 206, 4 x DC-3, 1 x Falcon 20

SALMON AIR 29 Hamner Drive, Salmon, ID 83467; +1 208 756 6211, Fax +1 208 756 6219, www.salmonair.com. JoAnn Wolters. On-demand passenger/cargo. 1 x Cessna 172, 1 x Cessna 206, 3 x Chieftain, 2 x Islander, 1 x Cessna 208

SAMOA AIR (Samoa Aviation dba) (SE) PO Box 280, Pago Pago International Airport, AS 96799; +1 684 699 9106, Fax +1 684 699 9751; James A Porter. Domestic/Flag passenger/cargo. 3 x Twin Otter

SEABORNE AIRLINES (Seaborne Virgin Islands dba) (BB) 34 Strand St, Christiansted, St Croix, VI 00820; +1 340 773 5991, Fax +1 340 773 8798, Res 1 866 359 8784. Maurice E Kurg. Commuter passenger/cargo. 5 x Twin Otter

SIERRA WEST AIRLINES (PKW/*Platinum West*) 8191 Laughlin Road, Oakdale, CA 95361; +1 209 848 0290, Fax +1 209 848 0299. Deborah Robinson. On-demand passenger/cargo. 1 x Metro II/Merlin IV, 4 x Metro III/Merlin IVC, 1 x Cheyenne, 2 x Lear 35

SKAGWAY AIR SERVICE (7J/SGY/493/*Skagway Air*) PO Box 357, Skagway, AK 99840; +1 907 983 2218, Fax +1 907 983 3318, www.skagwayair.com. Ben Lingle. Commuter passenegr/cargo. 2 x Cherokee, 7 x Cherokee SIX/Saratoga, 1 x Seneca, 1 x Islander, 1 x Piper T-1020

SKYWAY ENTERPRISES (SKZ/*Skyway Inc*) 3031 West Patrick Road, Kissimmee, FL 34741; +1 407 932 0600, Fax +1 407 932 4600. Thomas Loumakin. On-demand passenger/cargo. 2 x Lear 23, 3 x Shorts 330, 15 x Shorts 360, 1 x DC-9-15F

SMOKEY BAY AIR (2E) PO Box 457, Homer, AK 99603; +1 907 235 1511, Fax +1 907 235 1501, www.xyz.net/~seldovia/sbayair.htm. Claire A McCann. On-demand passenger/cargo. 1 x Cessna 172, 2 x Cessna 206

SUBURBAN AIR FREIGHT (SUB/*Sub Air*) PO Box 19090, Omaha, NE 68119; +1 402 344 4100, Fax +1 402 344 0415, www.subair.com. James Armstrong. On-demand passenger/cargo. 7 x Commander 680FL, 2 x Cessna 208, 4 x Beech 99, 2 x Beech 1900C

SUNDANCE AIR (BNC/*Barnacle Air*) 2209 South Olive Street, Denver, CO 80224; +1 303 782 9788, Fax +1 303 753 4647. Bert Vantoornburg. On-demand passenger/cargo. 4 x Chieftain, 1 x Beech 99, 3 x Beech 1900

SUPERIOR AVIATION (AB/HKA/*Spend Air*) 250 Riverhills Road, Kingsford, MI 49802; +1 906 774 0400, Fax +1 906 774 4118, www.superioraviation.com. Stephen Van Beek. On-demand passenger/cargo. 4 x Cessna 402, 11 x Cessna 404, 1 x Cessna 441, 11 x Cessna 208, 13 x Metro II/Merlin IV, 6 x Metro III

TANANA AIR SERVICE (Bidzy Ta Hot' Aana dba) (4E/TNR/*Tan Air*) PO Box 60713, Fairbanks, AK 99706; +1 907 474 0301, Fax +1 907 474 9311. Harold Esmailka. Commuter passenger/cargo. 12 x Cherokee SIX/Lance, 1 x Navajo

TAQUAN AIR (Venture Travel dba) (K3/TQN/*Taquan*) 1007 Water Street, Ketchikan, AK 99901; +1 907 225 8800, Fax +1 907 228 4616, Res 1 800 770 8800, www.taquanair.com. Brien Salazar. On-demand passenger/cargo. 5 x Beaver

TATONDUK FLYING SERVICE (Tatonduk Outfitters dba) (3K) PO Box 61680, Fairbanks, AK 99706; +1 907 474 4697, Fax +1 907 474 4687, www.tatondukflying.com. Robert Everts. Supplemental cargo. 4 x Piper Lance, 1 x Piper T-1020, 3 x Cessna 208

TELFORD AVIATION (TEL/*Telford*) 189 Odlin Road, Bangor, ME 04401; +1 207 945 3517, Fax +1 207 945 0992, www.telfordaviation.com. Telford Allen. On-demand passenger/cargo. 4 x Cessna 206, 14 x Cessna 208, 1 x Beech 99

TMC AIRLINES (TMM/*Willow Run*) 836 Willow Run Airport, Ypsilanti, MI 48198-0836; +1 734 485 8907, Fax +1 734 481 9182. James Loree. Part 125 cargo. 2 x Electra

TOLAIR SERVICES (TI/TOL/*Tol Air*) PO Box 37670, San Juan, PR 00937-0670; +1 787 791 5235, Fax +1 787 791 8385, www.tolair.com. Jorge Toledo. Supplemental cargo/on-demand cargo. 2 x Cessna 402, 5 x Beech 18, 5 x DC-3, 1 x Convair 240

TRANS AIR (P6/MUI/356/*Maui*) PO Box 29239, Honolulu, HI 96820; +1 808 833 5557, Fax +1 808 833 2636. Telmour Riahi. On-demand passenger/cargo. 3 x Cessna 402, 2 x Shorts 360

TRANS-AIR-LINK (GJB/*Sky Truck*) 3305 SW 9th Avenue Suite 110, Fort Lauderdale, FL 33315; +1 954 523 2123, Fax +1 954 523 2665. Hernando Gutierrez. Supplemental cargo. 3 x Convair 580, 1 x Electra

TRANS FLORIDA AIRLINES (TFA/*Trans Florida*) PO Box 10150, Daytona Beach, FL 32120-0150; +1 904 252 3053, Fax +1 904 252 0037. Robert Willman. Supplemental cargo. 2 x Convair 240

TRANS NORTH AVIATION (HX) PO Box 1445, Eagle River, WI 54521; +1 715 479 6777, Fax +1 715 479 8178, www.transnorth.com. Ronald Schaberg. On-demand passenger/cargo. 2 x Cessna 340, 1 x Chieftain

UNION FLIGHTS (UNF/*Union Flights*) 134 Lakes Boulevard, Dayton Valley, NV 89403; +1 775 246 4060, Fax +1 775 246 4077. Jay Paynter. On-demand passenger/cargo. 3 x Navajo/Chieftain, 11 x Cessna 208

VIEQUES AIR LINK (VI/VES/381/*Vieques*) PO Box 487, Vieques, PR 00765; +1 787 741 3266, Fax +1 787 741 0545, Res 1 888 901 9247, www.vieques-island.com/val/. Osvaldo Gonzalez. Commuter passenger/cargo. 6 x Islander, 3 x Trislander

VIKING EXPRESS (WCY/*Titan Air*) 43W518 Route 30, Sugar Grove, IL 60554; +1 630 466 7500, Fax +1 630 466 7041, www.vikjet.com. Robert Burwell. On-demand passenger/cargo. 5 x Cessna 208

VILLAGE AVIATION (dba Camai Air)(R9/CAM/451/*Air Camai*) PO Box 787, Bethel, AK 99559; +1 907 543 4040, Fax +1 907 543 2369. Don King. Commuter passenger/cargo. 1 x Cessna 206, 5 x Cessna 207

VISION AIR 2634 Airport Drive, Suite 106, North Las Vegas, NV 89032; +1 702 647 7700, Fax +1 702 646 6871. William Acor. On-demand passenger/cargo. 2 x Cessna 421, 12 x Chieftain, 1 x Piper T-1040, 1 x Cheyenne III, 2 x Dornier 228

WARBELOW'S AIR VENTURES (4W/VNA/*Ventaire*) 3758 University Avenue South, Fairbanks, AK 99709; +1 907 474 0518, Fax +1 907 479 5054, www.warbelows.com. Arthur Warbelow. Commuter passenger/cargo. 1 x Super Cub, 1 x Cessna 172, 2 x Cessna 206, 2 x Cessna 207, 10 x Chieftain

WEST AIR (PCM/*Pac Valley*) 5005 East Anderson, Fresno, CA 93727; +1 559 454 7843, Fax +1 559 454 7840. Beth Wood. On-demand cargo/operates FedEx Feeder flights in western USA. 35 x Cessna 208

WEST ISLE AIR (W6/WIL/590/*West Isle Air*) 4000 Airport Road, Suite A, Anacortes, WA 98221; +1 360 293 4691, Fax +1 360 293 0517, Res 1 800 474 4434, www.westisleair.com. James R Burton. Commuter passenger/cargo. 4 x Cessna 172, 5 x Cessna 206, 3 x Cessna 207, 2 x Chieftain

WESTERN AIR EXPRESS (WAE/*Western Express*) 3669 West Wright Street, Boise, ID 83705; +1 208 343 2756, Fax +1 208 343 2878, www.westernairexpress.com. Eugene Heil. On-demand passenger/cargo. 3 x Cessna 402, 5 x Metro II

WIGGINS AIRWAYS (WIG/*Wiggins*) One Garside Way, Manchester, NH 03108; +1 603 629 9191, Fax +1 603 665 9643, www.wiggins-air.com. David Ladd. On-demand cargo/operates FedEx Feeder flights in northeastern US. 33 x Cessna 208, 7 x Beech 99, 1 x Twin Otter

WINGS OF ALASKA (Alaska Juneau Aeronautics dba) (K5/WAK/*Wings Alaska*) 8421 Livingston Way, Juneau, AK 99801; +1 907 789 0790, Fax +1 907 789 2021, www.wingsofalaska.com. Robert Jacobsen. Commuter passenger/cargo. 3 x Cessna 206, 3 x Cessna 207, 7 x Beaver, 6 x Otter, 4 x Cessna 208

WRIGHT AIR SERVICE (8V) PO Box 60142, Fairbanks, AK 99706; +1 907 474 0502, Fax +1 907 474 0375. Robert Bursiel. Commuter passenger/cargo. 2 x Cessna 185, 2 x Helio Courier, 1 x Cessna 206, 1 x Bonanza, 2 x Cessna 207, 4 x Navajo/Chieftain, 4 x Cessna 208B

YUTE AIR ALASKA (Flight Alaska dba) (4Y/UYA/*Yute Air*) 3600 West International Airport Road, Anchorage, AK 99502; +1 907 243 3000, Fax +1 907 243 2811, www.yuteair.com. Skip Nelson. On-demand passenger/cargo. 2 x Cessna 206, 7 x Cessna 207, 1 x Chieftain, 2 x CASA 212

NOTES

AIRBUS A330-343 (X) *(Ian Bowley)*

AIR CANADA

IATA: AC   **ICAO:** ACA   **IATA/ARC:** 014   **RADIO:** *Air Canada*

CONTACTS

Mail
PO Box 14000
Station Airport
Dorval, QC H4Y 1H4

Telephone/Fax
Admin: +1 514 422 5000
Fax: +1 514 422 7741
Res: 1 888 422 7533

Internet: www.aircanada.ca

OPERATION

Type: Scheduled/charter passenger/cargo
Cities served: Canada: YEG YHZ YOW YQB YQM YQR YQT YUL YVR YWG
YXE YXY YYC YYG YYJ YYT YYZ (seasonal: YDF YLW YQX YQY) **US:** ATL BNA
BOS CHS CLT DCA DEN EWR FLL GSO HNL HPN IAD IAH IND JFK LAS LAX
LGA MCI MCO MIA MKE MSP MSY OGG ORD PHL PHX RDU SAN SEA SFO
STL TPA (seasonal: ANC PBI RSW) **Caribbean:** ANU BDA BGI FDF KIN MBJ
NAS PAP POS PTP UVF (seasonal/some charter: AVI GCM HOG PLS SJU
VRA) **México:** CUN MEX PVR **South America:** EZE GRU **Europe:** CDG
FRA LHR MAD MXP ZRH (seasonal: AMS CPH DUB FCO GLA MAN MUC
SNN) **Asia:** BJS HKG ICN KIX NRT PVG TLV TPE **Oceania:** MEL SYD
Global alliance: Star
Code-share: Air Canada Regional, Air Creebec, Air Georgian, Air Labrador, Air
New Zealand, Alitalia, All Nippon Airways, Atlantic Coast Airlines, Austrian
Airlines Group, Aviation Québec Labrador, BMI British Midland, Calm Air, Central
Mountain Air, EVA Air, First Air, Korean Air, Lufthansa, Mexicana, Royal
Jordanian, SAS, Singapore Airlines, Thai International, United Airlines/United
Express
FFP: Aeroplan

HISTORY/STRUCTURE

Founded: April 10, 1937 (as Trans-Canada Air Lines)
Start date: September 1, 1937
Chairman: John F Fraser
President/COO: Robert A Milton
Ownership: Publicly held (80% institutional, 14% retail, 6% employees)
(TSE/NASDAQ: AC)

BOEING 767-300 (ER) *(Brian Losito)*

FLEET

Type	No	Seats	Engines
Bombardier CRJ100ER	25	CY50	GE CF34-3A1/3B1
Boeing 737-200	42*	C12Y88 or C48 or Y117	PW JT8D-9A/17/17A
Airbus A319-100	37	C16Y96	CFM56-5A5
Airbus A320-200	47**	C20Y120 or Y1591	CFM56-5A1
Airbus A321	5		
Boeing 767-200	12	C36Y162	PW JT9D-7R4D
Boeing 767-200 (ER)	11	C36Y162	PW JT9D-7R4D
Boeing 767-300 (ER)	14	C35Y168 or C35Y175 or C36Y181	PW PW4060
Boeing 767-300 (ER)	19	C25Y180	GE CF6-80C2B6F
Airbus A330-300	8	C44Y228	RR Trent 772B-60
Airbus A340-300	11	C32Y252	CFM56-5C4
Boeing 747-400	3	C42Y379 or C42Y383	GE CF6-80C2B1F
Boeing 747-400 (SCD)	3	C43Y253	PW PW4056

* 3 operated by AC Jetz (C48), 8 operated by Tango by Air Canada (Y120),
10 stored, 20 earmarked for Zip
** 8 operated by Tango by Air Canada (Y170)

23 DC-9-32s, 3 747-200 Combis, 1 747-400, 3 767-200s, 5 767-300ERs stored

Ordered	
Airbus A319-100	11
Airbus A320-200	3
Airbus A321-200	7
Airbus A330-300	5 options
Airbus A340-300	9 options
Airbus A340-500	5
Airbus A340-600	3 (+10 options)

CANADA

BOMBARDIER DHC-8-311 *(John R Davies)*

AIR CANADA REGIONAL

IATA: QK   **ICAO:** ARN   **IATA/ARC:** 014   **RADIO:** *Transcan*

CONTACTS

Mail
310 Goudey Drive
Enfield, NS B2T 1E4

Telephone/Fax
Admin: +1 902 873 5000
Fax: +1 902 873 3897

OPERATION

Type: Scheduled/charter passenger/cargo
Cities served: Canada: YAM YBC YBG YBL YCD YCG YDF YEG YFC YGK YGP YGR YHZ YJT YKA YLW YMM YOJ YOP YOW YPR YQB YQG YQI YQL YQM YQQ YQR YQU YQX YQY YQZ YSB YSJ YSL YTS YTZ YUL YUY YVO YVR YWG YWK YWL YXC YXE YXJ YXS YXT YXU YYB YYC YYD YYE YYF YYJ YYR YYT YYY YYZ YZP YZR YZV ZBF **US:** BDL BOS BWI CLE CMH DTW PDX PIT PVD RIC SEA
All service operated for Air Canada; flights operated by AirBC, Air Nova, and Canadian Regional use QK flight numbers in 7650-8999 range
Code-share: Lufthansa, United Airlines
FFP: Aeroplan

HISTORY/STRUCTURE

Founded: January 1, 2001
CEO: Joseph Randell

Start date: January 31, 2001
Ownership: Air Canada (100%)

FLEET

Type	No	Seats	Engines
Beech 1900D	5	Y18	PWC PT6A-67D
DHC-8-100	63	Y37 or Y21/Combi or Y29/Combi	PWC PW120A
DHC-8-300	26	Y50	PWC PW123
Bombardier CRJ200ER	6	Y50	GE CF34-3B1
F28 Mk 1000	*11	Y63	RR Spey 555-15/15H/15N
BAe 146-200A	10	C8Y68 or C10Y67	LY ALF502R-5
* to be retired in 2002; 8 others stored			

NOTES   Beech 1900Ds flown as Air Alliance. Pending the announcement of a permanent name in 2002, AirBC, Air Nova, Air Ontario, and Canadian Regional-Canadien Régional names are worn by aircraft.

BOMBARDIER DHC-8-102 DASH 8 *(MAP)*

AIR CREEBEC

IATA: YN   **ICAO:** CRQ   **IATA/ARC:** 219   **RADIO:** *Cree*

CONTACTS

Mail
PO Box 430
Val D'Or, QC
J9P 4P4

Email: info@aircreebec.ca
Internet: www.aircreebec.ca

Telephone/Fax
Admin: +1 819 825 8355
Fax: +1 819 825 0208
Res: 1 800 567 6567

OPERATION

Type: Scheduled/charter passenger/cargo
Cities served: YAT YFA YGL YGW YKQ YKU YMO YMT YNC YNS YPO YTS YUL YVO ZEM ZKE
Bases: YGL YUL YMO YTS YVO
Code-share: Air Canada (flight numbers in 7200-7649 range)
FFP: Aeroplan

HISTORY/STRUCTURE

Founded: June 1982
Start date: July 1, 1982
CEO: Albert Diamond
Ownership: Creeco (100%)

FLEET

Type	No	Seats	Engines
Beech King Air A100	1	Y10	PWC PT6A-28
EMB-110P1	3	Y14	PWC PT6A-34
Beech 1900D	2	Y18	PWC PT6A-67D
DHC-8-100	1	Y37	PWC PWC PW120A
HS 748-2A	2	Y47	RR Dart 534-2

RAYTHEON BEECH 1900D *(John R Davies)*

AIR GEORGIAN (dba Air Alliance)

IATA: none   **ICAO:** GGN   **IATA/ARC:** none   **RADIO:** *Georgian*

CONTACTS

Mail
2450 Derry Road East
Mississauga, ON L5S 1B2

Internet: www.airalliance.ca

Telephone/Fax
Admin: +1 905 676 1221
Fax: +1 905 676 1176
Res: 1 800 996 9953

OPERATION

Type: Scheduled/charter passenger/cargo
Cities served: Canada: YGK YUL YYZ YZR **US:** ABE ALB DAY GRR HAR
MDT ROC SDF SYR
All scheduled service (with Beech 1900s) operated/flown for Air Canada using
only AC flight numbers (in 7200-7649 range)
Global alliance: Star, Air Canada Tier 3 operator
FFP: Aeroplan

HISTORY/STRUCTURE

Founded: 1994
Start date: 1994
CEO: Paul Mulrooney
Ownership: Western Regional Airlines (100%)

FLEET

Type	No	Seats	Engines
Beech King Air F90	1	Y9	PWC PT6A-135
Beech 1900C-1	1	Y18	PWC PT6A-65B
Beech 1900D	12	Y18	PWC PT6A-67D

BRITISH AEROSPACE (HAWKER SIDDELEY) HS 748 SERIES 2A *(Henry Tenby)*

AIR INUIT

IATA: 3H   **ICAO:** AIE   **IATA/ARC:** 875   **RADIO:** *Air Inuit*

CANADA

CONTACTS

Mail
547 Meloche Ave
Dorval, QC H9P 2W2

Telephone/Fax
Admin: +1 514 636 9445
Fax: +1 514 636 8916
Res: 1 800 361 2965

Email: info@airinuit.com
Internet: www.airinuit.ca

OPERATION

Type: Scheduled/charter passenger/cargo
Cities served: AKV XGR YGL YGW YIK YKG YPH YPJ YPX YQC YSK YTQ YUD YUL YVP YWB YZG
Code-share: First Air
FFP: Air Inuit Reward Program

HISTORY/STRUCTURE

Founded: 1978
CEO: Mark T Gordon

Start date: 1979
Ownership: Makivik Corporation

FLEET

Type	No	Seats	Engines
Beech King Air A100	1	Y10	PWC PT6A-28
DHC-6-300	5	Y18/Combi	PWC PT6A-27
DHC-8-100	2	Y37	PWC PW120A
HS 748-2A	4	Y40/Combi/Frtr	RR Dart 534-2
Convair 580	4	Y43/Y49	AN 501-D13
DHC-8-300	1	Y50	PWC PW123

Convair 580 & DHC-8-300 operated on behalf of Hydro-Québec; 580s to be
retired in favor of 2 Dash 8-Q400s

Subsidiaries Johnny May Air Charter and Nunavik Rotors operate one DHC-2
Beaver and two DHC-3 Otters, and one AS350B Astar, respectively

RAYTHEON BEECH 1900D *(Karl Hayes)*

AIR LABRADOR (Labrador Airways dba)

IATA: WJ   **ICAO:** LAL   **IATA/ARC:** 927   **RADIO:** *Lab Air*

CONTACTS

Mail
PO Box 310
Station A
Goose Bay, NF A0P 1S0

Email: sales@airlabrador.com
Internet: www.airlabrador.com

Telephone/Fax
Admin: +1 709 896 3658
Fax: +1 709 896 8905
Res: 1 800 665 1177

OPERATION

Type: Scheduled/charter passenger/cargo
Cities served: YAY YBI YBX YDI YDP YFX YHA YHG YHO YHR YIF YJT YMH YMN YQX YRF YRG YSO YYR YYT YZV
Some scheduled service operated for Air Canada Regional using AC flight numbers (in 7200-7649 range)
FFP: Aeroplan

HISTORY/STRUCTURE

Founded: 1948 (as Newfoundland Airways)
Start date: 1948
CEO: Roger W Pike
Ownership: Provincial Investments (Pike family)

FLEET

Type	No	Seats	Engines
DHC-3T Otter	1	Y9/Freighter	PWC PT6A-135A
Cessna 208B	1	Freighter	PWC PT6A-114
Beech 1900D	2	Y18	PWC PT6A-67D
DHC-6-100	1	Y19/Combi	PWC PT6A-20
DHC-6-300	4	Y19/Combi	PWC PT6A-27

BRITISH AEROSPACE (HAWKER SIDDELEY) 748 SERIES 2A *(Stephen Wilcox)*

AIR NORTH (Air North Charter & Training dba)

IATA: 4N   **ICAO:** ANT   **IATA/ARC:** 287   **RADIO:** *Air North*

CONTACTS

Mail
PO Box 4998
Whitehorse, YT
Y1A 6E6

Email: airnorth@yknet.yk.ca
Internet: www.airnorth.yk.net

Telephone/Fax
Admin: +1 867 668 2228
Fax: +1 867 668 6224
Res: 1 800 661 0407 (Canada)
Res: 1 800 764 0407 (US)

OPERATION

Type: Scheduled/charter passenger/cargo
Cities served: Canada: YDA YEG YEV YOC YXY YYC **US:** FAI JNU

HISTORY/STRUCTURE

Founded: 1977
Start date: January 17, 1986 (scheduled)
CEO: Joseph T Sparling
Ownership: Joseph T Sparling & Thomas A Wood

FLEET

Type	No	Seats	Engines
Beech 99	1	Y12	PWC PT6A-27
HS 748-2A	3	Y40	RR Dart 534-2
Ordered			
Boeing 737	2		

CESSNA 208B GRAND CARAVAN *(Henry Tenby)*

AIR TINDI

IATA: 8T   **ICAO:** none   **IATA/ARC:** 744   **RADIO:** none

CONTACTS

Mail
PO Box 1693
Yellowknife NT
X1A 2P3

Email: airtindi@airtindi.com
Internet: www.airtindi.com

Telephone/Fax
Admin: +1 867 669 8200
Fax: +1 867 669 8210

OPERATION

Type: Scheduled/charter passenger/cargo
Cities served: YFJ YFS YLE YRA YSG YZF

HISTORY/STRUCTURE

Founded: 1988
Start date: November 1, 1988
CEO: Peter Arychuk
Ownership: Arychuk family (100%)

FLEET

Type	No	Seats	Engines
Aviat A-1 Husky	1	Y1	LY O-360-A1P
Cessna A185F	3	Y3	CO IO-520-D
Beech King Air C90	1	Y6	PWC PT6A-20
Cessna 208	1	Y7	PWC PT6A-114A
Cessna 208B	2	Y9	PWC PT6A-114A
DHC-3 Otter	1	Y9	PWC PT6A-135A
Beech King Air B200C	1	EMS	PWC PT6A-42
Beech CATPASS 250	1	Y11	PWC PT6A-41
DHC-6-300	6	Y19	PWC PT6A-27

LOCKHEED L-1011-385-3 TRISTAR 500 *(Ian Bowley)*

AIR TRANSAT

IATA: TS   **ICAO:** TSC   **IATA/ARC:** 649   **RADIO:** *Transat*

CONTACTS

Mail
11600 rue Cargo A-1
Aéroport International de Montréal (Mirabel)
QC J7N 1G9
Internet: www.airtransat.com

Telephone/Fax
Admin: +1 514 476 1011
Fax: +1 514 476 6710
Res: 1 800 470 1011

OPERATION

Type: Scheduled/charter passenger
Cities served: Canada: YEG YHZ YMX YQB YQX YUL YVR YYC YYT YYZ **US:**
FLL HNL LAS MCO MIA MLB OGG PBI PIE RSW SRQ **Caribbean:** ANU AVI
CMW CYO FDF GCM HOG LRM MBJ NAS PLS POP PTP PUJ SCU SDQ SJU
SXM VRA **México:** ACA AUA CUN HUX MID MZT PVR ZIH ZLO **Central
America:** ADZ LIR MGA PTY SJO **South America:** BLA CFG CTG PMV
Europe: ABZ AMS ATH BFS BHX BOD BRU BSL CDG CWL DUB DUS EDI
EXT FAO FCO FRA GLA LGW LIS LYS MAN MRS NCE NCL NTE OPO PDL
SXF TER TLS WAW **Bases:** YMX YVR YYZ
Many destinations are served on a seasonal basis

HISTORY/STRUCTURE

Founded: December 1986
Chairman: Jean-Marc Eustache
Ownership: Transat AT (100%)

Start date: November 14, 1987
CEO: Denis Jacob

FLEET

Type	No	Seats	Engines
Boeing 757-200	4	Y228	RR RB211-535E4
Airbus A310-300	4	C20Y239	GE CF6-80C2A8
L-1011 TriStar 1	1	C19Y343	RR RB211-22B
L-1011 TriStar 100	3	C19Y343	RR RB211-22B
L-1011 TriStar 150	3	C19Y343	RR RB211-22B
L-1011 TriStar 500	6	C19Y290	RR RB211-524B4-02
Airbus A330-200	2	C21Y342	RR Trent 772B-60
Airbus A330-300	2	C21Y349	RR Trent 772-60
Ordered			
Airbus A310-300	2		

BOEING 727-200 (F) *(Paul Giannico)*

ALLCANADA EXPRESS (ACE)

IATA: none **ICAO:** CNX **IATA/ARC:** none **RADIO:** *Canex*

CONTACTS

Mail
603-50 Burnhamthorpe Road West
Mississauga, ON
L5B 3C2

Email: ace@allcanadaexpress.com
Internet: www.allcanadaexpress.com

Telephone/Fax
Admin: +1 905 896 7175
Fax: +1 905 896 1549

OPERATION

Type: Charter cargo
Bases: YHM YMX YVR YYZ
Cities served: Canada: YHM YMX YVR YWG YYC YYZ **US:** CVG TOL
Operates primarily contract service, including on behalf of BAX Global and UPS
(3 727-200s each); 4 727-200s wet-leased to CargoJet Canada

HISTORY/STRUCTURE

Founded: September, 1992
Start date: October 1992
CEO: John MacKenzie
Ownership: John MacKenzie and Murray Lautz

FLEET

Type	No	Engines
Boeing 727-100F	1	PW JT8D-7B
Boeing 727-200F	10	PW JT8D-9A/-15/-17/17R

EMBRAER EMB-110P1 BANDEIRANTE

AVIATION QUÉBEC LABRADOR

IATA: QC   **ICAO:** QLA   **IATA/ARC:** none   **RADIO:** *Québec Labrador*

CONTACTS

Mail
CP 575
Sept-Îles QC
G4R 4K7

Telephone/Fax
Admin: +1 418 962 7901
Fax: +1 418 962 9202

Email: aqladm@bbsi.net

OPERATION

Type: Scheduled/charter passenger/cargo
Cities served: YBX YGV YHR YIF YKL YNA YPN YZV
FFP: Aeroplan

HISTORY/STRUCTURE

Founded: 1983
Start date: 1983
CEO: Jacques Cleary
Ownership: Groupe Gamac (100%)

FLEET

Type	No	Seats	Engines
PA-31-350 Chieftain	1	Y9	LY TIO-540-J2BD
EMB-110P1	6	Y15	PWC PT6A-34
DHC-6-300	1	Y19	PWC PT6A-27

CANADA

FAIRCHILD SA-227AC METRO III *(John R Davies)*

BEARSKIN AIRLINES (Bearskin Lake Air Service dba)

IATA: JV   **ICAO:** BLS   **IATA/ARC:** 632   **RADIO:** *Bearskin*

CONTACTS

Mail
PO Box 1447
Sioux Lookout, ON
P8T 1C1

Telephone/Fax
Admin: +1 807 474 2635
Fax: +1 807 474 2645
Res: 1 800 465 5039 (Canada)
Res: 1 800 465 2327 (US)

Email: administration@bearskinairlines.com
Internet: www.bearskinairlines.com

OPERATION

Type: Scheduled/charter passenger/cargo
Cities served: KEW KIF MSA SUR WNN XKS YAC YAG YAM YAX YBE YER YFH YFO YHD YHP YKZ YLH YNO YOW YPL YPM YQD YQK YQT YRL YSB YTL YTS YVZ YWG YWP YXL YYB YYU ZPB ZRJ ZSJ
Bases: YXL YQT
FFP: Aeroplan

HISTORY/STRUCTURE

Founded: 1963 (as Bearskin Lake Air Service)
Start date: July 17, 1963
CEO: Harvey Friesen
Ownership: Privately held

FLEET

Type	No	Seats	Engines
PA-23-250 Aztec	1	Y5	LY IO-540-C4B5
Pilatus PC-12	6	Y9	PWC PT6A-67B
Beech King Air A100	4	Y12	PWC PT6A-28
Beech 99	6	Y14	PWC PT6A-28
Metro III	5	Y19	GA TPE331-11U-612G
Metro 23	2	Y19	GA TPE331-12U-701G

DOUGLAS DC-3 *(Steve Kinder)*

BUFFALO AIRWAYS

IATA: J4   **ICAO:** BFL   **IATA/ARC:** none   **RADIO:** *Buffalo*

CANADA

CONTACTS

Mail
1000 Buffalo Drive
Hay River Airport NT
X0E 0R9

Email: buffalo@ssimicro.com
Internet: www.buffaloairways.com

Telephone/Fax
Admin: +1 867 874 3333
Fax: +1 867 874 3572

OPERATION

Type: Scheduled/charter passenger/cargo
Cities served: YHY YZF

HISTORY/STRUCTURE

Founded: 1970
Start date: 1970
CEO: Joe McBryan
Ownership: Privately held

FLEET

Type	No	Seats	Engines
Beech Travel Air 95/B95	3	Y/Combi	LY O-360-A1A
Beech Baron C55/D55	2	Y/Combi	CO IO-520-C
Beech King Air A90	2	Y/Combi	PWC PT6A-20
PBY-5A Canso	3	Tanker	PW R-1830-92/-92S
CL-215-1A10	4	Tanker	PW R-2800-CA3
DC-3	10	Y27/Combi/Freighter	PW R-1830
Curtiss C-46	3	Freighter	PW R-2000
DC-4	5	Freighter/Tanker	PW R-2000

BRITISH AEROSPACE (HAWKER SIDDELEY) 748 SERIES 2A *(Matthew Lee)*

CALM AIR (Calm Air International dba)

IATA: MO   **ICAO:** CAV   **IATA/ARC:** 622   **RADIO:** *Calm Air*

CONTACTS

Mail
90 Thompson Drive
Thompson, MB
R8N 1Y8

Telephone/Fax
Admin: +1 204 778 6471
Fax: +1 204 778 6954
Res: 1 800 839 2256

Email: calmair@gatewest.net
Internet: www.calmair.com

OPERATION

Type: Scheduled/charter passenger/cargo
Cities served: XPK XSI YBK YCS YEK YFO YGX YLR YQD YRT YTH YUT YWG YXN YYL YYQ ZTM
Most scheduled service operated for Air Canada using AC flight numbers (in 7200-7649 range)
FFP: Aeroplan

HISTORY/STRUCTURE

Founded: 1962
Start date: 1976 (scheduled service)
CEO: Arnold Morberg
Ownership: Privately held

FLEET

Type	No	Seats	Engines
PA-31-350 Chieftain	1	Y9	LY TIO-540-J2BD
Cessna 208B	1	Y9	PWC PT6A-114A
DHC-6-100	1	Y19	PWC PT6A-20
SAAB 340B	4	Y34	GE CT7-9B
HS 748-2A/2B	6	Y36/Frtr	RR Dart 534-2/535-2

BOEING 737-200C *(Henry Tenby)*

CANADIAN NORTH (Air NorTerra dba)

IATA: 5T   **ICAO:** none   **IATA/ARC:** 518   **RADIO:** none

---

CONTACTS

Mail
300-5201 50th Avenue
Yellowknife NT
X1A 3S9

Telephone/Fax
Admin: +1 867 669 4000
Fax: +1 867 669 4040
Res: 1 800 661 1505

Email: email@cdn-north.com
Internet: www.canadiannorth.com

OPERATION

Type: Scheduled/charter passenger/cargo
Cities served: YCB YEG YEV YFB YHY YOW YRT YSM YVQ YYC YZF
FFP: Aeroplan

HISTORY/STRUCTURE

Founded: 1989 (as a division of Canadian Airlines)
Start date: September 1998
CEO: Michael King
Ownership: NorTerra Inc (Inuvialuit Development Corp & Nunasi Corp)

FLEET

Type	No	Seats	Engines
Fokker F28 Mk 1000	2	C6Y45	RR Spey 555-15N
Boeing 737-200C	3	Y112/Combi	PW JT8D-17/-17A

RAYTHEON BEECH 1900D *(Henry Tenby)*

CENTRAL MOUNTAIN AIR

IATA: 9M   **ICAO:** GLR   **IATA/ARC:** 634   **RADIO:** *Glacier*

CONTACTS

Mail
PO Box 998
Smithers, BC
V0J 2N0

Email: info@cmair.bc.ca
Internet: www.cmair.bc.ca

Telephone/Fax
Admin: +1 250 847 4780
Fax: +1 250 847 3744

OPERATION

Type: Scheduled/charter passenger/cargo
Hubs: YVR YYC
Cities served: Canada: YBL YCG YDQ YEG YLL YOJ YPE YQL YQQ YVR YWL YXC YXD YXH YYC YYD **US:** GEG
All scheduled service operated for Air Canada using only AC flight numbers (in 7200-7649 range)
FFP: Aeroplan

HISTORY/STRUCTURE

Founded: 1987
Start date: 1987
CEO: Doug McCrea
Ownership: 580741 BC Ltd (100%)

FLEET

Type	No	Seats	Engines
Beech 1900C-1	1	Y19	PWC PT6A-65B
Beech 1900D	11	Y18	PWC PT6A-67D

NOTES
Several Beech 1900Ds leased to Air Georgian

SAAB SF340A (Mike Reyno)

CORPORATE EXPRESS (Corpac Canada dba)

IATA: none   **ICAO:** CPB   **IATA/ARC:** none   **RADIO:** *Penta*

CONTACTS

Mail
575 Palmer Road NE
Calgary AB
T2E 7G4

Telephone/Fax
Admin: +1 403 216 4050
Fax: +1 403 216 4055
Res: 1 800 661 8151

Email: charter@corpxair.com
Internet: www.corpxair.com

OPERATION

Type: Scheduled/charter passenger/cargo
Hubs: YVR YYC
Cities served: YMM YXD YYC

HISTORY/STRUCTURE

Founded: 1975
Start date: 1975
CEO: Gordon Peariso
Ownership: Corpac Canada Ltd

FLEET

Type	No	Seats	Engines
BAe Jetstream 31	4	Y16/Y18	GA TPE331-10UG-513H/10UGR-514H
SAAB 340A	1	Y33	GE CT7-5A2

ATR42-300 *(John R Davies)*

FIRST AIR (Bradley Air Services dba)

IATA: 7F   **ICAO:** FAB   **IATA/ARC:** 245   **RADIO:** *First Air*

CONTACTS

Mail
3257 Carp Road
Carp, ON K0A 1L0
Email: reservat@firstair.ca
Internet: www.firstair.ca

Telephone/Fax
Admin: +1 613 839 3340
Fax: +1 613 839 5690
Res: 1 800 267 1247

OPERATION

Type: Scheduled/charter passenger/cargo
Cities served: YBB YCB YCO YCY YEG YEV YFB YFS YGT YHI YHK YHY YIO YLC YOW YRB YRT YSM YSR YTE YUL YUX YVM YVP YWG YXP YXY YYH YZF **Bases:** YOW **Hubs:** YEG YFB YRB YUL YVP YZF
Code-share: Air Canada (AC8950-8999 flight numbers), Air Inuit
FFP: Aeroplan

HISTORY/STRUCTURE

Founded: 1946 (as Bradley Air Services)   **Start date:** 1973 (scheduled)
Chairman: Pita Aatami   **CEO:** Robert Davis
Ownership: Makivik Corporation

FLEET

Type	No	Seats	Engines
DHC-2 Beaver	1	Y5	PW R-985
Beech 99	1	Y15	PWC PT6A-20
DHC-6-300	5	Y19	PWC PT6A-27
ATR42-300	4	Y40	PWC PW120
HS 748-2A/2B	7	Y44/Combi	RR Dart 534/535-3
DHC-7-150	1	Ice Patrol	PWC PT6A-50
Boeing 737-200C	3	Combi	PW JT8D-9A
Lockheed L-100-30	1	Freighter	AN 501-D22A
Boeing 727-100C	2	Y129/Combi/Frtr	PW JT8D-7B
Boeing 727-200F	3	Freighter	PW JT8D-7B/-9A/-15
Boeing 727-200F	1	Y170/Combi/Frtr	PW JT8D-15

NOTES Bradley Air Services also holds title to the names Ptarmigan Airways, Northwest Territorial Airways, and NWT Air

DE HAVILLAND CANADA DHC-3 TURBO OTTER *(John Wegg)*

HARBOUR AIR

IATA: H3 **ICAO:** none **IATA/ARC:** 458 **RADIO:** *Harbour*

CONTACTS

Mail
4760 Inglis Drive
Richmond, BC
V7B 1W4

Email: harbour@harbour-air.com
Internet: www.harbour-air.com

Telephone/Fax
Admin: +1 604 278 3478
Fax: +1 604 278 5271
Res: 1 800 665 0212
SITA: YVRRMH3

OPERATION

Type: Scheduled/charter passenger/cargo
Cities served: BA3 CXH YAJ YAQ YAV YBQ YBW YGG YMF YPI YTB YVR YWH YZP ZMT ZNA ZSW

HISTORY/STRUCTURE

Founded: 1981 (as Windoak Air Service)
Start date: 1982 (as Harbour Air)
CEO: Greg McDougall
Ownership: Privately held

FLEET

Type	No	Seats	Engines
Cessna A185F	2	Y3	CO IO-520-D
DHC-2 Beaver	15	Y6	PW R-985
DHC-3 Otter	7	Y13	PWC PT6A-34/-135A
DHC-6-300	*	Y17	PWC PT6A-27
*Twin Otters wet-leased from Kenn Borek as required			

BOMBARDIER DHC-8-102 DASH 8 *(Henry Tenby)*

HAWKAIR AVIATION SERVICES

IATA: BH   **ICAO:** none   **IATA/ARC:** none   **RADIO:** *none*

CONTACTS

Mail
Site 16 C-5 RR4 Bristol Road
Terrace BC
V8G 4V2

Email: reservations@hawkair.net
Internet: www.hawkair.net

Telephone/Fax
Admin: +1 250 635 4295
Fax: +1 250 635 7852
Res: 1 866 429 5247 (Canada)

OPERATION

Type: Scheduled/charter passenger/cargo
Cities served: YPR YVR YXT YYD

HISTORY/STRUCTURE

Founded: 1994
Start date: September 8, 2000 (scheduled passenger)
CEO: Paul Hawkins
Ownership: Privately held

FLEET

Type	No	Seats	Engines
DHC-8-100	2	Y37	PWC PW120A

SIKORSKY S-76A *(John Wegg)*

HELIJET INTERNATIONAL

IATA: JB   **ICAO:** JBA   **IATA/ARC:** 613   **RADIO:** *Helijet*

CONTACTS

Mail
5911 Airport Road South
Richmond, BC
V7B 1B5

Email: info@helijet.com
Internet: www.helijet.com

Telephone/Fax
Admin: +1 604 273 4688
Fax: +1 604 273 5301
Res: 1 800 665 4354

OPERATION
Type: Scheduled/charter passenger
Cities served: Canada: CXH YLY YVR YWH YXX **US:** BFI

HISTORY/STRUCTURE
Founded: September 1986 (as Helijet Airways)
Start date: November 27, 1986
Chairman: Alistair M R MacLennan
CEO: Danny Sitnam
Ownership: Publicly traded company (CDNX: HJI)

FLEET

Type	No	Seats	Engines
Bell 206B	1	Y4	AN 250-C20
AS350BA	1	Y5	TU Arriel 1B
AS355F1	1	Y5	AN 250-C20F
Sikorsky S-76A+	1	Y12	TU Arriel 2S1
Sikorsky S-76A	4	Y12/EMS	AN 250-C30S

AIRBUS A300B4-203 (F) *(Rurik Enriquez D)*

ICC CANADA (ICC AirCargo)
(ICC International Cargo Charters Canada dba)

IATA: none   **ICAO:** CIC   **IATA/ARC:** none   **RADIO:** *Air Trader*

CONTACTS

Mail
3220 Orlando Drive
Mississauga, ON
L4V 1N3

Telephone/Fax
Admin: +1 905 672 8731
Fax: +1 905 672 8732

OPERATION

Type: Scheduled/charter cargo primarily under contract to Tigress Cargo Airlines (Canada) and AeroUnion (México)
Cities served: Canada: YYZ **US:** DAY JFK **México:** MEX MTY
Caribbean: GEO POS

HISTORY/STRUCTURE

Founded: 1986 (as ACS Canada)
Start date: November 16, 1998
President/CEO: Edward C C Peagram
Ownership: Privately held (Edward Peagram)

FLEET

Type	No	Engines
A300B4-200 (F)	5	GE CF6-50C2

BOEING 727-100C *(Gary Tahir)*

KELOWNA FLIGHTCRAFT AIR CHARTER

IATA: none   **ICAO:** KFA   **IATA/ARC:** none   **RADIO:** *Flightcraft*

CONTACTS

Mail
1-5655 Kelowna Airport Road
Kelowna, BC
V1V 1S1

Email: info@flightcraft.ca
Internet: www.flightcraft.ca

Telephone/Fax
Admin: +1 250 491 5500
Fax: +1 250 765 1489

OPERATION

Type: Scheduled/charter passenger/cargo
Bases: YHM YHZ YMX (passenger) YVR YYC YYT
Hubs: YHM YVR
Operates for Purolator Courier and Canada Post; passenger charters for Neo Air Tours using name Vacances Air Columbus

HISTORY/STRUCTURE

Founded: March 20, 1970
Start date: June 1974
CEO: Barry Lapointe
Ownership: Barry Lapointe & Jim Rogers

FLEET

Type	No	Seats	Engines
Cessna 402B	1	Freighter	CO TSIO-520E
PA-42-720	1	Corporate	PWC PT6A-41
Convair 580	16	Y52/Frtr/Tanker	AN 501-D13
Boeing 727-100C/F	5	Freighter	PW JT8D-7B
Boeing 727-200F	13	Freighter	PW JT8D-9A
Boeing 727-200	1	C14Y137	PW JT8D-9A

BEECH KING AIR 200 *(John R Davies)*

KENN BOREK AIR

IATA: 4K   **ICAO:** KBA   **IATA/ARC:** 652   **RADIO:** *Borek Air*

CONTACTS

Mail
290 McTavish Road NE
Calgary, AB
T2E 7G5

Telephone/Fax
Admin: +1 403 291 3300
Fax: +1 403 250 6908

Email: borekair@cadvision.com
Internet: www.borekair.com

OPERATION

Type: Scheduled/charter passenger/cargo
Cities served: YAB YFB YGZ YIO YRB YSR YTE YVM YXP
Operates as Aklak from Inuvit, NT; operations on behalf of Harbour Air and Maldivian Air Taxi, MEDEVAC, plus contract services in Arctic and Antarctic and extensive worldwide charter and leasing

HISTORY/STRUCTURE

Founded: 1971   **Start date:** 1971
CEO: Kenn Borek   **Ownership:** Privately held

FLEET

Type	No	Seats	Engines
Cessna A185	2	Y3	CO IO-520-D
Beech King Air B90/C90	2	Y8	PWC PT6A-20
Beech 99/B99	3	Y15	PWC PT6A-20
Beech King Air 100/A100	5	Y13/EMS	PWC PT6A-28
Beech King Air 200	3	Y13	PWC PT6A-41
EMB-110P1 Bandeirante	2	Y18	PWC PT6A-34
DHC-6-100/200/300	34	Y19/Combi	PWC PT6A-20/-27
Douglas C-117D	1	Freighter	WR R-1820

PIPER PA-31-350 CHIEFTAIN *(Paul Giannico/Pegasus)*

KEYSTONE AIR SERVICE

IATA: BZ **ICAO:** KEE **IATA/ARC:** none **RADIO:** *Keystone*

CONTACTS

Mail	**Telephone/Fax**
PO Box 2140	Admin: +1 204 734 9351
Swan River MB	Fax: +1 204 734 9181
R0L 1Z0	Res: 1 800 665 3975 (Canada)

Internet: www.keystoneair.mb.ca

OPERATION

Type: Scheduled/charter passenger/cargo
Cities served: YDN YWG ZJN

HISTORY/STRUCTURE

Founded: 1984 (as Gabrielle Air Service)
Start date: 1985
CEO: Clifford R Arlt
Ownership: Privately held

FLEET

Type	No	Seats	Engines
PA-34 Seneca	1	Y5	LY IO-360-C1E6
PA-31-310 Navajo	1	Y7	LY TIO-540-A1A
PA-31-350 Chieftain	3	Y9	LY TIO-540-J2BD
Beech King Air 200	1	F9	PWC PT6A-41
Beech B99	1	Y14	PWC PT6A-27

CONVAIR 580 *(Ken Swartz)*

NOLINOR AVIATION (Les Investissements Nolinor dba)

IATA: none   **ICAO:** none   **IATA/ARC:** none   **RADIO:** none

CONTACTS

Mail
10105 Avenue Ryan
Dorval QC
H9P 1A2

Email: wings@nolinor.com
Internet: www.nolinor.com

Telephone/Fax
Admin: +1 514 631 0018
Fax: +1 514 631 0027
Res: 1 888 505 7025

OPERATION

Type: Charter passenger/cargo

HISTORY/STRUCTURE

Founded: 1992
Start date: 1992
CEO: Jean-Claude Tremblay
Ownership: Les Investissements Nolinor (100%)

FLEET

Type	No	Seats	Engines
Convair 580	4	Y32-50/Combi/Frtr	AN 501-D13

BRITISH AEROSPACE BAe 3112 JETSTREAM 31 *(Henry Tenby)*

NORTHWESTERN AIR LEASE

IATA: J3   **ICAO:** PLR   **IATA/ARC:** 325   **RADIO:** *Polaris*

CONTACTS

Mail
PO Box 23
Fort Smith, NWT
X0E 0P0

Email: nwal@auroranet.nt.ca
Internet: www.nwal.net

Telephone/Fax
Admin: +1 867 872 2216
Fax: +1 867 872 2214
Res: 1 877 872 2216

OPERATION

Type: Scheduled/charter passenger/cargo
Cities served: YMM YPY YSM YZF

HISTORY/STRUCTURE

Founded: 1965
Start date: 1965
CEO: Terry Harrold
Ownership: Privately held (Terry & Brian Harrold)

FLEET

Type	No	Seats	Engines
Cessna 401	1	Y7	CO TS10-520-E
Beech King Air A90	1	Y8	PWC PT6A-20
Beech 99	1	Y15	PWC PT6A-20
BAe Jetstream 31	2	Y19	GA TPE331-10UGR-514H

CESSNA 208B GRAND CARAVAN *(North-Wright Airways)*

NORTH-WRIGHT AIRWAYS

IATA: HW   **ICAO:** NWL   **IATA/ARC:** none   **RADIO:** *Northwright*

CANADA

CONTACTS

Mail
Bag Service 2200
Norman Wells, NWT
X0E 0V0

Telephone/Fax
Admin: +1 403 587 2288
Fax: +1 403 587 2962
Res: 1 800 661 0702

OPERATION

Type: Scheduled/charter passenger/cargo
Cities served: YCK YEV YGH YVQ YWJ YZF ZFN
FFP: Aeroplan

HISTORY/STRUCTURE

Founded: 1986
Start date: 1987
CEO: Warren Wright
Ownership: Privately held

FLEET

Type	No	Seats	Engines
Helio H-295	1	Y5	LY GO-480-G1D6
Cessna U206G	1	Y5	CO IO-520-F
Cessna 207	2	Y5	CO IO-520-F
Cessna 337C	1	Y5	CO IO-360-C
PC-6/B1-H2 Porter	1	Y6	PWC PT6A-20
BN-2A-26 Islander	1	Y9	LY O-540-E4C5
Cessna 208B	2	Y9	PWC PT6A-114A
Beech King Air 100	1	Y9	PWC PT6A-28
Beech 99	1	Y15	PWC PT6A-20
DHC-6-100	2	Y19	PWC PT6A-20
DHC-6-300	1	Y19	PWC PT6A-27

EMBRAER EMB-110P1 BANDEIRANTE *(Henry Tenby)*

PACIFIC COASTAL AIRLINES

IATA: 8P   **ICAO:** PCO   **IATA/ARC:** 905   **RADIO:** *Pasco*

CONTACTS

Mail
117-4440 Cowley Crescent
Richmond, BC
V7B 1B8

Internet: www.pacific-coastal.com

Telephone/Fax
Admin: +1 604 273 8666
Fax: +1 604 273 4485
Res: 1 800 663 2872

OPERATION

Type: Scheduled/charter passenger
Cities served: QBC YAA YBL YKT YPW YQQ YRD YVR YYJ YZT ZEL

HISTORY/STRUCTURE

Founded: 1979
Start date: 1979
CEO: Daryl Smith
Ownership: Smith family

FLEET

Type	No	Seats	Engines
Cessna A185F	1	Y4	CO IO-520-D
DHC-2 Beaver	3	Y6	PW R-985
G-21A Goose	4	Y9	PW R-985
Beech King Air 200	1	Y13	PWC PT6A-41
EMB-110P1	2	Y15	PWC PT6A-34
Beech 1900C	1	Y19	PWC PT6A-65B
Shorts 360 (300)	6	Y30	PWC PT6A-65AR/-65R

BRITISH AEROSPACE BAe 3112 JETSTREAM 31 *(Stephen Emmins)*

PEM-AIR (dba Trillium Air)

IATA: PD   **ICAO:** PEM   **IATA/ARC:** 329   **RADIO:** *Pem Air*

CONTACTS

Mail
RR # 6
Pembroke ON
K8A 6W7

Telephone/Fax
Admin: +1 613 687 8139
Fax: +1 613 687 5166
Res: 1 800 267 3131

Internet: www.pemair.on.ca, www.trilliumair.com

OPERATION

Type: Scheduled/charter passenger/cargo
Cities served: YKF YOW
All scheduled service operated as Trillium Air
FFP: Aeroplan

HISTORY/STRUCTURE

Founded: 1970
Start date: June 21, 1999 (as Trillium Air)
CEO: Delbert A O'Brian
Ownership: Privately held

FLEET

Type	No	Seats	Engines
BAe Jetstream 31	1	Y19	GA TPE331-10UG-513H

FAIRCHILD SA226-TC METRO II *(Henry Tenby)*

PERIMETER AIRLINES (INLAND)

IATA: UW　　**ICAO:** PAG　　**IATA/ARC:** 711　　**RADIO:** *Perimeter*

CONTACTS

Mail
626 Ferry Road
Winnipeg, MB
R3H 0T7

Telephone/Fax
Admin: +1 204 786 7031
Fax:　　+1 204 783 7911
Res:　　 1 800 665 8986
Res:　　+1 204 783 8000

OPERATION

Type: Scheduled/charter passenger/cargo
Cities served: YBR YBV YCR YDN YGO YIV YNE YOH YRS YST YWG ZGI ZTM

HISTORY/STRUCTURE

Founded: 1960
Start date: 1960
CEO: William J Wehrle
Ownership: Perimeter Aviation Ltd (100%)

FLEET

Type	No	Seats	Engines
Merlin IV	1	Y18	GA TPE331-10UA-511G
Metro II	13	Y18	GA TPE331-10UA-511G

SAAB SF340A *(SAAB)*

PROVINCIAL AIRLINES

IATA: AG   **ICAO:** PAL   **IATA/ARC:** 967   **RADIO:** *Speed Air*

CONTACTS

Mail
PO Box 29030
St John's, NF
A1A 5B5

Telephone/Fax
Admin: +1 709 576 1800
Fax: +1 709 576 1802
Res: 1 800 563 2800   **Internet:** www.provair.com

OPERATION

Type: Scheduled/charter passenger/cargo and maritime surveillance/remote sensing and environmental monitoring
Cities served: Provincial: YAY YBX YJT YDF YYR YYT ZUM **Innu Mikun:** YDI YDP YMN YHO   Twin Otter scheduled service operates as Innu Mikun Airlines, a joint venture between Provincial and Innu Development LP   **FFP:** Aeroplan

HISTORY/STRUCTURE

Founded: August 1972   **Start date:** 980 (scheduled)
Chairman: Thomas W Collingwood   **President:** Gus Ollerhead
Ownership: Air Canada (100%)

FLEET

Type	No	Seats	Engines
PA-23-250 Aztec	1	Y5	LY IO-540-C4B5
DHC-2 Beaver	1	Survey	LY R-985
BN-2A Islander	1	Y9/Survey	LY IO-540-K1B5
PA-31-310 Navajo	1	Y6	LY TIO-540-A
PA-31-350 Chieftain	1	Y8	LY TIO-540-J2BD
Beech King Air 200	4	Y8/Survey	PWC PT6A-41
Merlin IV	1	Freighter	GA TPE331-3UW-303G
DHC-6-300	2	Y19	PWC PT6A-27
Metro III	2	Y19/Freighter	GA TPE331-11U-601G
SAAB 340A	2	Y33	GE CT7-5A2
Ordered			
SAAB 340A	4		

NOTES Holds title to name Interprovincial Airlines

AIRBUS A330-322 *(Ian Bowley)*

SKYSERVICE AIRLINES

IATA: none   **ICAO:** SSV   **IATA/ARC:** 884   **RADIO:** *Skytour*

CONTACTS

Mail
9785 Ryan Avenue
Dorval, QC
H9P 1A2

Telephone/Fax
Admin: +1 514 636 3300
Fax: +1 514 636 4855

Internet: www.skyserviceairlines.com

OPERATION

Type: Passenger charters, mainly on behalf of Alba Tours & Sunquest Vacations, and also for Air Transat Holidays, Conquest Vacations, Signature Vacations, and World of Vacations

HISTORY/STRUCTURE

Founded: 1986
Start date: October 1994 (IT operations)
CEO: L Russell Payson
Ownership: Skyservice Investments

FLEET

Type	No	Seats	Engines
Boeing 727-200	1*	F66	PW JT8D-9A
Airbus A319-100	2	Y144	CFM56-5B5-2
Airbus A320-200	9	Y180	CFM56-5A3/-5B5, IAE V2527-A1/-A5
Airbus A330-300	1	Y363	PW PW4168

*operated for Sport Hawk International Airlines
Additional aircraft leased as required for northern winter season

NOTES

Skyservice Aviation offers cargo, EMS, and executive services with a fleet of Jetstream 31s and biz-jets

CANADA

CESSNA 421C GOLDEN EAGLE II *(Henry Tenby)*

SKYWARD AVIATION

IATA: K9   **ICAO:** SGK   **IATA/ARC:** 470   **RADIO:** *Skyward*

CONTACTS

Mail
PO Box 1207
Thompson MB
R8N 1P1

Email: skyinfo@skyward.mb.ca
Internet: www.skyward.mb.ca

Telephone/Fax
Admin: +1 204 778 7088
Fax: +1 204 677 5945
Res: 1 888 759 9273

OPERATION

Type: Scheduled/charter passenger/cargo
Cities served: XLB XSI XTL YBK YCS YEK YGO YIV YNE YOH YRT YST YTH YWG YXN YYQ ZAC ZGI ZTM

HISTORY/STRUCTURE

Founded: 1986 (as Len's Flying Service)   **Start date:** 1986
CEO: Frank P Behrendt   **Ownership:** Privately held

FLEET

Type	No	Seats	Engines
Cessna U206F/G	2	Y5	CO IO-520-F
Cessna 207A	1	Y5	CO IO-520-F
Cessna 310R	1	Y5	CO IO-520-M
Cessna 414	1	Y6	CO TSIO-520-J
Cessna 421C	1	Y6/EMS	CO GTSIO-520-L
Cessna 402B	1	Y7	CO TSIO-520-E
Cessna 441	3	Y8/EMS	GA TPE331-8-401S
Cessna 402C	1	Y9	CO TSIO-520-VB
Cessna 208B	2	Y9	PWC PT6A-114A
Beech King Air 100/A100	3	Y12/EMS	PWC PT6A-28
Beech CATPASS 200	1	Y12	PWC PT6A-41
EMB-110P1	4	Y18	PWC PT6A-34

DE HAVILLAND CANADA DHC-7-102 DASH 7 *(Gary Tahir)*

TRANS CAPITAL AIR

IATA: none   **ICAO:** none   **IATA/ARC:** none   **RADIO:** none

CONTACTS

Mail
Hangar #1
Toronto City Centre Airport
Toronto, ON M5V 1A1

Internet: www.transcapitalair.com

Telephone/Fax
Admin: +1 416 203 1144
Fax: +1 416 203 1120
Res: 1 888 644 6144

OPERATION

Type: Charter passenger

HISTORY/STRUCTURE

Founded: 1994
Start date: September 13, 1994
CEO: Victor P Pappalardo
Ownership: Stolport Corp

FLEET

Type	No	Seats	Engines
DHC-7-100	2	Y50	PWC PT6A-50

BRITISH AEROSPACE BAe 3112 JETSTREAM 31 *(Henry Tenby)*

TRANSWEST AIR

IATA: 9T   **ICAO:** none   **IATA/ARC:** 909   **RADIO:** *Air Sask*

CONTACTS

Mail
PO Box 100
Prince Albert, SK S6V 5R4
Internet: www.transwestair.com

Telephone/Fax
Admin: +1 306 764 1404
Fax: +1 306 763 1313
Res: 1 800 667 9356

OPERATION

Type: Scheduled/charter passenger/cargo
Cities served: YBE YNL YPA YQR YSF YVC YXE ZFD ZWL

HISTORY/STRUCTURE

Founded: August 2, 2000 (merger of Air Sask & Athabaska Airways)
Start date: September 11, 2000
CEO: Pat Campling Jr & Jim Glass   **Ownership:** Transwest Air LP

FLEET

Type	No	Seats	Engines
Cessna A185F	6	Y4	CO IO-520-D
DHC-2 Beaver	4	Y5	PW R-985
Cessna 310R	2	Y5	CO IO-520-M
Beech Baron E55	1	Y5	CO IO-520-C
PA-31-310 Navajo	2	Y7	LY TIO-540-A2C
PA-31-325 Navajo	1	Y7	LY TIO-540-F2BD
PA-31-350 Chieftain	4	Y8	LY TIO-540-J2BD
Cessna 441	1	Y8/EMS	GA TPE331-8-401S
DHC-3 Otter	2	Y9	PW R-1340
DHC-3T Otter	1	Y9	PWC PT6A-135A
MU-2N	1	Y9	GA TPE331-5-252M
Beech King Air A100	1	Y11	PWC PT6A-28
Beech 99A	1	Y14	PWC PT6A-27
DHC-6-100/200	3	Y17	PWC PT6A-20
Beech 1900D	2	Y18	PWC PT6A-67D
BAe Jetstream 31	4	Y19	GA TPE331-10UR-513H

DE HAVILLAND CANADA DHC-7-102 DASH 7 *(John R Davies)*

VOYAGEUR AIRWAYS

IATA: 4V   **ICAO:** VAL   **IATA/ARC:** 908   **RADIO:** *Voyageur*

CONTACTS

Mail
1500 Airport Road
North Bay ON
P0H 1P0

Telephone/Fax
Admin: +1 705 476 1750
Fax: +1 705 476 6773

Email: info@voyageurairways.com
Internet: www.voyageurairways.com

OPERATION
Type: Charter passenger/cargo, MEDEVAC

HISTORY/STRUCTURE
Founded: 1968
Start date: 1974
CEO: Max Shapiro
Ownership: Voyageur Airport Services

FLEET

Type	No	Seats	Engines
Beech King Air A100	7	Y9/EMS	PWC PT6A-28
Beech King Air 200/200C	4	Y9/EMS	PWC PT6A-41/42
DHC-7-100	7	Y48	PWC PT6A-50

CANADA

PILATUS PC-12/45 *(Henry Tenby)*

WASAYA AIRWAYS

IATA: WG   **ICAO:** WSG   **IATA/ARC:** 093   **RADIO:** *Wasaya*

CONTACTS

Mail
RR #4, 300 Anemki Place, Suite B
Thunder Bay, ON
P7J 1H9

Email: information@wasaya.com
Internet: www.wasaya.com

Telephone/Fax
Admin: +1 807 473 1200
Fax: +1 807 577 1549
Res: 1 877 492 7292

OPERATION

Type: Scheduled/charter passenger/cargo
Cities served: (scheduled) YQT YXL

HISTORY/STRUCTURE

Founded: 1986 (as Kelner Airways)
Start date: October 1987 (scheduled)
CEO: Tom Morris
Ownership: Wasaya Airways LP

FLEET

Type	No	Seats	Engines
Cessna 208B	5	Y9/Freighter	PWC PT6A-114A
PC-12	5	Y9	PWC PT6A-67B
Beech 1900D	1	Y18	PWC PT6A-67D
HS 748-2A/B	5	Frtr/Tanker	RR Dart 534-2/536-2/550-2

DE HAVILLAND CANADA DHC-6-100 TWIN OTTER *(John Wegg)*

WEST COAST AIR

IATA: 8O   **ICAO:** none   **IATA/ARC:** 222   **RADIO:** *Coast Air*

CONTACTS

Mail
PO Box 48197
Bentall Centre
Vancouver, BC
V7X 1N8

Email: info@westcoastair.com
Internet: www.westcoastair.com

Telephone/Fax
Admin: +1 604 606 6800
Fax: +1 604 606 6820
Res: 1 800 347 2222

OPERATION

Type: Scheduled/charter passenger
Cities served: CXH YWH

HISTORY/STRUCTURE

Founded: 1995
Start date: January 25, 1996
CEO: Al Baydala
Ownership: Privately held

FLEET

Type	No	Seats	Engines
DHC-2 Beaver	2	Y6	PW R-985
DHC-6-100	4	Y18	PWC PT6A-20
DHC-6-200	1	Y18	PWC PT6A-20

FAIRCHILD F-27F *(James Helbock)*

WESTERN EXPRESS AIR LINES (Westex)

IATA: none   **ICAO:** WES   **IATA/ARC:** none   **RADIO:** *Westex*

CONTACTS

Mail	**Telephone/Fax**
Box 24259 APO	Admin: +1 604 273 1500
Vancouver International Airport	Fax: +1 604 273 3863
Richmond, BC	Res: 1 877 882 2746
V7B 1Y4	

Email: ops@westex.ca
Internet: www.westex.ca

OPERATION

Type: Scheduled/charter/contract cargo
Cities served: Canada: YEG YVR YXT YXY YYC **US:** BFI SEA
Also operates for DHL, Loomis, & Purolator Courier & Canada Post

HISTORY/STRUCTURE

Founded: 1984 (as Aviation Business Flights)
Start date: 1994 (as Western Express Air Lines)
CEO: David J Oliver
Ownership: David J Oliver

FLEET

Type	No		Engines
Merlin IVA	1		GA TPE331-10UA-511G
Metro III	2		GA TPE331-11U-611G
Beech King Air B200	2	EMS	PWC PT6A-42
Fairchild F-27F	1		RR Dart 529-7E
Fokker F27 Mk 300M	1		RR Dart 514-7
Fokker F27 Mk 400	1		RR Dart 532-7

NOTES

Currently in the process of merging cargo operations with North American Airlines

BOEING 737-700 *(Gary Tahir)*

WESTJET AIRLINES

IATA: WS   **ICAO:** WJA   **IATA/ARC:** none   **RADIO:** *Westjet*

CONTACTS

Mail
5055 11ᵗʰ Street NE
Calgary, AB
T2E 8N4

Internet: www.westjet.com

Telephone/Fax
Admin: +1 403 444 2600
Fax: +1 403 444 2301
Res: 1 800 538 5696

OPERATION

Type: Scheduled/charter passenger/cargo
Cities served: YAM YEG YHM YLW YMM YOW YQM YQQ YQR YQT YQU YSB YTH YVR YWG YXE YXS YXU YXX YYC YYJ

HISTORY/STRUCTURE

Founded: 1995
Start date: February 29, 1996
Chairman: Clive Beddoe
Ownership: Publicly traded (TSE: WJA)

FLEET

Type	No	Seats	Engines
Boeing 737-200	23	Y125	PW JT8D-9A/-15/-15A/-17
Boeing 737-700	4	Y140	CFM56-7B24
Ordered			
Boeing 737-700	34	+56 options	

BOEING 727-100 (F) *(Henry Tenby)*

WINNPORT LOGISTICS

IATA: W8 **ICAO:** WNT **IATA/ARC:** 489 **RADIO:** *Winnport*

CONTACTS

Mail
103-1821 Wellington Avenue
Winnipeg MB
R3H 0G4

Email: winnport@winnport.com
Internet: www.winnport.com

Telephone/Fax
Admin: +1 204 954 9210
Fax: +1 204 954 9214

OPERATION

Type: Scheduled/charter cargo

HISTORY/STRUCTURE

Founded: 1998
Start date: February 1, 2000
CEO: Lynn F L Bishop
Ownership: Winnport Logistics

FLEET

Type	No	Engines
Boeing 727-100F	1	PW JT8D-7B

Canada Addenda

AIR MIKISEW Box 5175, Fort McMurray, AB T9H 3G2; +1 780 743 8218, Fax +1 780 743 8225, Res 1 888 268 7112, www.air-mikisew@home.com. Allan Prouix. Scheduled/charter passenger/cargo. 1x Cessna A185F, 1 Cessna U206G, 2 x Cessna 207, 2 x Beaver, 2 x Chieftain, 1 x Islander, 1 x King Air, 1 x Beech 99, 2 x Jetstream 32

AIR NOOTKA Box 19, Gold River, BC V0P 1G0; +1 250 283 2255, Fax +1 250 283 2256, www.airnootka.com, Grant Howatt. Scheduled/charter passenger/cargo. 1 x Cessna 180, 1 x Beaver, 1 x Otter

AIR SATELLITE (ASJ/*Satellite*) Aéroport de Baie Comeau, Pointe-Lebel QC, G5C 2S6; +1 418 589 8923, Fax +1 418 589 6895, Res 1 800 463 8512 (Canada 418), 1 800 231 7718, airsat@globetrotter.net, www.air-satellite.com. Edith Fournier. Scheduled/charter passenger/cargo. 2 x Cessna 310R, 1 x Cessna 335, 3 x Cessna 402/402B, 1 x Trislander

AIRSPEED AVIATION (SPD/*Speedline*) 3-30440 Liberator Avenue, Abbotsford, BC V2T 6H5; +1 604 852 9245, Fax +1 604 852 9295, Res 1 866 359 6837, www.airspeed-abby.com. John Giesbrecht. Scheduled/charter passenger/cargo. 1 x Cessna 402B, 1 x Cessna 414

AIRWAVE TRANSPORT (812971 Ontario Inc dba) (AWV/*Airwave*) 2450 Derry Road East, Hangar 5, Bay 3, Mississauga, ON L5S 1B2; +1 905 405 8622, Fax +1 905 405 9228. Chris Dunn. Charter cargo. 1 x Gulfstream I

ALBERTA CITYLINK (Palliser Air) (650584 Alberta Inc dba)(ABK/*Alberta Citylink*) PO Box 161, Medicine Hat, AB T1A 7E8; +1 403 527 3328, Fax +1 403 527 4721, Les N Little. Charter passenger/cargo. 2 x Jetstream 31, 1 x Jetstream 32EP

ALKAN AIR (AKN/*Alkan Air*) 105 Lodestar Lane, Whitehorse, YT Y1A 6E6; +1 867 668 2107, Fax +1 867 6117, alkanair@yknet.yk.ca, www.alkanair.com. Barry Watson. Charter passenger/cargo. 1 x Cessna U206G, 1 x Cessna T207A, 2 x Chieftain, 2 x Beech 200

ALTA FLIGHTS (CHARTERS)(Quikair) (ALZ) PO Box 9831, Edmonton International Airport, Edmonton, AB T5J 2T2; +1 780 890 1330, Fax +1 780 890 1331, Res 1 800 668 4766, admin@altaflights.com, www.altaflights.com, David Robertson. Scheduled (Quikair)/charter passenger/cargo. 2 x Cessna 402C, 1 x Cessna 414A, 4 x Cessna 208B, 2 x King Air B100, 1 x CATPASS 200, 1 x IAI 1125SPX, 15 x Metro III/23, 2 x Dornier 228-200

BAXTER AVIATION PO Box 1110, Nanaimo, BC V9R 6E7; +1 250 754 1066, Fax +1 250 754 1075, www.baxterair.com, Thomas Baxter. Scheduled/charter passenger/cargo. 2 x Cessna A185F, 9 x Beaver

BEAVER AIR SERVICES Box 2557, The Pas, MB R9A 1M3; +1 204 623 7160, Fax +1 204 623 3635. Shirley Castel. Scheduled/charter passenger/cargo. 1 x Cessna A185F, 2 x Chieftain, 1 x Cheyenne II, 1 x King Air 200

CANADIAN WESTERN AIRLINES Penthouse, 6081 No 3 Rd, Richmond, BC V6Y 2B2; +1 604 233 9292, Fax +1 604 214 9925, Res: 1 866 835 9292, info@cwair.com, www.cwair.com. Patrick Fowler. Scheduled/charter passenger/cargo. 2 x Cessna 401

COMMANDO AIR TRANSPORT PO Box 196, Gimli, MB R0C 1B0; +1 204 642 3414, Fax +1 204 642 3416, catinc@mb.sympatico.ca. Jeff Schroeder. Charter cargo. 1 x C-46

GEORGIAN EXPRESS CARGO (Georgian Express dba) 2833-16th Avenue, Main Terminal, Toronto-Buttonville Airport, Markham, ON L3R 0P8; +1 905 676 1221, Fax +1 905 676 1176, www.georgianexpress.com. Paul Mulrooney. Charter/contract cargo (operates for Dynamex). 1 x Cessna 208, 6 x Cessna 208B

INTEGRA AIR 101-417 Stubb Ross Rd, Lethbridge, AB T1K 7N3; +1 403 381 8359, Fax +1 403 320 9993, Res 1 877 213 8359, office@integraair.com, www.integraair.com. Brent Gateman. Scheduled/charter passenger/cargo. 1 x Navajo, 2 x King Air 100

K D AIR (XC/KDC/*Kay Dee*) RR 2, Site 225, C-11, Port Alberni, BC V9Y 7L6; +1 250 752 5884, Fax +1 250 752 5750, Res 1 800 665 4244, info@kdair.com, www.kdair.com. Ketty and Diana Banke. Scheduled passenger. 1 x Cessna 172, 1 x Navajo, 1 x Chieftain

KEEWATIN AIR (KIVALLIQ AIR) (FK) 15-20 Hangar Line Rd, Winnipeg, MB R3J 3Y8; +1 204 888 0100, Fax +1 204 888 3300, rklym@kivalliqair.com, www.kivalliqair.com. F Robert May. Scheduled/charter passenger/cargo (Aeroplan). 3 x PC-12, 1 x CATPASS 200, 1 x Lear 35; ordered: SJ30-2

KNIGHTHAWK AIR EXPRESS (2734141 Canada Inc dba)(KNX/*Knight Flite*) 100 Service Rd, Gloucester, ON K1V 9B4; +1 613 736 0048, Fax +1 613 736 0789, www.knighthawk.ca. Hugh MacMillan. Charter/contract cargo (operates for Airborne Express, Dynamex, FedEx). 1 x Beech 1900C, 4 x Falcon 20

LITTLE RED AIR SERVICE (LRA/*Little Red*) PO Box 584, Fort Vermilion, AB T0H 1N0; +1 780 927 4630, Fax +1 780 927 3667. Henry Grandjambe. Charter passenger/cargo. 4 x Cessna U206F, 2 x Chieftain, 1 x Beaver, 2 x Islander, 3 x King Air 100

MONTAIR AVIATION (UJ) Boundary Bay Airport, 4400-72 St, Delta, BC V4K 5B3; +1 604 946 6688, Fax +1 604 946 6508, Res 1 888 666 8247, montair@montair.com, www.montair.com. Al Neufeld. Scheduled/charter passenger/cargo. 2 x PC-12

MORNINGSTAR AIR EXPRESS (MAL/*Morningstar*) Edmonton City Centre Airport, Box 14, 29 Airport Road, Edmonton, AB T5G 0W6; +1 780 453 3022, Fax +1 780 453 6057, disp@maei.ca, www.maei.ca. Kim Ward & Don Wheaton Jr. Charter/contract cargo (operates as a FedEx Feeder). 4 x Cessna 208B, 4 x Boeing 727-100F

NAKINA OUTPOSTS CAMPS & AIR SERVICE 181 Cordingley Lake Rd, PO Box 126, Nakina, ON P0T 2H0; +1 807 329 5341, Fax +1 807 329 5876, nakinaop@astrocom.on.ca. Don & Millie Bourdignon. Scheduled/charter passenger/cargo. 1 x Turbo Otter, 1 x PC-12, 2 x Cessna 208B, 1 x Twin Otter

NORTH AMERICAN AIRLINES (NTM/*Northam*) Box 10, 575 Palmer Rd NE, Calgary, AB T2E 7G4; +1 403 275 7700, Fax +1 403 275 5947, Res 1 888 669 6649, northam@naairlines.com, www.naairlines.com. Don G Hollier. Charter passenger/cargo. 4 x Chieftain, 2 x Cessna 208, 3 x Metro III, 1 x King Air B300, 1 x Falcon 20, 2 x Westwind

NORTH CARIBOO FLYING SERVICE (NCB/*North Cariboo*) PO Box 6789, Fort St John, BC V1J 4J2; +1 250 787 0311, Fax +1 250 787 6086, sales@northcaribooair.com, www.northcaribooair.com. Dan O Wuthrich. Charter passenger/cargo. 3 x Cessna U206, 1 x Navajo, 1 x King Air B90, 1 x King Air 100, 2 x Twin Otter, 2 x CATPASS 200, 1 x Beech 1900C

NORTH VANCOUVER AIR (North Vancouver Airlines dba) (VL/NRV/*Norvan*) 311-5360 Airport Road South, Richmond, BC V7B 1B4; +1 604 278 1608, Fax +1 604 278 2608, Res 1 800 228 6608, travelinfo@northvanair.com, www.northvanair.com. Zoltan Kuun. Scheduled/charter passenger/cargo. 2 x Navajo, 1 x Chieftain, 2 x King Air A100

NORTHERN DENE AIRWAYS (NorcanAir) PO Box 2106, Prince Albert, SK S6V 6K1; +1 306 764 0550, Fax +1 306 953 0070, ndaypa@sk.sympatico.ca. David Webster. Scheduled/charter passenger/cargo. 1 x Cessna A185, 2 x Baron, 2 x Navajo, 4 x Chieftain, 3 x Beaver, 1 x Otter, 2 x Metro III

NORTHERN SKY AVIATION (Smart Sky) (477470 Alberta Inc dba) Box 205, High Level, AB T0H 1Z0; +1 780 926 3672, Fax +1 780 926 4460, www.smartair.ca. David Steer. Scheduled/charter passenger/cargo. 3 x PC-12

NORTHWAY AVIATION (NAL/*Northway*) PO Box 119, Arnes, MB R0C 0C0; +1 204 276 2045, Fax +1 204 276 2069, Res 1 888 536 5353, www.northwayav.com. Jim Johnson. Scheduled/charter passenger/cargo. 1 x Cessna A185E, 1 x Cessna U206F, 1 Cessna 207A, 1 x Beaver, 1 x Navajo, 1 x Chieftain, 1 x Islander, 1 x Cessna 208, 1 x Otter

NT AIR (THUNDERBIRD)(Northern Thunderbird Air dba) (NTA/*Thunderbird*) 4245 Hangar Road, Prince George BC, V2N 4M6; +1 250 963 9611, Fax +1 250 963 8422, Res 1 800 963 9611, www.ntair.ca. Doug McCrea. Scheduled/charter passenger/cargo. 1 x Cessna 208B, 1 x CATPASS 200, 3 x Beech 1900C-1

PASCAN AVIATION (PSC/*Pascan*) 222, 2ème Avenue, Aéroport International Jean-Lesage, Sainte-Foy, QC G2E 5W1; +1 418 877 8777, Fax +1 418 877 8781, Res 1 888 813 8777, pascan@pascan.com, www.pascan.com. Serge Charron. Scheduled/charter passenger/cargo. 3 x PC-12

PEACE AIR PO Box 6036, Peace River, AB T8S 1S1; +1 780 624 3060, Fax +1 780 624 3063, Res 1 800 563 3060, www.peaceair.com. Albert G Cooper. Scheduled/charter passenger/cargo. 2 x Cessna 210, 1 x Seneca, 2 x Chieftain, 3 x PC-12, 1 x Jetstream 32

POINTS NORTH AIR (Points North Air Services dba) Bag 7000, La Ronge, SK S0J 1L0; +1 306 633 2137, Fax +1 306 633 2152, points.north@sk.sympatico.ca, www.pointsnorthair.com. George Eikel. Charter passenger/cargo. 1 x Beaver, 2 x Cessna 402, 1 x Otter, 1 x Turbo Otter, 1 x Cessna 208B

PRINCE EDWARD AIR (CME/*Comet*) 250 Brackley Point Rd, PO Box 2349, Charlottetown, PEI C1A 8C1; +1 902 566 4488, Fax +1 902 368 3573, Res 1 800 565 5359, peair@aurora.com, www.peair.com. Robert M Bateman. Charter passenger/charter & contract cargo. 7 x Chieftain, 2 x Beech 99, 1 x CATPASS 250, 1 Beech 1900C

PROPAIR (PRO/*Propair*) B G 20, RR #1, Aéroport de Rouyn, QC J9X 5B7; +1 819 762 0811, Fax +1 819 762 1852, propair@lino.com. Jean Pronovost. Charter passenger/cargo. 1 x Cessna A185F, 1 x Beaver, 1 x Otter, 1 x Turbo Otter, 4 x King Air A100, 1 x King Air 200, 1 x Merlin IVA, 1 x Gulfstream I

REGENCY EXPRESS FLIGHT OPERATIONS (International Express Air Charter dba) 100-4400 72nd St, Boundary Bay Airport, Delta, BC V4K 5B3; +1 604 940 8841, Fax +1 604 940 8499, www.regencyexpress.com. Ranj Gill. Scheduled/charter cargo. 2 x Chieftain, 2 x Islander, 2 x Cessna 208B

SHUSWAP AIR (Shuswap Flight Center dba) (SFC/*Shuswap*) PO Box 1887, Salmon Arm, BC V1E 4P9; +1 250 832 8830, Fax +1 250 832 2825, Res: 1 800 663 4074, sair@shuswapair.com, www.shuswapair.com. Stephen W Raffel. Charter passenger/cargo. 1 x King Air 100

SKYLINK EXPRESS 1027 Yonge Street, Toronto, ON M4W 2K9; +1 416 922 7000, Fax +1 416 924 9006. Dan Rocheleau. Charter/contract cargo. 4 x Cessna 208B, 6 x Beech 1900C

SOUTH NAHANNI AIRWAYS (3119378 Canada Inc dba) PO Box 407, Fort Simpson, NT X0E 0N0; +1 867 695 2007, Fax +1 867 695 2943. Jacques J Harvey. Charter passenger/cargo. 1 x Twin Otter 100

STAGE AIR 3390 Airport Road, Penticton, BC V2A 8X1; +1 250 492 0074, Fax +1 250 493 7733, fly@stageair.com, www.stageair.com. Michelle Tuckwood. Scheduled/charter passenger/cargo. 1 x Cessna 210, 1 x PA-44, 1 x Duke, 1 x Navajo, 1 x Cessna 208B

SUMMIT AIR CHARTERS #27 Yellowknife Airport, Yellowknife, NT X1A 3T2; +1 867 669 9789, Fax +1 867 669 9649, infor@summitair.net, www.summitair.net. James B Tait. Charter passenger/cargo. 1 x Cessna 207, 3 x Skyvan, 1 x Dornier 228

SUNWEST HOME AVIATION (CNK/*Chinook*) 230 Aviation Place NE, Calgary, AB T2E 7G1; +1 403 275 8121, Fax +1 403 275 4637, Res 1 888 291 4566, info@sunwesthome.com, www.sun-westhome.com. Mark Eberl & Richard Hotchkiss. Charter passenger/cargo. 1 x Cessna A185F, 3 x Navajo, 2 x Chieftain, 1 x Cessna 208B, 1 x Beech 18, 2 x King Air B100, 3 x Metro II, 2 x Metro 23, 1 x King Air 200, 2 x Cessna 550, 1 x Cessna 560, 2 x Lear 35, 1 x Lear 55, 1 x Hawker 800, 1 x Falcon 900EX

THUNDER AIRLINES (THU/*Air Thunder*) 310 Hector Dougall Way, Thunder Bay, ON P7E 6M6; +1 807 475 4211, Fax +1 807 475 5841, contact@thunderair.com, www.thunderair.com. Ken Bittle. Charter passenger/cargo & EMS. 1 x Cessna 208B, 4 x MU-2, 3 x King Air A100

WEST WIND AVIATION (WEW/*Westwind*) Hangar 3, John G Diefenbaker Airport, Saskatoon SK, S7L 5X4; +1 306 652 9121, Fax +1 306 652 3958, www.westwindservices.com. Dennis Goll. Charter passenger/cargo & EMS. 1 x Cessna 414, 4 x Cessna 401, 1 x Cessna 402C, 1 x Cessna 500, 4 x King Air 200/B200, 1 x Lear 25B, 2 x Jetstream 31, 2 x HS748A/B

CANADA

NOTES

DE HAVILLAND CANADA DHC-7-102 DASH 7 *(Wolfgang Hut)*

GRØNLANDSFLY (GREENLANDAIR)

IATA: GL   **ICAO:** GRL   **IATA/ARC:** 631   **RADIO:** *Greenlandair*

CONTACTS

Mail
PO Box 1012
DK-3900 Nuuk
Greenland

Telephone/Fax
Admin: +299 34 34 34
Fax: +299 32 72 88

Email: glahq@greenlandair.gl
Internet: www.greenland-guide.dk/gla/

OPERATION

Type: Scheduled/charter passenger/cargo
Cities served: Greenland: AGM CNP GOH JAV JCH JEG JFR JGO JGR JHS JJU JNN JNS JSU JUV KUS NAQ OBY SFJ THU UAK UMD **Europe:** CPH Service to Canada offered in cooperation with First Air (Bradley Air Services) and to Iceland with Flugfelag Íslands; charter service operated as Greenlandair Charter (GLACE)

HISTORY/STRUCTURE

Founded: November 7, 1960   **Start date:** 1963
Chairman: Peter Grønvold Samuelsen   **CEO:** Finn Øelund
Ownership: Greenland government (37.5%), SAS (37.5%), Danish government (25%)

FLEET

Type	No	Seats	Engines
MD 500D	4	Y4	AN 250-C20B
AS350B2	5	Y6	TU Arriel 1D1
Beech 200	1	Y7	PWC PT6A-41
Bell 212	4	Y9	PWC PT6T-3B
DHC-6-300	2	Y18/Combi	PWC PT6A-27
Sikorsky S-61N	3	Y25	GE CT58-140-2
DHC-7-100	6	Y50/Combi	PWC PT6A-50
Boeing 757-200	1	CY200	RB211-535E4

Greenland Addenda

AIR ALPHA GREENLAND (Air Alpha) (GD) PO Box 1, DK-3952 Ilulissat; +299 94 30 04, Fax +299 94 34 00, www.airalpha.com. Ib Sørensen. Scheduled helicopter operations on behalf of Home Rule Government in East Greenland and charter. 2 x JetRanger/LongRanger, 5 x Bell 222

NOTES

ATR42-320 *(Pierre Lacombe)*

AIR SAINT-PIERRE

IATA: PJ　　**ICAO:** SPM　　**IATA/ARC:** 638　　**RADIO:** *Saint Pierre*

CONTACTS

Mail
BP 4225
18 rue Albert Briand
F-95700 Saint-Pierre et Miquelon

Email: asp@cancom.net
Internet: http:// 209.205.50.254/aspweb

Telephone/Fax
Admin: +508 41 00 00
Fax:　　+508 41 00 02

OPERATION

Type: Scheduled/charter passenger/cargo
Cities served: FSP MQD **Canada:** YHZ YQY YUL YYT (seasonal: YQM)

HISTORY/STRUCTURE

Founded: March 6, 1964
Start date: 1965 (with own aircraft)
CEO: Rémy L Briand
Ownership: Briand family

FLEET

Type	No	Seats	Engines
PA-31-350 Chieftain	1	Y7	LY TIO-540-J2BD
ATR42-320	1	Y48	PWC PW121

ANTONOV AN-24B *(Steve Kinder)*

AEROCARIBBEAN

IATA: 7L   **ICAO:** CRN   **IATA/ARC:** 164   **RADIO:** *Aerocaribbean*

CONTACTS

Mail
Calle 23, #113
Vedado
Ciudad de La Habana, Cuba

Telephone/Fax
Admin: +53 7 33 5017
Fax: +53 7 33 5016

OPERATION

Type: Scheduled/charter passenger/cargo
Cities served: Caribbean: BCA CCC FPO HOG MBJ SCU SDQ TND VRA
Central America: MGA
Code-share: Cubana

HISTORY/STRUCTURE

Founded: 1982
Start date: December 2, 1982
Chairman: Julian Alvarez Infiesta
CEO: Arturo Mirabal
Ownership: Cuban government

FLEET

Type	No	Seats	Engines
Yakovlev Yak-40	6	Y32/Freighter	IV AI-25
ATR42-300	3	Y46	PWC PW120
Antonov An-24B	1	Y50	IV AI-24-II
Antonov An-26	3	Freighter	IV AI-24-VT
Ilyushin Il-18D/V	5	Y100/Freighter	IV AI-20M

ATR42-300 *(P Loeuillet/JM Magendie/Avimage)*

AEROGAVIOTA

IATA: none   **ICAO:** GTV   **IATA/ARC:** none   **RADIO:** *Gaviota*

CONTACTS

Mail
Avenida 47, Playa, 2814
Reparto Kolhy, Playa
Ciudad de La Habana, Cuba

Telephone/Fax
Admin: +53 7 81 3068
Fax: +53 7 33 2621

OPERATION

Type: Charter passenger/cargo, mostly on behalf of Cuban tourist industry

HISTORY/STRUCTURE

Founded: 1994
Start date: 1994
Ownership: Cuban government

FLEET

Type	No	Seats	Engines
PZL An-2	1	Y11	ASh-621R
Mil Mi-8/8P/8T	15	Y24/Cargo	IS TV2-117A
Yakovlev Yak-40	4	Y32	IV AI-25
ATR42-300	3	Y46	PWC PW120
Antonov An-26/26B	23	Combi/Y44	IV AI-24-VT
Antonov An-30	2	Survey	IV AI-24T
Ordered			
ATR42-500	4		

All operated by Cuban Air Force

EMBRAER EMB-145MP *(Carlos Aleman)*

AIR CARAÏBES

IATA: TX   **ICAO:** FWI   **IATA/ARC:** 427   **RADIO:** *French West*

CONTACTS

Mail
Immeuble le Caducée
Morne Vergain
F-97139 Abymes, Guadeloupe, FWI
Email: info@aircaraibes.com
Internet: www.aircaraibes.com

Telephone/Fax
Admin: +590 82 47 47
Fax: +590 82 47 49
Res: +590 82 47 00

OPERATION

Type: Scheduled passenger/charter
Bases: FDF PTP
Cities served: Caribbean: DSD FDF GBJ LSS PAP PTP SBH SDQ SFG SJU SLU SXM   **South America:** CAY **USA:** MIA
Charter operations (9-19 seats) under the name Caraïbes Air Transport
Alliance: CaribSky
Code-share: Air France, LIAT   **FFP:** Frequence Plus

HISTORY/STRUCTURE

Founded: 1969 (as Société Antillaise de Transport Aérien/Air Guadeloupe)
Start date: July 2000
President: JP Dubreuil   **CEO:** Phillippe Chevallier
Ownership: Société Caribéenne des Transports Aériens (70% held by Groupe Dubreuil)

FLEET

Type	No	Seats	Engines
Cessna 208B	6	Y9	PWC PT6A-114A
Dornier 228-200	4	Y19	GA TPE331-5/-5A/-5AB/-5B/-10GP/-10T
ATR42-500	2	Y46	PWC PW127E
ATR72-200	1	Y70	PWC 127
ATR72-500	1	Y70	PWC 127F
EMBRAER ERJ 145MP	2	Y50	AN AE3007A
Ordered			
EMBRAER 170	2		

AIRBUS A340-312 *(Ian Bowley)*

AIR JAMAICA

IATA: JM **ICAO:** AJM **IATA/ARC:** 201 **RADIO:** *Jamaica*

CONTACTS

Mail
72-76 Harbour Street
Kingston, Jamaica

Internet: www.airjamaica.com

Telephone/Fax
Admin: +1 876 922 3460
Fax:　　 +1 876 967 3125
Res:　　 1 800 523 5585

OPERATION

Type: Scheduled passenger/cargo
Hub: MBJ
Cities served: Caribbean: BGI BON CUR GCM GND HAV KIN MBJ NAS SLU
US: ATL BOS BWI EWR FLL IAH JFK LAX MCO MIA ORD PHL **Europe:** LHR
MAN
Code-share: Cubana, Delta Air Lines
FFP: 7th Heaven

HISTORY/STRUCTURE

Founded: October 1968 **Start date:** April 1, 1969
Chairman: Gordon (Butch) Stewart **CEO:** Christopher Zacca
President: Albert P Chappell
Ownership: Air Jamaica Acquisition Group (55%), Jamaican government (45%)

FLEET

Type	No	Seats	Engines
MD-83	2*	F12Y135	PW JT8D-219
Airbus A320-200	8	F12Y138	CFMI FM56-5A3/5B4/P
Airbus A321-200	3	F12Y177	CFMI CFM56-5B3/P
Airbus A310-300 (ET)	4	F18Y200	PW4152
Airbus A340-300	1**	F12C28Y251	CFMI CFM56-5C3
*to be retired in 2002			
**to be returned to lessor in May02			
Ordered			
Airbus A320-200	2		
Airbus A340-300	2	F12C14Y252	CFM56-5C4 (ex-Air Canada)

BOMBARDIER DHC-8-102 DASH 8 *(Tom Sheridan)*

AIR JAMAICA EXPRESS

IATA: JQ   **ICAO:** JMX   **IATA/ARC:** 100   **RADIO:** *Jamaica Express*

CONTACTS

Mail
72-76 Harbour St
Kingston
Jamaica

Telephone/Fax
Admin: +1 876 923 6664
Fax: +1 876 937 3807
Res: 1 800 523 5585

Internet: www.airjamaica.com/express.htm

OPERATION

Type: Scheduled passenger
Hub: MBJ
Cities served: GCM HAV KIN KTP MBJ NAS NEG OCJ PAP PLS POT SDQ
(seasonal: SCU)
All service operated for Air Jamaica using only JM flight numbers
FFP: 7th Heaven

HISTORY/STRUCTURE

Founded: 1973 (as Jamaica Air Taxi)
Start date: April 18,1996
Chairman: Gordon (Butch) Stewart
Ownership: Air Jamaica (100%)

FLEET

Type	No	Seats	Engines
DHC-6-300	2	Y19	PWC PT6A-27
DHC-8-100	6	Y37	PWC PW120A/121

RAYTHEON BEECH 1900D *(Carlos Aleman)*

AIR SANTO DOMINGO (Aerolíneas Santo Domingo)

IATA: EX   **ICAO:** SDO   **IATA/ARC:** 309   **RADIO:** *Aero Domingo*

CONTACTS

Mail
Edificio JP, Av 27 de Febrero 272
Esq Calle Seminario
Santo Domingo, Dominican Republic

Telephone/Fax
Admin: +1 809 683 4535
Fax: +1 809 381 0080
Res: +1 809 683 8006

Internet: www.airsantodomingo.com

OPERATION

Type: Scheduled passenger
Cities served: ABA BRX EPS HEX LRM POP PUJ SIG SJU

HISTORY/STRUCTURE

Founded: 1996
Start date: 1996
CEO: Henry William Azar
Ownership: SAP Group

FLEET

Type	No	Seats	Engines
Let 410	3	Y17	WA M-601E
Beech 1900D	1	Y19	PWC PT6A-67D

BOEING 737-200 *(Gianfranco Beting)*

BAHAMASAIR

IATA: UP **ICAO:** BHS **IATA/ARC:** 111 **RADIO:** *Bahamas*

CONTACTS

Mail
Coral Harbour Road
N4881, Nassau, Bahamas

Internet: www.bahamasair.com

Telephone/Fax
Admin: +1 242 377 8451
Fax: +1 242 377 8550
Res: 1 800 222 4262

OPERATION

Type: Scheduled passenger/cargo
Cities served: Caribbean: ASD ATC AXP CRI ELH FPO GGT GHB IGA LGI MAY MHH MYG PLS RSD SAQ SML TBI TCB TZN ZSA **US:** FLL MCO MIA
Some services operated by Sky Unlimited

HISTORY/STRUCTURE

Founded: 1973
Start date: June 7, 1973
Chairman: Anthony C Miller
MD: Glenn Pickard
Ownership: Bahamasair Holdings (Bahamas government)

FLEET

Type	No	Seats	Engines
DHC-8-300	5	Y50	PWC PW123
Boeing 737-200	2	Y120	PW JT8D-9A

BOEING 737-800 *(Jonathan W Holmes)*

BWIA WEST INDIES AIRWAYS

IATA: BW   **ICAO:** BWA   **IATA/ARC:** 106   **RADIO:** *West Indian*

CONTACTS

Mail
Administration Building
Golden Grove Road
PO Box 604
Piarco International Airport
Port of Spain, Trinidad

Email: mail@bwee.com
Internet: www.bwee.com

Telephone/Fax
Admin: +1 868 669 3000
Fax: +1 868 669 0453
Res: 1 800 538 2942

OPERATION

Type: Scheduled/charter passenger/cargo
Cities served: Caribbean: ANU BGI GND KIN POS SLU SXM TAB
South America: CCS GEO **US:** IAD MIA JFK **Canada:** YYZ **Europe:** LHR
Code-share: LIAT, Tobago Express
FFP: BWee Miles

HISTORY/STRUCTURE

Founded: 1939 (as British West Indian Airways)
Start date: November 27, 1940
Chairman: Lawrence Duprey   **CEO:** Conrad Aleong
Ownership: Private investors (51%); Trinidad & Tobago government (33.5%),
employees (15.5%)

FLEET

Type	No	Seats	Engines
DHC-8-300	4*	Y50	PWC PW123
MD-83	4**	F12Y108	PW JT8D-219
Boeing 737-800	6	F16Y138	CFM56-7B26
L-1011-500	4***	F28Y210	RR RB211-524B4
*operated as BWee Express **3 to be returned to lessors ***2 stored			
Ordered			
Airbus A340-300	2		

LET 410 *(MAP)*

CARIBAIR

IATA: B9   **ICAO:** CBC   **IATA/ARC:** none   **RADIO:** *Caribair*

CONTACTS

Mail
Aeropuerto de Herrera
Av Luperon
Santo Domingo, Dominican Republic

Email: caribair@wowmail.com
Internet: www.caribair.net

Telephone/Fax
Admin: +1 809 542 6688
Fax: +1 809 567 7033

OPERATION

Type: Charter passenger/cargo; operates domestic and international services

HISTORY/STRUCTURE

Founded: 1983
Start date: 1983
CEO: Rafael Rosado Fermin
Ownership: Privately held

FLEET

Type	No	Seats	Engines
Bell 206B	1	Y4	AN 250-C20
PA-32-300 Cherokee	1	Y3	LY IO-540-K1G5
PA-31-310 Navajo	2	Y	LY TIO-540-A2C
BN-2A Islander	1	Y9	LY O-540-E4C5
Let 410	5	Y19	WA M-601
BAe Jetstream 31	1	Y19	GA TPE331-10UG-513H

DE HAVILLAND CANADA DHC-6-300 TWIN OTTER VISTALINER *(Edward Felleson)*

CARIB AVIATION

IATA: K7   **ICAO:** DEL   **IATA/ARC:** none   **RADIO:** *Red Tail*

CONTACTS

Mail
PO Box 318
St John's
Antigua, West Indies

Telephone/Fax
Admin: +1 268 462 3147
Fax: +1 218 462 3125

Email: carib@candoo.com
Internet: www.candoo.com/carib

OPERATION

Type: Scheduled/charter passenger/cargo
Cities served: ANU AXA DCF NEV SKB
All scheduled service operated by Twin Otter for LIAT
Alliance: CaribSky
Code-share: LIAT

HISTORY/STRUCTURE

Founded: 1973 (as Barbuda Wings)
Start date: 1973
CEO: Bruce Kaufman
Ownership: Bruce Kaufman

FLEET

Type	No	Seats	Engines
Queen Air Excalibur	1	Y6	LY IO-720-A1B
Cessna 402B	1	Y7	CO TSIO-520-E
BN-2A Islander	3	Y8	LY O-540-E4C5
DHC-6-300	1	Y19	PWC PT6A-27
Ordered			
DHC-6-300	1		

BOMBARDIER DHC 8-103 DASH 8 *(Edward Felleson)*

CARIBBEAN STAR AIRLINES
(Caribbean Star Ltd dba)

IATA: 8B	ICAO: GFI	IATA/ARC: 557	RADIO: *Carib Star*

CONTACTS

Mail
Coolidge Industrial Estate
PO Box 1628W
Airport Road
St John's
Antigua, West Indies

Telephone/Fax
Admin: +1 268 480 2500
Fax: +1 268 480 2592
Res: +1 268 480 2561

Email: marketing@flycaribbeanstar.com
Internet: www.flycaribbeanstar.com

OPERATION

Type: Scheduled/charter passenger
Cities served: Caribbean: ANU AXA BGI DOM EIS GND NEV POS SKB SLU SVD SXM TAB **South America:** GEO

HISTORY/STRUCTURE

Founded: January 19, 2000
Start date: October 18, 2000
Chairman: R Allen Stanford
CEO: Paul Moreira
Ownership: Caribbean Star Holdings (R Allen Stanford)

FLEET

Type	No	Seats	Engines
DHC-8-100	7	Y37	PWC PW 120A/121
DHC-8-300	2	Y50	PWC PW 123B
Ordered			
DHC-8	7		

NOTES

Plans to form Caribbean Star Inc to operate from San Juan

BOEING 737-200 *(Gianfranco Beting)*

CAYMAN AIRWAYS

IATA: KX   **ICAO:** CAY   **IATA/ARC:** 378   **RADIO:** *Cayman*

CONTACTS

Mail
PO Box 1101
Georgetown
Grand Cayman, Cayman Islands

Telephone/Fax
Admin: +1 345 949 8200
Fax: +1 345 949 7607
Res: 1 800 422 9626 (USA)

Internet: www.caymanairways.com

OPERATION

Type: Scheduled/charter passenger/cargo
Cities served: Caribbean: CYB GCM KIN **US:** IAH MIA TPA
Code-share: United Airlines
FFP: Sir Turtle Rewards Programme

HISTORY/STRUCTURE

Founded: 1955 (as Cayman Brac Airways)
Start date: July 1968
Chairman: Roy McTaggart
President: Michael Adam
Ownership: Cayman Islands government (100%)

FLEET

Type	No	Seats	Engines
Boeing 737-200	2	Y108/Y113	PW JT8D-15A/-17A
Boeing 737-200C	1	Y119	PW JT8D-17

AIRBUS 320-233 *(Gary Tahir)*

CUBANA (Cubana de Aviación)

IATA: CU   **ICAO:** CUB   **IATA/ARC:** 136   **RADIO:** *Cubana*

CONTACTS

Mail
Calle 23 No 64 esq a Infanta
Vedado, Ciudad de La Habana 10400, Cuba

Telephone/Fax
Admin: +53 7 33 4949
Fax: +53 7 33 3323

Email: ecadcom@iacc3.get.cma.net
Internet: www.cubana.cu

OPERATION

Type: Scheduled/charter passenger/cargo. Cubana also operates many flights for the Cuban military.
Cities served: Caribbean: AVI AUA BCA BYM CMW CYO FDF GAO GER HOG MOA MZO PTP SCU SDQ **México:** CUN MEX **Central America:** SJO **South America:** BOG EZE GRU MVD SCL **Canada:** YMX YYZ **Europe:** BCN FCO LPA MAD ORY
Code-share: Aerocaribbean, Aeropostal, Aeroflot, Air Jamaica, COPA, Ecuatoriana, Lauda Air Italy

HISTORY/STRUCTURE

Founded: October 8, 1929 (as Compañía Nacional Cubana de Aviación Curtiss)
Start date: October 30, 1930
Administrator: Marcos Reloba   **Ownership:** Cuban government

FLEET

Type	No	Seats	Engines
Antonov An-24RV	5	Y44	IV AI-24-VT
Yakovlev Yak-42D	4	Y120	LO D-36
Ilyushin Il-62M	6	C12Y150	SO D-30KU
Ilyushin Il-76MD	2	Freighter	SO D-30KP-2

Cubana uses DC-10-30s (C28Y275) operated by Air Lib (France) on many European flights, and A320s (C18Y150) operated by TACA (El Salvador) on many North American flights.

BOMBARDIER DHC-8-311 DASH 8 (John van den Berg)

DUTCH CARIBBEAN EXPRESS
(Dutch Caribbean Airlines dba)

IATA: K8   **ICAO:** DCE   **IATA/ARC:** 559   **RADIO:** *Dutch Caribbean*

CONTACTS

Mail
Aeropuerto Hato
Curaçao, Netherlands Antilles

Email: info@flydce.com
Internet: www.flydce.com

Telephone/Fax
Admin: +599 833 8888
Fax: +599 833 8300
Res: +1 800 327 7230

OPERATION

Type: Scheduled/charter passenger/cargo
Cities served: Caribbean: AUA BON CUR KIN POS SXM
South America: CCS MAR PBM VLN **Europe:** AMS

HISTORY/STRUCTURE

Founded: December 28, 2000
Start date: September 2001
Chairman: Bas Kooijman
Ownership: Island Territory of Curaçao

FLEET

Type	No	Seats	Engines
DHC-8-300	2	Y48	PWC PW123
MD-82	2	C8Y131	PW JT8D-217/-217C

Boeing 767-300ER (Y272) operated by SOBELAIR (Belgium) for AMS service

BOEING 727-200 *(Tom Sheridan)*

L B LTD

IATA: 7Z   **ICAO:** LBH   **IATA/ARC:** 569   **RADIO:** *Laker Bahamas*

CONTACTS

Mail
1170 Lee Wagner Boulevard, Suite 200
Fort Lauderdale, FL 33315

Email: lblimited@laker.net

Telephone/Fax
Admin: +1 954 359 0199
Fax: +1 954 359 7698
Res: +1 800 545 1300

OPERATION

Type: Charter passenger, primarily on behalf of Princess Vacations/Grand
Bahama Vacations and UNEXSO between the Bahamas and the US
Cities served: Caribbean: FPO **US:** BDL BNA BWI CLE CLT CMH CVG FLL
GSP MEM ORD RDU RIC TYS (some seasonal)

HISTORY/STRUCTURE

Founded: 1992 (as Laker Airways [Bahamas])
Start date: May 18, 1992
CEO: Sir Freddie Laker
Ownership: Sir Freddie Laker (34%), Sir Jack Hayward (33%), Oscar
Wyatt (33%)

FLEET

Type	No	Seats	Engines
Boeing 727-200	4	Y175	PW JT8D-15

BOMBARDIER DHC-8-110 DASH 8 *(Tom Sheridan)*

LIAT (LIAT (1974))

IATA: LI   **ICAO:** LIA   **IATA/ARC:** 140   **RADIO:** *Liat*

CONTACTS

Mail
V C Bird International Airport
PO Box 819
St John's, Antigua, West Indies

Telephone/Fax
Admin: +1 268 480 5665
Fax: +1 268 480 5625
Res: +1 268 480 5600

Email: reservations@liatairline.com
Internet: www.liatairline.com

OPERATION

Type: Scheduled/charter passenger/cargo
Cities served: Caribbean: ANU AXA BGI DOM EIS GND NEV POS SJU SKB
SLU STT STX SVD SXM TAB **South America:** GEO
Code-share: Air Caraïbes, BWIA, Carib Aviation, Trans Island Air 2000, Winair
Alliances: BWIA, CaribSky

HISTORY/STRUCTURE

Founded: September 20, 1956 (as Leeward Islands Air Transport Services)
Start date: September 20, 1974
Chairman: Wilbur Harrigan
CEO: Gary Cullen
COO: Louis Harkin
Ownership: 1 Caribbean governments (30.8%), BWIA (29.2%), private investors
(26.7%), employees (13.3%)

FLEET

Type	No	Seats	Engines
DHC-8-100	7	Y37	PWC PW120A/121
DHC-8-300	3	Y50	PWC PW123

BEECH 1900C-1 AIRLINER *(Carlos Aleman)*

NEVIS EXPRESS (Daystar Airways dba)

IATA: VF   **ICAO:** none   **IATA/ARC:** none   **RADIO:** *none*

CONTACTS

Mail
PO Box 682
Charlestown, Nevis
St Kitts & Nevis, West Indies

Telephone/Fax
Admin: +1 869 469 9065
Fax: +1 869 469 9751
Res: +1 869 469 9755/9756

Email: reservations@nevisexpress.com
Internet: www.nevisexpress.com

OPERATION

Type: Scheduled/charter passenger/cargo
Cities served: NEV SJU SKB

HISTORY/STRUCTURE

Founded: 1993 (as Daystar Airways, AK)
Start date: 1993
CEO: Allen Haddadi
Ownership: Privately held

FLEET

Type	No	Seats	Engines
BN-2A	3	Y9	LY O-540-E4C5
Beech 1900C-1	1	Y19	PWC PT6A-65B

RAYTHEON BEECH 1900D *(Carlos Aleman)*

SAP (Servicios Aéreos Profesionales)

IATA: 5S   **ICAO:** PSV   **IATA/ARC:** none   **RADIO:** *Proservicios*

CONTACTS

Mail
Aeropuerto de Herrera
Santo Domingo
Dominican Republic

Telephone/Fax
Admin: +1 809 565 2448
Fax: +1 809 540 4667

Email: sap.air@codetel.net.do
Internet: www.sapair.com

OPERATION

Type: Charter passenger/cargo

HISTORY/STRUCTURE

Founded: 1981
Start date: 1981
President: José Miguel Patín Hernandez
Ownership: SAP Group

FLEET

Type	No	Seats	Engines
Cessna 172K	3	Y3	LY O-320
Cessna 206	1	Y5	LY IO-540
BN-2A Islander	3	Y9	LY O-540-K1B5/E4C5
G-159 Gulfstream	1	Y14	RR Dart 529-8
Let 410	7	Y17/Y19	WA M-601D/E
DHC-6-200	2	Y20	PWC PT6A-20
Beech 1900C	1	Y18	PWC PT6A-67B
Beech 1900D	4	Y18	PWC PT6A-67D
EMB-120 Brasília	1	Y28	PWC PW118
Shorts 360-200	2	Y38	PWC PT6A-65AR

BEECH 1900C-1 AIRLINER *(Tom Sheridan)*

SKYKING AIRLINES (TCI Skyking dba)

IATA: RU   **ICAO:** SKI   **IATA/ARC:** 025   **RADIO:** *Skyking*

CONTACTS

Mail
P O Box 398
Providenciales
Turks & Caicos Islands, BWI

Email: king@tciway.tc
Internet: www.skyking.tc

Telephone/Fax
Admin: +1 (649) 941-5464
Fax: +1 (649) 941-4264

OPERATION

Type: Scheduled/charter passenger/cargo
Cities served: CAP GDT PLS POP SDQ XSC

HISTORY/STRUCTURE

Founded: 1995 (as TCI Skyking)
Start date: 1995
President: Charles Harold
Ownership: Privately held

FLEET

Type	No	Seats	Engines
Cessna 404	1	Y10	CO GTSIO-520-M
Beech 1900C-1	3	Y19	PWC PT6A-65B

BOMBARDIER DHC-8-315 DASH 8-Q300 *(Nigel Steele)*

TOBAGO EXPRESS

IATA: none   **ICAO:** none   **IATA/ARC:** none   **RADIO:** none

CONTACTS

Mail
Piarco International Airport
Crown Point, Tobago

Telephone/Fax
Admin: +868 631 8015
Res: +868 627 2942

Internet: www.tobagoexpress.com

OPERATION

Type: Scheduled passenger/cargo
Cities served: POS TAB
All scheduled service operated using only BW flight numbers (in 1500 range)
FFP: Bwee Miles

HISTORY/STRUCTURE

Founded: 2001
Start date: June 24, 2001
General Manager: Tom Yew
Ownership: BWIA (25%), BWIA shareholders (45%), Tobago Business Inc
(20%), individual investors (15%)

FLEET

Type	No	Seats	Engines
DHC-8-300	1	Y50	PWC PW123
Ordered			
DHC-8-300	1		

DE HAVILLAND CANADA DHC 6-300 TWIN OTTER *(Hernán Matos)*

WINAIR (Windward Islands Airways International)

IATA: WM   **ICAO:** WIA   **IATA/ARC:** 295   **RADIO:** *Winair*

CONTACTS

Mail
PO Box 2088
Princess Juliana International Airport
St Maarten, Netherlands Antilles

Telephone/Fax
Admin: +599 545 2568
Fax: +599 545 5229
Res: +599 545 4237

Email: reservations@fly-winair.com
Internet: www.fly-winair.com

OPERATION

Type: Scheduled/charter passenger/cargo
Cities served: ANU AXA EIS EUX NEV SAB SBH SKB SXM
Code-share: LIAT
Alliance: CaribSky

HISTORY/STRUCTURE

Founded: August 24, 1961 (as Windward Islands Airways)
Start date: August 5, 1962
Chairman: Michael Ferrier
MD: John Strugnell
Ownership: Netherlands Antilles government

FLEET

Type	No	Seats	Engines
DHC-6-300	4	Y20	PWC PT6A-27

Caribbean Addenda

ABACO AIR Marsh Harbour International Airport, PO Box AB20492, Marsh Harbour, Abaco, BS; +1 242 367 2266, Fax +1 242 367 3256, http://oii.net/abacoair/index.htm, abacoair@oii.net. Andrew Kelly. Charter passenger. 3 x Commander 500, 1 x Islander

AEROMAR AIRLINES (BQ/ROM/926/*Bravo Quebec*) Aeropuerto Internacional Las Américas, DO; +1 809 549 0281, Fax +1 809 542 0152, www.aeromarairlines.com. Scheduled/charter passenger/cargo. Boeing 727-200s wet-leased from Falcon Air Express

AEROTAXI (CNI/*Seraer*) Calle 27, Numero 102, Vedado, Ciudad de La Habana, CU; +53 732 2515, Fax +53 733 3082. Benigno Miranda. Charter passenger. 41 x An-2, 4 x DC-3

AIR D'AYITI (Haiti Aviation)(Air D'Ayiti Express) (H9/008) 8034 NE2nd Ave, Miami, FL 33138, USA; +1 305 751 3434, Fax +1 305 751 2424. Charles Voight. Scheduled/charter passenger/cargo. Wet-leases Boeing 727s and Cessna 208Bs.

AIR ST KITTS & NEVIS (Kingfisher Air Services dba) PO Box 529, Basseterre, KN; +1 869 469 9241, Fax +1 869 465 9833. Richard V Hurley. Charter passenger. 2 x Cessna 402B

APA INTERNATIONAL AIR (7P/APY/917/*APA International*) PO Box 524039, Miami, FL 33152-4039 USA; +1 305 345 0567, Fax +1 305 223 1141. Rafael Trujillo. Scheduled/charter passenger/cargo using wet-leased equipment from US carriers.

AVIA AIR (3R/ARB/*Aviair*) PO Box 69, Aeropuerto Internacional Reina Beatrix, Aruba; +297 8 34600, Fax +297 8 26355. Episanyo (Efi) Tromp. Scheduled/charter passenger/cargo. 1 x Cessna 402B, 2 x Bandeirante

CANCUN EXPRESS PO Box 30117 SMB, Georgetown, Grand Cayman, CYM; +1 345 949 0241, Fax +1 345 946 3301. Jeff Walsh. Charter passenger. 1 x Jetstream 32EP

CAT ISLAND AIR PO Box CB-11150, Nassau, BS; +1 242 377 3318, Fax +1 242 377 3320. Albert Rolle. Charter passenger. 1 x Aztec, 2 x Bandeirante

CHEROKEE AIR PO Box AB 20485, Marsh Harbour, Abaco, BS; +242 367 2089, Fax +242 367 2530, cherokeeair@oii.net, www.oii.net/cherokeeair. Faron S Sawyer. Charter passenger. 3 x Aztec

COTURISCA Av Nuñez de Caceres Esq, Guarocuya, Santo Domingo, DO; +809 683 3660, Fax +809 683 3651, info@coturisca.com, www.coturisca.com. Huascar M Rodriguez. 2 x Bell 206, 2 x BO 105, 1 x Chieftain

EAGLE AIR SERVICES PO Box 838, Castries, LC; +758 452 1900, Fax +758 452 9683, eagleairslu@candw.lc, www.eagleairslu.com. Ewart F Hinkson. 2 x Islander

FLY BVI PO Box 3347, Roadtown, Tortola, BVI; 1 800 435 9284 (US), +1 284 495 1747, Fax +1 284 495 1973, info@fly-bvi.com , www.fly-bvi.com. Nikki Abrams. Charter passenger. 1 x Aztec, 1 x Cessna 404

GLOBAL AIRWAYS PO Box 359, Providenciales, TC; +1 649 941 3222, Fax +1 649 946 7290, global@tciway.tc. Charter passenger. 1 x Aztec, 1 x Cessna 402

INTERISLAND AIRWAYS (JY/IWY/*Islandways*) PO Box 191, Providenciales, TC; +1 649 946 4181, Fax +1 649 946 4040, fly@tciway.tc, www.interislandairways.com. Lyndon R Gardiner. Scheduled/charter passenger. 1 x Aztec, 1 x Cessna 401, 1 x Cessna 402, 1 x Twin Otter, 1 x Beech 1900D

ISLAND AIR (G5) PO Box 2433, Georgetown, Grand Cayman, CYM; +1 345 949 0241, Fax +1 345 949 7044, Res +1 345 949 5252, www.islandaircayman.com, iair@candw.ky. Mirvin Cumber. Scheduled/charter passenger/cargo. 1 x Islander, 1 x Navajo, 1 x Twin Otter

LEAIR CHARTER PO Box CB-13007, Nassau International Airport, Nassau, BS; +242 377 2356, Fax +242 377 2357, www.bahamasnet.com/leair. Larry Brown. Charter passenger. 3 x Aztec, 1 x Navajo

MAJOR'S AIR SERVICES PO Box F-41282, Freeport, Grand Bahama, BS; +1 242 352 5778, Fax +1 242 352 5788. Roosevelt Major. Charter passenger. 2 x Beech C99

MUSTIQUE AIRWAYS (Q4/MAW/*Mustique*) E T Joshua Airport, VC; +1 784 458 4380, Fax +1 784 456 4586, www.mustique.com, info@mustique.com. Jonathan Palmer. Scheduled/charter passenger/cargo. 2 x Commander 500, 2 x Islander, 1 x Bandeirante

ST BARTH COMMUTER (PV/SBU/*Commuter*) Aéroport Gustave III, F-97133 St Barthélemy, GP; +590 27 54 54, Fax + 590 27 54 58, www.st-barths.com/stbarth-commuter/index.html. Bruno Masens. Scheduled/charter passenger. 4 x Islander

SANDPIPER AIR (4 Way Charter Co dba) PO Box CB-13838, Nassau, BS; +242 377 5751, Fax +242 377 3143, www.sandpiperair.com. Kevin Turnquest. Charter passenger. 3 x Cessna 402B, 2 x Cessna 402C

SKY UNLIMITED PO Box N-10859, Nassau, BS; +1 242 377 8993, Fax +1 242 377 3107, www.bahamas.mall.bs/skyunlimited. Heuter B Rolle. Scheduled (for Bahamasair)/charter passenger. 1 x Aztec, 1 x Beech C99, 1 x Beech 1900C

SOUTHERN AIR CHARTER PO Box N8912, Nassau, BS; +1 242 377 2014, Fax +1 242 377 1066. Nathaniel Tibbs. Charter passenger. 1 x Beech 1900C

SVG AIR (St Vincent & The Grenadines Air) (SVD/*Grenadines*) PO Box 39, Kingstown, VC; +1 784 457 5124, Fax +1 784 457 5077, info@svgair.com, www.svgair.com. Martin Barnard. Scheduled/charter passenger/cargo. 2 x Cessna 402, 3 x Commander 500, 5 x Islander

TIMAIR Sangster International Airport, Montego Bay, JM; +1 876 952 2516, Fax +1 876 979 1113, timair@usa.net, www.timair.com. Fraser McConnell. 2 x Cessna 182, 3 x Cessna 206, 1 x Cessna 337, 1 x Islander

TRANS ANGUILLA PO Box 1329, Wallblake Airport, AI; +1 264 497 8690, Fax +1 264 497 8689, transang@anguillanet.com, www.trans.ai. Lincoln Gumbs. Scheduled/charter passenger/cargo. 2 x Islander, 1 x King Air 200, 1 x Twin Otter

TRANS CARIBBEAN AIRWAYS Herrara International Airport, Ave Luperon, Santo Domingo, DO; Charter passenger/cargo. 1 x Beech 1900C

TRANS ISLAND AIR 2000 (TIA) (TRD/*Trans Island*) South Ramp, Grantley Adams International Airport, Christ Church, BB; +1 246 418 1650, Fax +1 246 428 0916, www.tia2000.com, info@tia2000.com. Bruce Kaufman. Scheduled/charter passenger (CaribSky). 1 x Islander, 2 x Commander 500, 1 x Bandeirante, 2 x Twin Otter

TROPICAL AIRWAYS (M7) 76 rue Panaméricaine, Pétionville, HT; +1 509 256 3626, Fax +1 509 256 3629, www.tropical-haiti.com. Philippe Gornail. Scheduled/charter passenger. 1 x Cessna 402B, 4 x Let 410, 2 x Shorts 360

TURKS & CAICOS AIRWAYS (QW/TCI/254/*Turk National*) PO Box 114, Providenciales, TC; +1 649 946 4255, Fax +1 649 946 5781. A V Butterfield Sr. Scheduled/charter passenger. 1 x Aztec, 2 x Islander

TYDEN AIR PO Box 107, The Valley, AI; +1 264 497 3419, Fax +1 264 497 3079, Res 1 800 842 0261. Lesley Lloyd. Charter passenger (CaribSky). 2 x Islander

WINDWARD EXPRESS AIRWAYS Princess Juliana International Airport, St Maarten, AN; +599 548 3085, Fax +1 599 548 3085, windwardexpress@hotmail.com. Jean Halley. Charter passenger/cargo. 1 x Islander

NOTES

DOUGLAS DC-9-32 *(Gary Jennings)*

AERO CALIFORNIA

IATA: JR   **ICAO:** SER   **IATA/ARC:** 078   **RADIO:** *Aerocalifornia*

CONTACTS

Mail
Aquiles Serdán 1995
La Paz, BCS 23000

Telephone/Fax
Admin: +52 612 112 0800
Fax: +52 612 123 5343
Res: +52 555 207 1392 (Mexico City)
Res: 01 800 237 6225 (México)
Res: 1 800 237 6225 (US/Can)

OPERATION

Type: Scheduled/charter passenger/cargo
Cities served: México: AGU CEN CJS CLQ CUL CUU CVM DGO GDL HMO
LAP LMM LTO MAM MEX MTY PBC SJD SLP TIJ TPQ TRC ZLO **US:** LAX TUS
Code-share: American Airlines
FFP: Club Altus

HISTORY/STRUCTURE

Founded: 1960
Start date: 1960
President/CEO: Raul A Aréchiga
Ownership: Privately held

FLEET

Type	No	Seats	Engines
DC-9-14	5	Y85	PW JT8D-7A/-7B
DC-9-15	6	Y85	PW JT8D-7A/-7B
DC-9-32	11	Y104	PW JT8D-9A/-15

FAIRCHILD FH-227D *(Flemming Løvenvig)*

AEROCARIBE

IATA: QA   **ICAO:** CBE   **IATA/ARC:** 723   **RADIO:** *Aerocaribe*

CONTACTS

Mail
Av Cobá 5
Local B1 y B3
Plaza América
Cancún, QR 77500

Email: info@aerocaribe.com.mx
Internet: www.aerocaribe.com

Telephone/Fax
Admin: +52 998 887 4002
Fax: +52 998 884 9996
Res: +52 998 884 2000 (Mexico City)
Res: 01 800 502 2000 (México))
Res: 1 800 531 7921 (US/Can)

OPERATION

Type: Scheduled/charter passenger/cargo
Cities served: México: CME CTM CUN CZA CZM HUX MEX MID MTY OAX PQM PXM SZT TAP TGZ VER VSA **Caribbean:** HAV
All scheduled service operated as Mexicana Inter using only MX flight numbers (7000 range); some flights operated by associated company Aerocozumel
FFP: Frecuenta

HISTORY/STRUCTURE

Founded: 1975
Start date: July 12, 1975
CEO: Jaime Valenzuela T
Ownership: CINTRA Holdings (IPC: CINTRA)(99.99%)

FLEET

Type	No	Seats	Engines
BAe Jetstream 32EP	5	Y19	GA TPE331-12UAR-704H
Fairchild FH-227D	1	Y50	RR Dart 532-7L
DC-9-14	2	Y83	PW JT8D-7B
DC-9-15	2	Y83	PW JT8D-7B
DC-9-31	5	Y110	PW JT8D-9A

MÉXICO

BOEING 727-200 *(Omar Muñoz Ledo Perez)*

AEROLINEAS INTERNACIONALES

IATA: N2   **ICAO:** LNT   **IATA/ARC:** 440   **RADIO:** *Internacionales*

CONTACTS

Mail
Blvd Vincente Guerrero 46
Col Lomas de la Selva,
Cuernavaca, Mórelos 62270

Telephone/Fax
Admin: +52 777 311 5114
Fax: +52 555 536 1549
Res: 01 800 990 9100 (México)

Email: admonai@central.edsa.net.mx
Internet: www.aerolineas.cc/index.html

OPERATION

Type: Scheduled/charter passenger
Cities served: ACA AGU BJX CJS CUL MEX REX TIJ
Charter operations to Mexican resort areas
FFP: Exclusive Card

HISTORY/STRUCTURE

Founded: June 24, 1993
Start date: March 25, 1994
Chairman: Jorge Rodríguez Marié
Ownership: Privately held (Jorge Rodríguez Marié)

FLEET

Type	No	Seats	Engines
Boeing 727-100	2	Y115	PW JT8D-7B
Boeing 727-200	4	Y180	PW JT8D-9

SAAB 340B *(SAAB)*

AEROLITORAL (Servicios Aéreos Litoral)

IATA: 5D   **ICAO:** SLI   **IATA/ARC:** 297   **RADIO:** *Litoral*

CONTACTS

Mail
Carretera Miguel Alemán, Km. 22.8
Apodaca, NL 66601

Email: comentarios@aerolitoral.com
Internet: www.aerolitoral.com

Telephone/Fax
Admin: +52 818 386 2070
Fax: +52 818 368 1601
Res: 01 800 021 4000 (México)
Res: 1 800 247 6639 (US/Can)

OPERATION

Type: Scheduled passenger/cargo
Cities served: México: ACA AGU BJX CEN CJS CME CUL CUU DGO GDL GUB GYM HMO LAP LMM LOV LTO MTY MXL MZT PAZ PDS PVR QRO REX SLP TAM TIJ TRC VER VSA ZIH ZLO **US:** ELP IAH PHX SAT TUS
All service operated on behalf of AeroMexico using only AM flight numbers
Code-share: Delta Air Lines
FFP: Club Premier

HISTORY/STRUCTURE

Founded: May 1989 (as Servicios Aéreos Litoral)
Start date: July 1989
Chairman: Alfonso Pasquel
President: Carlos Treviño
Ownership: CINTRA Holdings (IPC: CINTRA)(99.5%)

FLEET

Type	No	Seats	Engines
Metro III	4	Y19	GA TPE331-11U-611G
Metro 23	12	Y19	GA TPE331-12U-701G
SAAB 340B	15	Y33	GE CT7-9B
Ordered			
SAAB 340B	7		

MÉXICO

ATR42-500 *(Gianfranco Beting)*

AEROMAR AIRLINES (Transportes Aeromar)

IATA: VW   **ICAO:** TAO   **IATA/ARC:** 590   **RADIO:** *Aeromar*

CONTACTS

Mail
Hangar 1, Zona D, Col. Federal AICM.
México, DF 15620

Telephone/Fax
Admin: +52 555 133 1107
Fax: +52 555 756 0174
Res: 5 133 1111 (Mexico City)
Res: 01 800 704 2900 (México)
Res: 1 210 829 1704 (US)

Internet: www.aeromar.com.mx

OPERATION

Type: Scheduled passenger/cargo
Cities served: México: CLQ CVM IZT JAL LZC MEX MIT MLM MTY PAZ PBC QRO SLP SZT TLC UPN **US:** SAT
Code-share: AeroMexico, Mexicana, United Airlines
FFP: Mileage Plus

HISTORY/STRUCTURE

Founded: January 29, 1987
Start date: November 7, 1987
Chairman: Carlos Autrey
MD: Juan Ignacio Steta
Ownership: Autrey Group

FLEET

Type	No	Seats	Engines
ATR42-320	5	Y48	PWC PW121
ATR42-500	9	Y48	PWC PW127E

BOEING 767-200 (ER) *(Luis Calvo)*

AEROMEXICO (Aerovías de México)

IATA: AM   **ICAO:** AMX   **IATA/ARC:** 139   **RADIO:** *Aeromexico*

CONTACTS

Mail
Paseo de la Reforma 445
México, DF 06500

Internet: www.aeromexico.com

Telephone/Fax
Admin: +52 555 133 4000
Fax: +52 555 133 4628
Res: 5 133 4010 (Mexico City)
Res: 01 800 021 4010 (México)
Res: 1 800 237 6639 (US/Can)

OPERATION

Type: Scheduled passenger
Cities served: México: ACA AGU BJX CEN CJS CPE CUL CUN CUU DGO GDL GYM HMO LAP LMM MAM MEX MID MTY MZT OAX PVR REX SJD TAP TIJ TRC VER VSA ZIH **US:** ATL DFW IAH JFK LAS LAX MIA MSY ONT ORD PHX SAN SLC **South America:** GRU LIM SCL **Europe:** CDG MAD
Global alliance: SkyTeam
Code-share: Aerolitoral, Aeromar, Air France, Atlantic Southeast, Austrian Airlines, Comair, Delta Air Lines, Grupo TACA, LAN Chile, Swissair
FFP: Club Premier

HISTORY/STRUCTURE

Founded: 1934 (as Aeronaves de México)
Start date: May 15, 1934
Chairman/President: Alfonso Pasquel
COO: Arturo Barahona
Ownership: CINTRA Holdings (IPC: CINTRA)(99.26%)

DOUGLAS DC 9-32 *(Omar Muñoz Ledo Perez)*

FLEET

Type	No	Seats	Engines
DC-9-31	1	C12Y85	PW JT8D-17
DC-9-32	15	C12Y85	PW JT8D-17
MD-87	8	C12Y100	PW JT8D-219
MD-82	14	C12Y130	PW JT8D-217A/-217C/-219
MD-83	9	C12Y130	PW JT8D-219
MD-88	10	C12Y130	PW JT8D-219
Boeing 757-200	9	C24Y156	PW PW2037
Boeing 767-200ER	4	C21Y160	PW PW4056
Boeing 767-300ER	1	C21Y188	PW PW4062

MÉXICO

BOEING 727-200 (F) *(Rurik Enriquez D)*

AEROMEXPRESS

IATA: QO   **ICAO:** MPX   **IATA/ARC:** 976   **RADIO:** *Aeromexpress*

CONTACTS

Mail
Av Texcoco esq Av Tahel
Col Peñón de los Baños
México, DF 15520

Telephone/Fax
Admin: +52 555 133 0237
Fax: +52 555 237 2226
Info: 01 800 706 9300 (México)
Info: 1 310 215 4200 (US)

Internet: www.aeromexpress.com.mx

OPERATION

Type: Scheduled/charter cargo
Cities served: México: BJX GDL MEX MID **Central America:** SJO **US:** DAY
DFW LAX
Operates in cooperation with Aerocaribe, Aerolitoral, AeroMexico, & Mexicana
Global alliance: SkyTeam Cargo

HISTORY/STRUCTURE

Founded: 1990
Start date: June 9, 1994
President: Javier Elizalde
Ownership: CINTRA Holdings (IPC: CINTRA)

FLEET

Type	No	Engines
Boeing 727-200F	1	PW JT8D-17

MÉXICO

BOEING 727-200 *(Gianfranco Beting)*

ALLEGRO AIR (Líneas Aéreas Allegro)

IATA: LL   **ICAO:** GRO   **IATA/ARC:** 902   **RADIO:** *Allegro*

CONTACTS

Mail
Av Cuba, Plaza América
Local 39
Cancún, QR 77500

Telephone/Fax
Admin: +52 998 887 9091
Fax: +52 998 884 8180
Res: 01 800 715 7640 (México)
Res: 1 877 443 7578 (US)

Email: info@allegroair.com.mx

OPERATION

Type: Scheduled/charter passenger
Cities served: México: CUN GDL MEX TIJ **US:** LAS
Charter operations for US tour operators including Apple Vacations, Club Med,
Funjet Vacations, TNT Vacations, & Vacation Express

HISTORY/STRUCTURE

Founded: 1992
Start date: December 26, 1992
President: Fernando Padilla
CEO: Jorge Nava
Ownership: Privately held

FLEET

Type	No	Seats	Engines
Boeing 727-200	7	Y167/Y170/Y172	PW JT8D-15/-17/-17R
Boeing 727-200	7	Y170/Y173	PW JT8D-217C/-15/-17

BOEING 737-200 *(Gianfranco Beting)*

AVIACSA (Aviación de Chiapas)

IATA: 6A   **ICAO:** CHP   **IATA/ARC:** 095   **RADIO:** *Aviacsa*

CONTACTS

Mail
Hangar No 13, Zona D
Aviación General AICM
México, DF 15520

Telephone/Fax
Admin: +52 555 756 0650
Fax: +52 555 758 3823
Res: 5 716 9004 (Mexico City)
Res: 01 800 711 6733 (México)
Res: 1 888 528 4227 (US/Can)

Internet: www.aviacsa.com.mx

OPERATION

Type: Scheduled/charter passenger
Cities served: México: ACA BJX CTM CUN GDL HMO MEX MID MLM MTY MXL OAX TAP TGZ VSA **US:** IAH LAS
Code-share: COPA, Grupo TACA
FFP: AviacsaPass

HISTORY/STRUCTURE

Founded: June 1990
Start date: September 20, 1990
President/CEO: Eduardo Morales
Ownership: Privately held (Consorcio Aviaxsa)

FLEET

Type	No	Seats	Engines
DC-9-15	3	Y90	PW JT8D-7A/7B
Boeing 727-200	9	Y120	PW JT8D-15/-15A/-17
Boeing 727-200	9	Y164	PW JT8D-15/-15A

MÉXICO

BOEING 737-700 *(Rurik Enriquez D)*

AZTECA AIRLINES (Líneas Aéreas Azteca dba)

IATA: ZE   **ICAO:** LCD   **IATA/ARC:** 994   **RADIO:** *Azteca*

CONTACTS

Mail
Hangar 27, Zona C
Col Federal AICM
México, DF 15620

Email: info@aazteca.com
Internet: www.aazteca.com

Telephone/Fax
Admin: +52 555 716 8960
Res: +52 55 716 8989 (Mexico City)
Res: 01 800 229 8322 (México)
Res: 1 888 754 0066 (US)

OPERATION

Type: Scheduled/charter passenger/cargo
Cities served: México: CJS CUN CUU GDL MEX TIJ **US:** ELP
FFP: OnePass

HISTORY/STRUCTURE

Founded: 2000
Start date: June 3, 2001
President: Leonardo Sánchez Avalos
CEO: Marcos Shuster
Ownership: Privately held (Leonardo Sánchez Avalos)

FLEET

Type	No	Seats	Engines
Boeing 737-300	2	Y136	CFMI CFM56-3B2
Boeing 737-700	2	Y136	CFMI CFM56-3B2

BOEING 737-200C *(H Gutierrez)*

ESTAFETA CARGA AEREA

IATA: none   **ICAO:** none   **IATA/ARC:** none   **RADIO:** *Estafeta*

CONTACTS

Mail
Cerrada Ceylán 539
Col Industrial Vallejo
México, DF 02300

Telephone/Fax
Admin: +52 555 242 9100
Admin: 1 956 717 3435 (US)

Internet: www.estafeta.com.mx

OPERATION

Type: Scheduled cargo
Cities served: CJS CUU HMO MEX MID MTY MZT SLP TIJ

HISTORY/STRUCTURE

Founded: August 1979
Start date: August 2000
CEO: José Antonio Armendáriz
Ownership: Estafeta Mexicana

FLEET

Type	No	Engines
Boeing 737-200C	2	PW JT8D-9A/-17
Ordered		
Boeing 737-200	1	

BOEING 737-200 *(Omar Muñoz Ledo Perez)*

MAGNICHARTERS

IATA: none   **ICAO:** GMT   **IATA/ARC:** none   **RADIO:** *Magnicharters*

CONTACTS

Mail
La Barca 1128
Col Mitras Sur 4
Monterrey, NL 64020

Telephone/Fax
Admin: +52 818 369 0855
Fax: +52 818 369 0977
Res: +52 818 356 0593
Res: +52 555 566 6788 (Mexico City)
Res: 01 800 201 1404 (México)

OPERATION

Type: Charter passenger
Cities served: ACA BJX CUN GDL HUX MEX MID MTY MZT PVR ZIH

HISTORY/STRUCTURE

Founded: 1994
Start date: January 1995
President: Gabriel Bojorques
Ownership: Magnitur (Grupo Turístico Magno)

FLEET

Type	No	Seats	Engines
Boeing 737-200	5	Y109	PW JT8D-9A/-17A

BOEING 767-300F *(Rurik Enriquez D)*

MASAIR CARGO (Aerotransportes Mas de Carga)

IATA: MY   **ICAO:** MAA   **IATA/ARC:** 865   **RADIO:** *Mas Carga*

CONTACTS

Mail
Almacen 22 AICM
Aduana Interior AICM
México, DF 15520

Email: my@masair.com
Internet: www.masair.com.mx

Telephone/Fax
Admin: +52 555 786 9555
Fax:　 +52 555 786 9543

OPERATION

Type: Scheduled/charter cargo
Cities served: México: GDL MEX MID **Central America:** GUA PTY SJO
South America: LIM MAO VCP **US:** JFK LAX MIA ORD

HISTORY/STRUCTURE

Founded: September 13, 1990
Start date: April 29, 1992
President/CEO: Luis Sierra
Ownership: LAN Chile (25%), Promotor Aéreo Latinoamericano

FLEET

Type	No	Engines
DC-8-71F	2	CFMI CFM56-2C
Boeing 767-300F	1	GE CF6-80C2B7F

MÉXICO

AIRBUS A320-231 *(Ben Wang)*

MEXICANA (Corporación Mexicana de Aviación)

IATA: MX **ICAO:** MXA **IATA/ARC:** 132 **RADIO:** *Mexicana*

CONTACTS

Mail	**Telephone/Fax**
Xola 535, Col del Valle	Admin: +52 555 448 3000
México, DF 03100	Fax: +52 555 523 2364
	Res: 5 448 0990 (Mexico City)
	Res: 01 800 502 2000 (México)
Internet: www.mexicana.com	Res: 1 800 531 7921 (US/Can)

OPERATION

Type: Scheduled/charter passenger/cargo
Cities served: México: ACA BJX CME CUN CZM GDL HMO HUX MEX MID MLM MTT MXL MZT NLD OAX PVR PXM SJD SLW TAM TIJ VER VSA ZCL ZIH ZLO **Caribbean:** HAV SCU SDQ **Central America:** GUA SAL SJO **South America:** BOG EZE **US:** DEN EWR LAS LAX LRD MDW MIA OAK ORD SAT SFO SJC **Canada:** YUL YYZ
Code-share: Aerocaribe, Aerolitoral, Aeromar, AeroMexico, Air Canada, Lufthansa, SERVIVENSA, United Airlines
FFP: Frecuenta

HISTORY/STRUCTURE

Founded: July 12, 1921 (as Compañía Mexicana de Transportación Aérea)
Start date: April 1928 (scheduled by Compañía Mexicana de Aviación)
President/CEO: Fernando Flores
Ownership: CINTRA Holdings (IPC: CINTRA)

FLEET

Type	No	Seats	Engines
Fokker 100	12	C8Y93	RR Tay 650-15
Airbus A319-112	2	C12Y120	CFMI CFM56-5B6/2P
Airbus A320-200	24	C12Y138 or Y174	IAE V2500-A1
Boeing 727-200	20	C12Y138 or Y156	PW JT8D-17R
Boeing 757-200	8	C12Y170/171	PW2040
Ordered			
Airbus A320-200	8		

BOEING 717-200 *(Michael Carter)*

VUELAMEX

IATA: **ICAO:**   **IATA/ARC:**   **RADIO:** *Vuelamex*

CONTACTS

Mail
Montes Urales 450, Piso 2
Lomas de Chapultepec
México, DF 11000

Telephone/Fax
Admin: +52 552 122 9999

Internet: www.vuelamex.com.mx

OPERATION

Type: Scheduled/charter passenger/cargo
Cities served: (planned) ACA BJX CJS CUN HMO MEX MLM OAX TIJ UPN
ZIH

HISTORY/STRUCTURE

Founded: 2001
Start date: 2002
CEO: Rodrigo Vásquez Colmenares
Ownership: Privately held (Miguel Abed)

FLEET

Type	No	Seats	Engines
Boeing 717-200	4	Y125	RR BR715
Ordered			
Boeing 717-200	8		

MÉXICO

México Addenda

AERO CUAHONTE (CUO/*Cuahonte*) Aeropuerto Federal de Uruapan Ignacio López Rayón, Col San José Obrero, Uruapan, Michoacán 60160; +52 452 524 0032, Fax +52 452 524 9360. Enrique Cuahonte Amezcua. Scheduled/charter passenger/cargo. 1 x Cessna T210N, 1 x Cessna 402C, 1 x Metro II, 1 x Metro III

AEROFERINCO (FEO/*Aeroferinco*) Calle 3 Sur, Esquina Con 15 Av, Col Centro, Playa del Carmen, QR 77710; +52 984 873 1919, Fax +52 984 873 0574, cozumel@aeroferinco.com, www.aeroferinco.com. Cap Fernando Quintín Vargas. Scheduled/charter passenger/cargo. 1 x Dornier 28D-2, 5 x Let 410

AERO UNION (Aerotransportes de Carga Unión) Aquiles Serdán 1995, La Paz, BCS 23000, www.aerounion.com.mx; +52 555 784 2125 Ext 111/113, Fax +52 555 785 2817. Carlos Hernández. Scheduled/charter cargo. 1 x A300B4-200F operated by ICC Canada

AVIOQUINTANA (Aviones de Renta de Quintana Roo) (AQT/*Avioquintana*) Av Juárez 90, Col Centro, Chetumal, QR 77000; +52 983 832 0664, Fax +52 983 832 8597. Cap Mario A Hermosillo Torres. Scheduled/charter passenger. 1 x Seneca, 1 x Metro II

HELIVAN (Helicopteros y Vehículos Aéreos Nacionales) Plaza Localo Local 2, Cancún, QR; +52 998 883 3104, helivan@caribe.net.mx, www.dutyfreemalls.com/helihawk/helicopter.htm. Charter passenger. 1 x Bell 206, 2 x Beech 1900D

TACSA (Transportes Aéreos de Coahuila) (*Transcoahuila*) Carretera Saltillo-Monterrey Km 30.5, Saltillo, Coahuila 25900; +52 844 488 1890, Fax +52 844 488 1811. 1 x Cessna 208B, 1 x Metro II

WESTAIR DE MEXICO Hangar 5 Fila 8, Aeropuerto Internacional de Guadalajara, Guadalajara, Jalisco; +52 333 688 5251, Fax +52 333 688 5013, Info: +1 805 777 8949 (US), jorgecor@earth-link.net, www.westairdemexico.com. Cap Jorge Corales. Charter/contract cargo. 7 x Metro III, 1 x Falcon 20

NOTES

MÉXICO

LET 410 *(Ito Noriyuki)*

AEROLINEAS SOSA

IATA: P4   **ICAO:** none   **IATA/ARC:** none   **RADIO:** *Sosa*

CONTACTS

Mail
Avenida San Isidro
Frente al Parque Central
La Ceiba
Honduras

Telephone/Fax
Admin: +504 443 1399
Fax: +504 443 1894

Email: aerososa@caribe.hn

OPERATION

Type: Scheduled/charter passenger/cargo
Cities served: GJA LCE RTB SAP UII

HISTORY/STRUCTURE

Founded: 1984
Start date: 1984
CEO: Juan Antonio Sosa B
Ownership: Privately held

FLEET

Type	No	Seats	Engines
Let 410	2	Y17	WA M-601D
Nord 262A	2	Y29	TU Bastan VIC
Fairchild F-27F	1	Y44	RR Dart 528-7E

SHORTS SD3-60 VARIANT 200 *(Michael Robison)*

AEROPERLAS
(Aerolíneas Pacífico Atlántico dba)

IATA: WL   **ICAO:** APP   **IATA/ARC:** 828   **RADIO:** *Aeroperlas*

CONTACTS

Mail
Aéropuerto Marcos A Gelabert
Albrook
Panamá

Telephone/Fax
Admin: +507 315 7555
Fax: +507 315 7537
Res: +507 315 7500

Email: info@aeroperlas.com
Internet: www.tacaregional.com/aeroperlas

OPERATION

Type: Scheduled/charter passenger/cargo
Cities served: ACU AFS BFQ BOC CHX CTD CTE CZJ DAV ELE GHE JQE MPP ONX OTD PLP PUE PYC SAX UTU
Some services operated under the name Aerolínas Pacífico Atlántico (APAIR)
Alliance: Grupo TACA
FFP: Distancia

HISTORY/STRUCTURE

Founded: 1969 (as Aerolíneas Islas de las Perlas)
Start date: June 1970
President: Eduardo Stagg
Ownership: Grupo TACA, private investors

FLEET

Type	No	Seats	Engines
Cessna 208B	3	Y9	PWC PT6A-114A
Beech King Air A100	1	Y10	PWC PT6A-27
DHC-6-300	3	Y20	PWC PT6A-27
Shorts 360 (200)	5	Y36	PWC PT6A-65AR

LET 410 *(Edward Felleson)*

ATLANTIC AIRLINES

IATA: none   **ICAO:** none   **IATA/ARC:** none   **RADIO:** none

---

CONTACTS

Mail
Busto José Marti 2 1/2 c al Este
Managua
Nicaragua

Telephone/Fax
Admin: +1 505 222 5787
Fax: +1 505 228 5614

Email: atlantic@nic.gbm.net
Internet: www.atlanticairlines.com.ni

OPERATION

Type: Scheduled/charter passenger/cargo
Cities served: BEF MGA PUZ RNI TGU

HISTORY/STRUCTURE

Founded: 1997
Start date: December 1997
CEO: Luis Arévalo Ramírez
Ownership: Privately held

FLEET

Type	No	Seats	Engines
Let 410	3	Y19	WA M-601E

DE HAVILLAND CANADA DHC-7-102 DASH 7 *(Kenneth Turley)*

AVCOM (Aviones Comerciales de Guatemala)

IATA: none   **ICAO:** none   **IATA/ARC:** none   **RADIO:** none

CONTACTS

Mail
Avenida Hincapié
Calle 18, Zona 13, Hangar 21
Aéropuerto La Aurora
Guatemala City 01013
Guatemala

Telephone/Fax
Admin: +1 502 331 5821
Fax: +1 5502 332 4946

OPERATION

Type: Charter passenger/cargo

HISTORY/STRUCTURE

Founded: 1954
Start date: 1954
CEO: James Callawan
Ownership: Privately held

FLEET

Type	No	Seats	Engines
Cessna 337E	1	Y5	CO IO-360-CID
Commander 500S	2	Y6	LY IO-540-E1B5
DHC-6-300	5	Y19	PWC PT6A-27
DHC-7-102	2	Y50	PWC PT6A-50

BOEING 737-200 *(Dave Campbell)*

AVIATECA

IATA: GU   **ICAO:** GUG   **IATA/ARC:** 240   **RADIO:** *Aviateca*

CONTACTS

Mail
Avenida Hincapié 12-22, Zona 13
Aéropuerto La Aurora
Guatemala City 01013, Guatemala

Telephone/Fax
Admin: +502 331 8261
Fax: +502 331 7412
Res: 1 800 327 9832

Internet: www.grupotaca.com

OPERATION

Type: Scheduled/charter passenger/cargo
Cities served: Central America: FRS GUA SAL SJO **México:** CUN MEX
US: DFW
Alliance: Grupo TACA
Code-share: American Airlines, LACSA, TACA
FFP: Distancia, LatinPass

HISTORY/STRUCTURE

Founded: March 14, 1945 (as Compañia Guatemalteca de Avíacíon)
Start date: March 1946
President: Ing Julio Obols Gomes
Ownership: Grupo TACA (30%), private investors (70%)

FLEET

Type	No	Seats	Engines
Boeing 737-200	5	Y122/Y125	PW JT8D-9A/-15

BOEING 737-700 *(Gianfranco Beting)*

COPA AIRLINES (Compañia Panameña de Aviación)

IATA: CM   **ICAO:** CMP   **IATA/ARC:** 230   **RADIO:** *Copa*

CONTACTS

Mail
Apartado, Postal 1572
Panamá 1
Panamá

Email: cserv@mail.copa.com.pa
Internet: www.copaair.com

Telephone/Fax
Admin: +507 227 2522
Fax: +507 227 1952
Res: 1 800 359 2672 (US)
PR: +1 507 227 0116

OPERATION

Type: Scheduled/charter passenger
Cities served: Central America: GUA MGA PTY SJO SAL **México:** CUN MEX
Caribbean: HAV KIN MBJ PAP SDQ SJU **South America:** BAQ BOG CCS
CLO CTG EZE GRU GYE LIM MDE SCL UIO **US:** LAX MIA MCO
Code-share: Continental Airlines
FFP: OnePass

HISTORY/STRUCTURE

Founded: August 30, 1944
Start date: May 5, 1947
Chairman: Alberto Motta
CEO: Pedro Heilbron
Ownership: Private investors (51%), Continental Airlines (49%)

FLEET

Type	No	Seats	Engines
Boeing 737-200	10	C8Y106	PW JT8D-15
Boeing 737-700	8	C12Y112	CFM56-7B24
Ordered			
Boeing 737-700	4		

ATR42-300 *(George G Fariñas)*

ISLEÑA AIRLINES (Isleña de Inversiones)

IATA: WC   **ICAO:** ISV   **IATA/ARC:** 282   **RADIO:** none

---

CONTACTS

Mail
PO Box 402
Avenida San Isidro,
Frente Parque Central
La Ceiba, Honduras

Email: info@flyislena.com
Internet: www.flyislena.com

Telephone/Fax
Admin: +504 443 0179
Fax: +504 441 2527
Res: +504 443 0179 ext 109

OPERATION

Type: Scheduled/charter passenger
Cities served: Central America: GJA LCE RTB PCH PEU SAP TGU TJI
Caribbean: GCM
Alliance: Grupo TACA
FFP: Distancia, LatinPass

HISTORY/STRUCTURE

Founded: 1981
Start date: March 31, 1981
President/CEO: Arturo Alvarado Wood
Ownership: Private investors (80%), Grupo TACA (20%)

FLEET

Type	No	Seats	Engines
Cessna 208B	4	Y9	PWC PT6A-114
Shorts 360 (100)	2	Y39	PWC PT6A-65R
ATR42-300	6	Y50	PWC PW120/121

SHORTS SD3-60 VARIANT 200 *(George G Fariñas)*

LA COSTEÑA

IATA: none   **ICAO:** none   **IATA/ARC:** none   **RADIO:** *Lacostena*

CONTACTS

Mail
Aeropuerto Internacional Augusto Cesar Sandino
Terminal Vuelos Nacionales
Managua, Nicaragua

Email: info@flylacostena.com
Internet: www.flylacostena.com

Telephone/Fax
Admin: +505 263 1228
Fax: +505 263 1281
Res: +505 263 2142

OPERATION

Type: Scheduled/charter passenger/cargo
Cities served: BEF MGA NCR PUZ RNI SIU WSP
All scheduled service operated for TACA using only TA flight numbers
Alliance: Grupo TACA
FFP: Distancia

HISTORY/STRUCTURE

Founded: 1991
Start date: 1991
President: Julio Caballero
Ownership: Grupo TACA (50%), Caballero/private investors (50%)

FLEET

Type	No	Seats	Engines
Cessna 208B	4	Y14	PWC PT6A-114A
Shorts 360 (200)	2*	Y36	PWC PT6A-65AR

*leased from Aeroperlas

AIRBUS A320-233 *(Gianfranco Beting)*

LACSA (Líneas Aéreas Costarricenses SA)

IATA: LR   **ICAO:** LRC   **IATA/ARC:** 133   **RADIO:** *Lacsa*

CONTACTS

Mail
Apartado 1531-1000
San José, Costa Rica

Telephone/Fax
Admin: +506 231 6064
Fax:　　+506 232 9185
Res:　　1 800 225 2272 (US/Canada)

Internet: www.centralamerica.com/cr/lacsa/lacsa.htm

OPERATION

Type: Scheduled/charter passenger/cargo
Cities served: Central America: GUA MGA PTY SAL SJO **México:** CUN MEX
South America: BOG CCS GYE LIM SCL UIO **US:** JFK LAX MIA MSY
Canada: YUL YYZ
Code-share: American Airlines, AVIATECA, SAM Colombia, SANSA, TACA
FFP: Distancia, LatinPass, LacsaPass

HISTORY/STRUCTURE

Founded: October 17, 1945
Start date: June 1, 1946
Chairman: Alonso Lara
President: José Guillermo Rojas
Ownership: Private investors (86.98%), ASA LACSA (3.02%), Grupo TACA (10%)

FLEET

Type	No	Seats	Engines
Boeing 737-200	5	C8Y111	PW JT8D-15/-17/-17A
Airbus A320-200	5	C8Y138	IAE V2527-A5/V2527E-A5

BRITTEN-NORMAN BN-2A-26 ISLANDER *(Edward Felleson)*

MAYA ISLAND AIR (Belize Air Maya dba)

IATA: MW   **ICAO:** MYD   **IATA/ARC:** none   **RADIO:** *Myland*

CONTACTS

Mail
PO Box 458
Municipal Airport
Belize City
Belize

Telephone/Fax
Admin: +501 2 35794
Fax: +501 2 62192
Res: 1 800 225 6732

Email: mayair@btl.net
Internet: www.mayaairways.com

OPERATION

Type: Scheduled/charter passenger/cargo
Cities served: BGK BZE CUK CYC CZH DGA FRS PBZ PND SPR TZA

HISTORY/STRUCTURE

Founded: 1962 (as Maya Airways)
Start date: December 1, 1997 (following merger with Island Air)
CEO: Brian Roe
Ownership: Privately held

FLEET

Type	No	Seats	Engines
Cessna 207A	2	Y6	CO IO-520-F17B
BN-2A	5	Y9	LY O-540-E4C5
Cessna 208B	1	Y14	PWC PT6A-114A

CESSNA 208B GRAND CARAVAN *(MAP)*

SANSA (Servicios Aéreos Nacionales SA)

IATA: RZ   **ICAO:** LRS   **IATA/ARC:** 503   **RADIO:** none

---

CONTACTS

Mail
Apartado 999-1007
Edificio Colon
San José, Costa Rica

Email: info@flysansa.com
Internet: www.flysansa.com

Telephone/Fax
Admin: +506 290 2727
Fax: +506 232 9185
Res: +1 506 221 9414

OPERATION

Type: Scheduled/charter passenger/cargo
Cities served: BCL GLF LIR NOB OTR PBP PJM PLD PMZ SJO TMU TNO TTQ XQP
All scheduled service operated for LACSA using only LR flight numbers
Alliance: Grupo TACA
FFP: Distancia

HISTORY/STRUCTURE

Founded: 1980
Start date: 1980
President: Carlos M Delgado
Ownership: LACSA

FLEET

Type	No	Seats	Engines
Cessna 208B	8	Y9	PWC PT6A-114

AIRBUS A320-233 *(Gary Tahir)*

TACA

IATA: TA   **ICAO:** TAI   **IATA/ARC:** 202   **RADIO:** *Taca*

CONTACTS

Mail
Edificio Caribe, 2 Piso
San Salvador, El Salvador

Telephone/Fax
Admin: +503 298 5055
Fax: +503 223 3757
Res: 1 800 535 8780

Internet: www.grupotaca.com

OPERATION

Type: Scheduled/charter passenger/cargo
Cities served: Central America: BZE GUA MGA PTY RTB SAL SAP SJO TGU
México: MEX **US:** IAD IAH JFK LAX MIA MSY SFO **Cargo:** GUA IAH LAX
MGA MIA SAL SAP SJO (operated by Florida West International Airlines)
Code-share: American Airlines, AVIATECA, Isleña, LACSA
FFP: Distancia, LatinPass

HISTORY/STRUCTURE

Founded: December 1931 (as Transportes Aéreos Centro-Americanos)
Start date: March 16, 1932
President/CEO: Federico Bloch
Ownership: Grupo TACA

FLEET

Type	No	Seats	Engines
Boeing 737-200	5	C8Y111	PW JT8D-17/-17A
Airbus A319-100	5	C12Y108	IAE V2524-A5
Airbus A320-200	21	C12Y138	IAE V2527E-A5/V2527-A5
Boeing 767-200ER	1*	Y234	GE CF6-80A2
*stored, for sale			
Ordered			
Airbus A319-100	11		
Airbus A320-200	12		

BAC ONE-ELEVEN SERIES 401/AK *(Chris Benesh)*

TIKAL JETS AIRLINES (Tikal Jets dba)

IATA: A5   **ICAO:** TKC   **IATA/ARC:**   **RADIO:** *Tikal*

CONTACTS

Mail
Avenida Hincapié y 18 Calle
Zona 13, Hangar 8
Aeropuerto La Aurora
Guatemala City 01013, Guatemala

Email: tikalair@guate.net
Internet: www.tikaljets.centroamerica.com

Telephone/Fax
Admin: +502 334 5631
Fax: +502 361 3343
Res: +502 332 5070

OPERATION

Type: Scheduled/charter passenger/cargo
Cities served: Central America: FRS GUA SAP **México:** CUN

HISTORY/STRUCTURE

Founded: 1990
Start date: 1992
President: Uri Roitman

FLEET

Type	No	Seats	Engines
EL-1 Gavilán	1	Y6	LY TIO-540-W2A
Let 410	2	Y19	WA M-601D/M-601E
BAC 1-11 400	2	Y79	RR Spey 511-14

LET 410 *(Steve Kinder)*

TRAVELAIR (Ace Air dba)

IATA: U3   **ICAO:** none   **IATA/ARC:** 585   **RADIO:**

CONTACTS

Mail
Apartado 8-4920
San José
Costa Rica

Telephone/Fax
Admin: +506 220 3054
Fax: +506 220 0413
Res: 1 800 948 3770

Email: travelair@centralamerica.com
Internet: www.centralamerica.com/cr/tran/travlair.htm

OPERATION

Type: Scheduled/charter passenger/cargo
Cities served: BCL GLF ISL LIR MRCE MRDK NOB PKM PMZ RIK SYQ TMU TNO TNQ XQP

HISTORY/STRUCTURE

Founded: 1991
Start date: December 15, 1991
CEO: Howard Solomon
Ownership: Conner Thomas & Charlie Warbelow

FLEET

Type	No	Seats	Engines
Cessna U206E	1	Y6	CO IO-520-F
BN-2A Islander	1	Y8	LY O-540-E4C5
Let 410	3	Y15	WA M-601D

CESSNA 208B GRAND CARAVAN *(Edward Felleson)*

TROPIC AIR

IATA: PM   **ICAO:** TOS   **IATA/ARC:** none   **RADIO:** *Tropiser*

CONTACTS

Mail
PO Box 20
San Pedro
Belize

Telephone/Fax
Admin: +501 26 2012
Fax:　+501 26 2338
Res:　 1 800 422 3435 (US)

Email: tropicair@btl.net
Internet: www.tropicair.com

OPERATION

Type: Scheduled/charter passenger/cargo
Cities served: BZE CUK CZH DGA FRS PBZ PND SPR TZA

HISTORY/STRUCTURE

Founded: 1979 (as Tropical Air Service)
Start date: 1979
CEO: Celi McCorkle
Ownership: Privately held

FLEET

Type	No	Seats	Engines
Cessna 207A	1	Y6	CO IO-520-F
Cessna 208B	6	Y14	PWC PT6A-114A

Central America Addenda

AEREO RUTA MAYA Avenida Hincapié, Rua 8, Hangar 13-1, Aeropuerto Internacional La Aurora, Guatemala City 01013, GT; +502 360 4920, Fax +502 331 4995, armsa@intelnet.net.gt, http://personales.com/guatemala/guatemala/armsa. Ricardo Callaway. Charter passenger/cargo. 1 x Baron, 2 x Cessna 208, 3 x Let 410

AEREO TAXI INTERNACIONAL Apartado 55-0960, Paitilla, Panamá; +507 264 2776, Fax +507 226 3422. José Ivanhoe de Roux. Charter passenger. 1 x Bell 206, 3 x Islander

AERO COSTA SOL (CSG) Apartado 782-4050, Alajuela, Aeropuerto Internacional Juan Santamaria, Hangar No 2, San José, CR; +506 440 14 44, Fax +506 441 26 71, Res 1 800 832 0474, 1 800 245 8420 (US/Can), www.hotelherradura.com/indexaero.htm. Alvaro Zamora Herrara. Charter passenger. 1 x Aztec, 3 x Navajo, 2 x Metro II, 1 x Let 410

AEROSEGOVIA (SGV/*Segovia*) Aeropuerto Internacional Augusto Cesar Sandino, Managua, NI; +505 2 787162, Fax +505 2 704134, asegovia@cablenet.com.ni. Walter R Castillo Sandino. Charter cargo. 1 x An-32 (other aircraft leased from Aerocaribbean as required)

AGUILAS MAYAS INTERNACIONAL (AMISA)(GME) Avenida Hincapié y 18 Calle, 14-01, Local 3, Zona 13, Aeropuerto Internacional La Aurora, Guatemala City 01013, GT; +502 385 4175, amisa@amigo.net.gt, www.dragonaviation.com/tours.html. Andre Anoshkin. Charter passenger. 2 x An-2P, 1 Yak-40

ATASA (Aerolíneas Turísticas de América SA) Terminal Aerea del Aeropuerto Internacional Tobías Bolaños, Pavas, San José, CR; +506 232 1125, Fax +506 232 5802. Rodrigo Chinchilla. Charter passenger.

AVIATUR (Aviación de Turismo) Apartado 0832-1658 WTC, Panama City, Panamá; +507 315 0311, Fax +507 315 0316, aviatur@sinfo.net, www.panamareservation.com/PAG/aviatur.html. Zosimo Guardia V. Scheduled/charter passenger. 1 x Cessna U206G, 1 x Commander 500S, 2 x Cessna 208B, 3 x Islander

AVIONES TAXI AEREO Aeropuerto Internacional Juan Santamaria, Apdo 605-4050, Alajuela, San José, CR; +506 41 27 13. Manuel E Guerra V. Charter passenger. 3 x Aztec, 1 x Navajo, 1 x Twin Otter (aircraft interchanged with TACSA)

DHL AERO EXPRESO (D5/DAE/992) Apartado Aéreo 11491, Panama City 6, Panamá; +507 238 4206, Fax: +507 238 4149, Steve Getzler. Scheduled cargo for DHL Worldwide Express. 3 x 727-200F

DHL DE GUATEMALA (L3/JOS/947) Air Operations Department, Blvd Juan Pablo II, 10 Avenida 6-75, Zona 13, Guatemala City 01013, GT; +502 361 7458, Fax: +502 361 7450. Enrique Salazar. Scheduled cargo for DHL Worldwide Express. 1 x Metro III, 1 x ATR42-300

INTER (Transportes Aéreos Inter) (TSP/*Transpo-Inter*) Hincapié 12-22, Zona 13, Aéropuerto La Aurora, Guatemala City 01013, GT; +502 361 2144, Fax +502 331 8768, info@flyinter.com, www.flyinter.com. Julio O Gomes. Scheduled/charter passenger/cargo (Grupo TACA). Scheduled domestic service for AVIATECA using only GU flight numbers. 3 x Cessna 208B

LAN HONDURAS (Líneas Aéreas Nacionales de Honduras) (ULD) Casilla Postal 35, La Ceiba, Honduras; + 504 242 2354. Rafael Nuñez. Scheduled/cargo passenger/cargo. 1 x An-24, 2 x An-26

MAPIEX AERO Aeropuerto Marcos A Gelabert de Albrook, Panamá; +507 3150291, Fax +507 315 0290, aero@sinfo.com, www.matiexaero.com. Scheduled passenger. 2 x Metro II

PANAVIA PANAMA (PNV) Apartado 8140030, Zona 14/1, Panama City, Panamá; +507 238 4503, Fax: +507 238 4509. Charter cargo. 1 x 727-100F

PARSA Apartado 9-001, Aeropuerto Marcos A Gelabert de Albrook, Casilla 87-1133, Panamá 7; + 507 226 3883, +507 226 3422. José Ivanhoe de Roux. Scheduled/charter passenger. 1 x Seneca, 3 x Islander, 1 x Trislander

RACSA (Rutas Aéreas Centro Americanas SA) Avenida Hincapié, Calle 18, Hangar 12, Aeropuerto La Aurora, Guatemala City 01013, GT; +502 334 7935, Fax +502 334 7935, Res: +502 332 5686, Fernando Castillo. Charter passenger. 1 x Nord 262A

ROLLINS AIR Aeropuerto CP 451, La Ceiba, HN; +504 441 2560, Fax +504 441 2172. Claudius Rollins. Scheduled/charter passenger/cargo. 5 x Let 410, 1 x Yak-40, 2 x FH-227B

TACSA (Taxi Aereo Centroaméricano) Aeropuerto Internacional Tobías Bolaños, Hangar 9, Apdo 3941-1000, San José; +506 232 1469. Manuel E Guerra V. Charter passenger. 3 x Cessna 206, 1 x Seneca, 2 x Aztec, 4 x Navajo (aircraft interchanged with Aviones Taxi Aereo)

TAG (Transportes Aereos Guatemaltecos) Avenida Hincapié y 18 Calle, Hangar 15, Zona 13, Aeropuerto La Aurora, Guatemala City, GT; +502 360-3038, Fax +502 334 7205. José Antonio Gonzalez Aparicio. 1 x Comanche, 1 x Cessna 185, 1 x Beech 18, 1 x Let 410

NOTES

CITY AND AIRPORT DECODE

A

ABA	Arroyo Barril, DO
ABE	Allentown, PA
ABI	Abilene, TX
ABQ	Albuquerque, NM
ABR	Aberdeen, SD
ABY	Albany, GA
ABZ	Aberdeen, UK
ACA	Acapulco, MX
ACK	Nantucket, MA
ACT	Waco, TX
ACU	Achutupo, PAN
ACV	Eureka/Arcata, CA
ACY	Atlantic City Intl, NJ
ADK	Adak Island, AK
ADQ	Kodiak, AK
ADZ	Isla de San Andrés, COL
AED	Aleneva, AK
AET	Allakaket, AK
AEX	Alexandria, LA
AFS	Panama City-Albrook (Marcos A Gelabert), PAN
AFW	Fort Worth-Alliance, TX
AGM	Tasiilaq, GL
AGS	Augusta, GA
AGT	Ciudad del Este, BR
AGU	Aguascalientes, MX
AHN	Athens, GA
AIA	Alliance, NE
AKI	Akiak, AK
AKK	Akhiok, AK
AKL	Auckland, NZ
AKN	King Salmon, AK
AKP	Anaktuvuk Pass, AK
AKV	Akulivik, QC
ALB	Albany, NY
ALM	Alamogordo, NM
ALO	Waterloo, IA
ALS	Alamosa, CO
ALW	Walla Walla, WA
ALZ	Alitak, AK
AMA	Amarillo, TX
AMS	Amsterdam-Schiphol, NLD
ANC	Anchorage, AK
ANI	Aniak, AK
ANU	V C Bird Intl, AG
AOO	Altoona, PA
AOS	Amook, AK
APF	Naples, FL
ARC	Arctic Village, AK
ARN	Stockholm-Arlanda, SE
ART	Watertown, NY

ASD	Andros Town, BS
ASE	Aspen, CO
ASU	Asunción, PY
ATC	Arthur's Town, BS
ATH	Athens, GR
ATL	Atlanta, GA
ATT	Atmautluak, AK
ATW	Appleton, WI
ATY	Watertown, SD
AUA	Aruba, AW
AUG	Augusta, ME
AUS	Austin, TX
AVI	Ciego de Avila, CU
AVL	Asheville, NC
AVP	Wilkes-Barre/Scranton, PA
AXA	Wallblake, AI
AXP	Spring Point, BS
AZO	Kalamazoo, MI

B

BAQ	Barranquilla, COL
BBQ	Barbuda, AG
BBR	Basse Terre, GP
BCA	Baracoa, CU
BCL	Barra del Colorado, CR
BCN	Barcelona, ES
BDA	Kindley Field, BM
BDL	Bradley Intl, CT
BDR	Bridgeport, CT
BEF	Bluefields, NI
BEH	Benton Harbor, MI
BET	Bethel, AK
BFD	Bradford, PA
BFF	Scottsbluff, NE
BFI	Seattle-Boeing Field, WA
BFL	Bakersfield, CA
BFM	Mobile, AL
BFQ	Bahia Piña, PAN
BFS	Belfast, UK
BGI	Barbados, BB
BGK	Big Creek, BZ
BGM	Binghamton, NY
BGR	Bangor, ME
BHB	Bar Harbor, ME
BHM	Birmingham, AL
BHX	Birmingham, UK
BIL	Billings, MT
BIM	Bimini, BS
BIS	Bismarck, ND
BJI	Bemidji, MN
BJS	Beijing-Capital, CN

BJX	León/Guanajuato, MX
BKK	Bangkok, TH
BKW	Beckley, WV
BKX	Brookings, SD
BLA	Barcelona, VE
BLF	Bluefield, WV
BLI	Bellingham, WA
BMG	Bloomington, IN
BMI	Bloomington, IL
BNA	Nashville, TN
BOC	Bocas Del Toro, PAN
BOD	Bordeaux, FR
BOG	Bogotá, COL
BOI	Boise, ID
BOM	Mumbai, IND
BON	Bonaire, AN
BOS	Boston, MA
BPT	Beaumont/Pt Arthur, TX
BQK	Glynco Jetport, GA
BQN	Aguadilla, PR
BQU	Port Elizabeth, Bequia, VC
BRD	Brainerd, MN
BRL	Burlington, IA
BRO	Brownsville, TX
BRU	Brussels, BE
BRW	Barrow, AK
BRX	Barahona-Habanero, DO
BSL	Basle, CH
BTI	Barter Island, AK
BTM	Butte, MT
BTR	Baton Rouge, LA
BTT	Bettles, AK
BTV	Burlington, VT
BUD	Budapest, HU
BUF	Buffalo, NY
BUR	Burbank, CA
BWD	Brownwood, TX
BWI	Baltimore, MD
BYM	Bayamo, CU
BZA	Bonanza, San Pedro, NI
BZE	Belize City-Phillip S W Goldson Intl, BZ
BZN	Bozeman, MT

C

CAE	Columbia, SC
CAI	Cairo, EG
CAK	Akron/Canton, OH
CAP	Cap-Haïtien, HT
CAY	Cayenne, GF
CBE	Cumberland, MD
CCC	Cayo Coco, CU

CCS	Caracas, VE
CDB	Cold Bay, AK
CDC	Cedar City, UT
CDG	Paris-Charles de Gaulle, FR
CDR	Chadron, NE
CDV	Cordova, AK
CEC	Crescent City, CA
CEN	Ciudad Obregon, MX
CEZ	Cortez, CO
CFG	Cienfuegos, CU
CFQ	Creston, BC
CGI	Cape Girardeau, MO
CGN	Cologne/Bonn, DEU
CGX	Meigs Field, IL
CHA	Chattanooga, TN
CHO	Charlottesville, VA
CHS	Charleston, SC
CHX	Changuinola, PAN
CIA	Rome-Ciampino, IT
CIC	Chico, CA
CID	Cedar Rapids, IA
CIU	Chippewa County, MI
CIW	Canouan Island, VC
CJS	Ciudad Juárez, MX
CKB	Clarksburg, WV
CLD	Carlsbad, CA
CLE	Cleveland, OH
CLL	College Station, TX
CLM	Port Angeles, WA
CLO	Cali, COL
CLQ	Colima, MX
CLT	Charlotte, NC
CME	Ciudad del Carmen, MX
CMH	Columbus, OH
CMI	Champaign, IL
CMW	Camaguey, CU
CMX	Hancock, MI
CNF	Belo Horizonte, BR
CNM	Carlsbad, NM
CNP	Nerlerit Inaat, GL
CNS	Cairns, AU
CNW	Waco-Connolly, TX
COD	Cody, WY
COS	Colorado Springs, CO
COU	Columbia, MO
CPE	Campeche, MX
CPH	Copenhagen-Kastrup, DK
CPR	Casper, WY
CRI	Crooked Island, BS
CRP	Corpus Christi, TX
CRU	Carriacou, GD
CRW	Charleston, WV
CSG	Columbus, GA
CTD	Chitré, PAN

CTE	Carti, PAN
CTG	Cartegena, COL
CTM	Chetumal, MX
CTO	Calverton, NY
CTS	Sapporo-Chitose, JP
CUK	Caye Caulker, BZ
CUL	Culiacán, MX
CUN	Cancún, MX
CUR	Curaçao, AN
CUU	Chihuahua, MX
CVG	Cincinnati, OH
CVJ	Cuernavaca, MX
CVM	Ciudad Victoria, MX
CVN	Clovis, NM
CWA	Central Wisconsin, WI
CWF	Lake Charles, LA
CWL	Cardiff, UK
CXH	Vancouver-Coal Harbour, BC
CXI	Christmas Island, Kiribati
CXL	Calexico, CA
CYB	Cayman Brac, CYM
CYF	Chefornak, AK
CYO	Cayo Lago, CU
CYS	Cheyenne, WY
CZA	Chichen Itza, MX
CZH	Corozal, BZ
CZJ	Coruzon de Jesus, PAN
CZM	Cozumel, MX

D

DAB	Daytona Beach, FL
DAL	Dallas-Love Field, TX
DAV	David, PAN
DAY	Dayton, OH
DBQ	Dubuque, IA
DCA	Washington-Ronald Reagan National, DC
DCF	Cane Field, DM
DDC	Dodge City, KS
DEC	Decatur, IL
DEL	Delhi, IND
DEN	Denver, CO
DFW	Dallas/Fort Worth, TX
DGA	Dangriga, BZ
DGO	Durango, MX
DHN	Dothan, AL
DIK	Dickinson, ND
DLG	Dillingham, AK
DLH	Duluth, MN
DOM	Melville Hall, DM
DPS	Denpasar, Bali, IDN
DRO	Durango, CO
DRT	Del Rio, TX

DSD	La Désirade, GP
DSM	Des Moines, IA
DTN	Shreveport-Downtown, LA
DTT	Detroit-City, MI
DTW	Detroit-Metro, MI
DUB	Dublin, IE
DUJ	Dubois, PA
DUS	Düsseldorf, DEU
DUT	Dutch Harbor, AK
DVL	Devils Lake, ND
DXB	Dubai, AE

E

EAT	Wenatchee, WA
EAU	Eau Claire, WI
EDI	Edinburgh, UK
EEK	Eek, AK
EEN	Keene, NH
EFD	Houston-Ellington, TX
EGE	Vail, CO
EGX	Egegik, AK
EIS	Tortola, VG
EKO	Elko, NV
ELD	El Dorado, AR
ELE	El Real, PAN
ELH	North Eleuthera, BS
ELM	Elmira/Corning, NY
ELP	El Paso, TX
EMA	East Midlands, UK
ENA	Kenai, AK
EPS	El Portillo, DO
ERI	Erie, PA
ESC	Escanaba, MI
EUG	Eugene, OR
EUX	St Eustatius, AN
EVV	Evansville, IN
EWR	Newark Intl, NJ
EXT	Exeter, UK
EYW	Key West, FL
EZE	Buenos Aires-Pistarini, ARG

F

FAI	Fairbanks, AK
FAO	Faro, PT
FAR	Fargo, ND
FAT	Fresno, CA
FAY	Fayetteville, NC
FCA	Kalispell, MT
FCO	Rome-Fiumicino, IT
FDF	Fort-de-FR, MQ
FHU	Fort Huachuca/Sierra Vista, AZ

FKL	Franklin, PA
FLG	Flagstaff, AZ
FLL	Fort Lauderdale, FL
FLO	Florence, SC
FMN	Farmington, NM
FMY	Fort Myers, FL
FNL	Fort Collins/Loveland, CO
FNT	Flint, MI
FOD	Fort Dodge, IA
FOE	Topeka-Forbes, KS
FPO	Freeport, BS
FRA	Frankfurt-Rhein/Main, DEU
FRD	Friday Harbor, WA
FRM	Fairmont, MN
FRS	Flores, GT
FSD	Sioux Falls, SD
FSM	Fort Smith, AR
FSP	St Pierre, PM
FUK	Fukuoka, JP
FWA	Fort Wayne, IN
FYU	Fort Yukon, AK
FYV	Fayetteville, AR

G

GAL	Galena, AK
GAO	Guantanamo, CU
GBD	Great Bend, KS
GBJ	Marie Galante, GP
GCC	Gillette, WY
GCK	Garden City, KS
GCM	Grand Cayman, CYM
GCN	Grand Canyon, AZ
GDL	Guadalajara, MX
GDT	Grand Turk, TC
GDV	Glendive, MT
GDX	Magadan, RU
GEG	Spokane, WA
GEO	Georgetown, GY
GER	Nueva Gerona, CU
GFK	Grand Forks, ND
GGG	Longview, TX
GGT	George Town, BS
GGW	Glasgow, MT
GHB	Governors Harbour, BS
GHC	Great Harbour Cay, BS
GHE	Garachiné, PAN
GIG	Rio de Janeiro-Intl, BR
GJA	Isla de Guanaja, HN
GJT	Grand Junction, CO
GLA	Glasgow, UK
GLD	Goodland, KS
GLF	Golfito, CR
GLH	Greenville, MS

GLS	Galveston, TX
GND	St Georges-Port Saline, GD
GNU	Goodnews Bay, AK
GNV	Gainesville, FL
GOH	Nuuk, GL
GON	New London/Groton, CT
GPT	Gulfport/Biloxi, MS
GPZ	Grand Rapids, MN
GRB	Green Bay, WI
GRI	Grand Island, NE
GRR	Grand Rapids, MI
GRU	São Paulo-Guarulhos, BR
GSO	Greensboro/High Pt/Winston-Salem, NC
GSP	Greenville/Spartanburg, SC
GST	Gustavus, AK
GTF	Great Falls, MT
GTR	Golden Triangle Regional, Columbus, MS
GUA	Guatemala City, GT
GUB	Guerrero Negro, MX
GUC	Gunnison, CO
GUM	Guam, GU
GUP	Gallup, NM
GVA	Geneva, CH
GYE	Guayaquil, EC
GYM	Guaymas, MX

H

HAM	Hamburg, DEU
HAR	Harrisburg, PA
HAV	Havana, CU
HDN	Steamboat Springs-Hayden, CO
HEL	Helsinki, FI
HEX	Santo Domingo-Herrera, DO
HGR	Hagerstown, MD
HHH	Hilton Head Island, SC
HIB	Hibbing/Chisholm, MN
HII	Lake Havasu City, AZ
HKG	Chek Lap Kok, HK
HKY	Hickory, NC
HLN	Helena, MT
HMO	Hermosillo, MX
HNL	Honolulu, HI
HNM	Hana, Maui, HI
HOB	Hobbs, NM
HOG	Holguín, CU
HOM	Homer, AK
HON	Huron, SD
HOT	Hot Springs, AR
HOU	Houston-Hobby, TX

HPB	Hooper Bay, AK
HPN	Westchester County, NY
HPV	Princeville, Kauai, HI
HRL	Harlingen, TX
HRO	Harrison, AR
HSH	Henderson Sky Harbor, NV
HSL	Huslia, AK
HSV	Huntsville/Decatur, AL
HTS	Huntington, WV
HUF	Terre Haute, IN
HUX	Huatulco, MX
HVN	New Haven, CT
HVR	Havre, MT
HYA	Hyannis, MA
HYS	Hays, KS

I

IAD	Washington-Dulles Intl, DC
IAH	Houston-Bush Intercontinental, TX
ICN	Seoul-Incheon, KR
ICT	Wichita, KS
IDA	Idaho Falls, ID
IFP	Bullhead City, AZ
IGA	Inagua, BS
IGG	Igiugig, AK
IGM	Kingman, AZ
ILE	Killeen, TX
ILG	Wilmington, DE
ILI	Iliamna, AK
ILM	Wilmington, NC
ILN	Wilmington, OH
IMT	Iron Mountain, MI
IND	Indianapolis, IN
INL	International Falls, MN
INT	Winston-Salem/Smith-Reynolds, NC
IPL	El Centro/Imperial, CA
IPT	Williamsport, PA
IQT	Iquitos, PE
ISL	Punta Islita, CR
ISN	Williston, ND
ISO	Kinston, NC
ISO	Kinston, NC
ISP	Long Island MacArthur, NY
IST	Istanbul, TR
ITH	Ithaca, NY
ITO	Hilo, HI
IWD	Ironwood, MI
IYK	Inyokern, CA
IZT	Ixtepec, MX

J

JAC	Jackson Hole, WY
JAL	Jalapa, MX
JAN	Jackson, MS
JAV	Ilulissat, GL
JAX	Jacksonville, FL
JBR	Jonesboro, AR
JCH	Qasigiannguit, GL
JEG	Aasiaat, GL
JFK	New York-JFK, NY
JFR	Paamiut, GL
JGO	Qeqertarsuaq, GL
JGR	Kangilinnguit, GL
JHM	Kapalua, Maui, HI
JHS	Sisimiut, GL
JHW	Jamestown, NY
JJU	Qaqortoq, GL
JLN	Joplin, MO
JMS	Jamestown, ND
JNB	Johannesburg, ZA
JNN	Nanortalik, GL
JNS	Narsaq, GL
JNU	Juneau, AK
JON	Johnston Island, USA
JQE	Jaque, PAN
JST	Johnstown, PA
JSU	Maniitsoq, GL
JUV	Upernavik, GL

K

KAL	Kaltag, AK
KCG	Fisheries, AK
KCL	Chignik, AK
KCQ	Chignik, AK
KEF	Keflavík, IS
KEK	Ekwok, AK
KES	Kelsey, MB
KEW	Keewaywin, ON
KGK	Koliganek, AK
KHH	Kaohsiung, TW
KHV	Khabarovsk, RU
KIB	Ivanof Bay, AK
KIF	Kingfisher Lake, ON
KIJ	Niigata, JP
KIN	Kingston-Norman Manley, JM
KIX	Osaka-Kansai, JP
KKB	Kitoi Bay, AK
KKH	Kongiganak, AK
KOA	Kona, Hawaii, HI
KOY	Olga Bay, AK
KOZ	Ouzinkie, AK
KPN	Kipnuk, AK

KSA	Kosrae, FSM
KSM	Saint Marys, AK
KTN	Ketchikan, AK
KTP	Tinson, JM
KUK	Kasigluk, AK
KUL	Kuala Lumpur, MY
KUS	Kulusuk, GL
KVC	King Cove, AK
KWA	Kwajalein, MH
KWK	Kwigillngok, AK
KWN	Quinhagak, AK
KWP	West Point, AK
KZB	Zachar Bay, AK

L

LAA	Lamar, CO
LAF	Lafayette, IN
LAM	Los Alamos, NM
LAN	Lansing, MI
LAP	La Paz, MX
LAR	Laramie, WY
LAS	Las Vegas, NV
LAW	Lawton, OK
LAX	Los Angeles, CA
LBA	Leeds/Bradford, UK
LBB	Lubbock, TX
LBE	Latrobe, PA
LBF	North Platte, NE
LBL	Liberal, KS
LCE	La Ceiba, HN
LCH	Lake Charles, LA
LCK	Columbus (Rickenbacker), OH
LEB	Lebanon, NH
LEX	Lexington, KY
LFT	Lafayette, LA
LGA	New York-LaGuardia, NY
LGB	Long Beach, CA
LGI	Long Island-Deadmans Cay, BS
LGW	London-Gatwick, UK
LHR	London-Heathrow, UK
LIH	Lihue, Kauai, HI
LIM	Lima, PE
LIR	Liberia, CR
LIS	Lisbon, PT
LIT	Little Rock, AR
LMM	Los Mochis, MX
LMT	Klamath Falls, OR
LNK	Lincoln, NE
LNS	Lancaster, PA
LNY	Lanai City, HI
LOV	Monclova, MX

LPA	Las Palmas, Gran Canaria, ES
LPB	La Paz, BO
LRD	Laredo, TX
LRM	La Romana, DO
LRU	Las Cruces, NM
LSE	La Crosse, WI
LSS	Les Saintes, Terre-de-Haut, GP
LTO	Loreto, MX
LWB	Greenbrier, WV
LWS	Lewiston, ID
LWT	Lewistown, MT
LYB	Little Cayman, CYM
LYH	Lynchburg, VA
LYS	Lyon-St Exupéry, FR
LYU	Ely, MN
LZC	Lazáro Cárdenas, MX

M

MAD	Madrid, ES
MAF	Midland/Odessa, TX
MAJ	Majuro, MH
MAM	Matamoros, MX
MAN	Manchester, UK
MAO	Manaus, BR
MAR	Maracaibo, VE
MAY	Mangrove Cay, BS
MAZ	Mayaguez, PR
MBJ	Montego Bay, JM
MBL	Mainstee, MI
MBS	Saginaw, MI
MCE	Merced, CA
MCG	McGrath, AK
MCI	Kansas City, MO
MCK	McCook, NE
MCN	Macon, GA
MCO	Orlando Intl, FL
MCW	Mason City, IA
MDE	Medellín, COL
MDS	Middle Caicos, TC
MDT	Harrisburg Intl, PA
MDW	Chicago-Midway, IL
MDY	Midway Atoll
MDZ	Mendoza, ARG
MEI	Meridian, MS
MEL	Melbourne-Tullamarine, AU
MEM	Memphis, TN
MEX	Mexico City, MX
MFE	McAllen, TX
MFR	Medford, OR
MGA	Managua, NI
MGM	Montgomery, AL
MGW	Morgantown, WV

MHH	Marsh Harbour, BS	MXP	Milan-Malpensa, IT	ORF	Norfolk, VA
MHK	Manhattan, KS	MYG	Mayaguana, BS	ORH	Worcester, MA
MHR	Sacramento-Mather, CA	MYR	Myrtle Beach, SC	ORI	Port Lions, AK
MHT	Manchester, NH	MYU	Mekoryuk, AK	ORY	Paris-Orly, FR
MIA	Miami, FL	MZO	Manzanillo, CU	OSA	Osaka-Metropolitan, JP
MID	Mérida, MX	MZT	Mazatlán, MX	OSH	Oshkosh, WI
MIT	Comitan, MX			OSL	Oslo, NO
MKC	Kansas City, MO			OTD	Contadora, PAN

N

O

P

MHH   Marsh Harbour, BS
MHK   Manhattan, KS
MHR   Sacramento-Mather, CA
MHT   Manchester, NH
MIA   Miami, FL
MID   Mérida, MX
MIT   Comitan, MX
MKC   Kansas City, MO
MKE   Milwaukee, WI
MKG   Muskegon, MI
MKK   Molokai/Hoolehua, HI
MKL   Jackson, TN
MLB   Melbourne, FL
MLI   Moline, IL
MLL   Marshall, AK
MLM   Morelia, MX
MLS   Miles City, MT
MLU   Monroe, LA
MMX   Malmö, SE
MNI   Montserrat-Blackburne, MSR
MNL   Manila, PH
MOA   Moa, CU
MOB   Mobile, AL
MOD   Modesto, CA
MOT   Minot, ND
MPB   Miami-Watson Island, FL
MPP   Malatupo, PAN
MQD   Miquelon, PM
MQS   Mustique, VC
MQT   Marquette, MI
MRCE Carate, CR
MRDK Drake Bay, CR
MRS   Marseille, FR
MRY   Monterey, CA
MSA   Muskrat Dam, ON
MSL   Muscle Shoals, AL
MSN   Madison, WI
MSO   Missoula, MT
MSP   Minneapolis/St Paul, MN
MSS   Massena, NY
MSY   New Orleans, LA
MTH   Marathon, FL
MTJ   Montrose, CO
MTO   Mattoon, IL
MTT   Minatitlán, MX
MTY   Monterrey, MX
MUC   Munich, DEU
MUE   Kamuela, HI
MVD   Montevideo, UY
MVN   Mt Vernon, IL
MVY   Martha's Vineyard, MA
MWA   Marion, IL
MWH   Moses Lake, WA
MXL   Mexicali, MX

N

NAN   Nadi, Fiji
NAQ   Qaanaaq, GL
NAS   Nassau, BS
NCA   North Caicos, TC
NCE   Nice, FR
NCL   Newcastle, UK
NCR   San Carlos, NI
NEG   Negril, JM
NEV   Nevis, KN
NGO   Nagoya, JP
NLD   Nuevo Laredo, MX
NLG   Nelson Lagoon, AK
NME   Nightmute, AK
NMG   San Miguel, PAN
NOB   Nosaria, CR
NRT   Tokyo-Narita, JP
NSB   Bimini North, BS
NTE   Nantes, FR
NUE   Nuremberg, DEU
NUI   Nuiqsut, AK
NUL   Nulato, AK
NUP   Nunapitchuk, AK
NVG   Nueva Guinea, NI

O

OAJ   Jacksonville, NC
OAK   Oakland, CA
OAX   Oaxaca, MX
OBY   Ittoqqortoormiit, GL
OCJ   Ocho Rios, JM
OFK   Norfolk, NE
OGG   Kahului, Maui, HI
OGS   Ogdensburg, NY
OKC   Oklahoma City, OK
OKJ   Okayama, JP
OLF   Wolf Point, MT
OLH   Old Harbor, AK
OMA   Omaha, NE
OME   Nome, AK
ONT   Ontario, CA
ONX   Colón, PAN
OOK   Toksook Bay, AK
OPO   Oporto, PT
ORD   Chicago-O'Hare International, IL

P

PAH   Paducah, KY
PAP   Port-au-Prince, HT
PAZ   Poza Rica, MX
PBC   Puebla, MX
PBI   West Palm Beach, FL
PBM   Paramaribo, SR
PBP   Punta Islita, CR
PBZ   Placentia, BZ
PCM   Playa del Carmen, MX
PDL   Ponta Delgada, PT
PDS   Piedras Negras, MX
PDT   Pendleton, OR
PDX   Portland, OR
PEN   Penang, MY
PFN   Panama City, FL
PGA   Page, AZ
PGV   Greenville, NC
PHF   Newport News/Williamsburg, VA
PHL   Philadelphia, PA
PHX   Phoenix, AZ
PIA   Peoria, IL
PIB   Laurel/Hattiesburg, MS
PID   Nassau Paradise Island, BS
PIE   St Petersburg Intl, FL
PIH   Pocatello, ID
PIK   Prestwick, UK
PIP   Pilot Point, AK
PIR   Pierre, SD
PIT   Pittsburgh, PA
PJM   Puerto Jiménez, CR
PKA   Napaskiak, AK
PKB   Parkersburg, WV
PKC   Petropavlovsk-Kamchatski, RU
PLB   Plattsburgh, NY
PLD   Samara, CR

ORF   Norfolk, VA
ORH   Worcester, MA
ORI   Port Lions, AK
ORY   Paris-Orly, FR
OSA   Osaka-Metropolitan, JP
OSH   Oshkosh, WI
OSL   Oslo, NO
OTD   Contadora, PAN
OTH   North Bend, OR
OTM   Ottumwa, IA
OTR   Coto 47, CR
OTZ   Kotzebue, AK
OWB   Owensboro, KY
OXR   Oxnard, CA

PLN	Pellston, MI
PLP	La Palma, PAN
PLS	Providenciales, TC
PMD	Palmdale/Lancaster, CA
PMV	Porlamar, VE
PMZ	Palmar Sur, CR
PNC	Ponca City, OK
PNI	Pohnpei, FSM
PNS	Pensacola, FL
POP	Puerto Plata, DO
POS	Port of Spain, TT
POT	Port Antonio, JM
POU	Poughkeepsie, NY
PPE	Puerto Penasco, MX
PPG	Pago Pago, AS
PPT	Papeete, Tahiti, PF
PQI	Presque Isle, ME
PQM	Palenque, MX
PRC	Prescott, AZ
PRG	Prague, CZ
PSC	Pasco, WA
PSE	Ponce, PR
PSG	Petersburg, AK
PSM	Portsmouth, NH
PSP	Palm Springs, CA
PSR	Pescara, IT
PTH	Port Heiden, AK
PTP	Pointe-à-Pitre, GP
PTU	Platinum, AK
PTY	Panama City-Tocumen International, PAN
PUB	Pueblo, CO
PUE	Puerto Obaldía, PAN
PUJ	Punta Cana, DO
PUW	Pullman, WA
PUZ	Puerto Cabezas, NI
PVD	Providence, RI
PVG	Shanghai-Pudong, CN
PVR	Puerto Vallarta, MX
PWM	Portland, ME
PXM	Puerto Escondido, MX
PYC	Playon Chico, PAN

Q

| QBC | Bella Coola, BC |
| QRO | Queretaro, MX |

R

RAP	Rapid City, SD
RBY	Ruby, AK
RDB	Red Dog, AK
RDD	Redding, CA
RDG	Reading, PA

RDM	Redmond, OR
RDU	Raleigh/Durham, NC
REK	Reykjavík, IS
REX	Reynosa, MX
RFD	Rockford, IL
RHI	Rhinelander, WI
RIC	Richmond/Williamsburg, VA
RIK	Carrillo, CR
RIW	Riverton, WY
RKD	Rockland, ME
RKS	Rock Springs, WY
RNI	Corn Island, NI
RNO	Reno, NV
ROA	Roanoke, VA
ROC	Rochester, NY
ROR	Koror, PW
ROW	Roswell, NM
RSD	Rock Sound, BS
RSH	Run Mission, AK
RST	Rochester, MN
RSW	Southwest Florida Regional, FL
RTB	Roatán, HN
RUH	Riyadh, SA
RUI	Ruidoso, NM
RUT	Rutland, VT
RWI	Rocky Mount/Wilson, NC

S

SAB	Saba, AN
SAF	Santa Fe, NM
SAL	San Salvador, SV
SAN	San Diego, CA
SAP	San Pedro Sula, HN
SAQ	San Andros, BS
SAT	San Antonio, TX
SAV	Savannah, GA
SAX	Sambú, PAN
SBA	Santa Barbara, CA
SBH	St Barthelémy, GP
SBN	South Bend, IN
SBP	San Luis Obispo, CA
SBS	Steamboat Springs, CO
SBY	Salisbury, MD
SCC	Prudhoe Bay/Deadhorse, AK
SCE	State College, PA
SCL	Santiago, CL
SCM	Scammon Bay, AK
SCQ	Santiago de Compostela, ES
SCU	Santiago, CU
SCX	Salina Cruz, MX
SDF	Louisville, KY

SDJ	Sendai, JP
SDP	Sand Point, AK
SDQ	Santo Domingo, DO
SDY	Sidney, MT
SEA	Seattle/Tacoma, WA
SEL	Seoul-Kimpo, KR
SFB	Sanford, FL
SFG	St Martin-Grand Case, GP
SFJ	Kangerlussuaq, GL
SFO	San Francisco, CA
SFS	Subic Bay, PH
SGF	Springfield, MO
SGU	Saint George, UT
SHA	Shanghai-Hong Qiao, CN
SHD	Shenandoah Valley, VA
SHJ	Sharjah, AE
SHR	Sheridan, WY
SHV	Shreveport, LA
SIG	San Juan-Isla Grande (Dominicci), PR
SIN	Singapore-Changi, SG
SIT	Sitka, AK
SIU	Siuna, NI
SJC	San Jose, CA
SJD	San José del Cabo/Los Cabos, MX
SJO	San José-Juan Santamaría Intl, CR
SJT	San Angelo, TX
SJU	San Juan-Luis Muñoz Marín Intl, PR
SKB	St Kitts, KN
SLC	Salt Lake City, UT
SLK	Saranac Lake, NY
SLN	Salina, KS
SLP	San Luis Potosí, MX
SLU	St Lucia-Vigie, LC
SLW	Saltillo, MX
SLX	Salt Cay, TC
SMF	Sacramento-Metropolitan, CA
SMK	St Michael, AK
SML	Stella Maris, Long Island, BS
SMX	Santa Maria, CA
SNA	John Wayne Orange County, CA
SNN	Shannon, IE
SNP	St Paul Island, AK
SOP	Pinehurst, NC
SOW	Show Low, AZ
SPI	Springfield, IL
SPK	Sapporo, JP
SPN	Saipan, MP
SPR	San Pedro, BZ
SPS	Wichita Falls, TX
SPW	Spencer, IA

SQI	Sterling/Rock Falls, IL	
SRQ	Sarasota/Bradenton, FL	
SSI	Brunswick, GA	
STC	St Cloud, MN	
STG	St George Island, AK	
STI	Santiago, DO	
STL	St Louis, MO	
STN	London-Stansted, UK	
STR	Stuttgart, DEU	
STT	St Thomas, VI	
STX	St Croix, VI	
SUF	Lamezia Terme, IT	
SUN	Sun Valley, ID	
SUR	Summer Beaver, ON	
SUX	Sioux City, IA	
SVC	Silver City, NM	
SVD	Saint Vincent, VC	
SVO	Moscow-Sheremetyevo, RU	
SWF	Newburgh, NY	
SXB	Strasbourg, FR	
SXF	Berlin-Schönefeld, DEU	
SXM	St Maarten-Juliana, AN	
SYB	Seal Bay, AK	
SYD	Sydney, AU	
SYP	Santiago, PAN	
SYQ	San José-Pavas, CR	
SYR	Syracuse, NY	
SZT	San Cristobal de las Casas, MX	

T

TAB	Tobago, TT
TAL	Tanana, AK
TAM	Tampico, MX
TAP	Tapachula, MX
TBI	The Bight, BS
TBN	Fort Leonard Wood, MO
TCB	Treasure Cay, BS
TCL	Tuscaloosa, AL
TER	Terceira, PT
TEX	Telluride, CO
TGU	Tegucigalpa, HN
TGZ	Tuxtla Gutierrez, MX
THU	Pituffik (Thule), GL
TIJ	Tijuana, MX
TKK	Truk (Chuuk), FSM
TLC	Toluca, MX
TLH	Tallahassee, FL
TLS	Toulouse, FR
TLT	Tuluksak, AK
TLV	Tel Aviv, ISR
TMU	Tambor, CR
TNK	Tununak, AK

TNO	Tamarindo, CR
TOG	Togiak, AK
TOL	Toledo, OH
TPA	Tampa/St Petersburg, FL
TPE	Taipei, TW
TPQ	Tepic, MX
TRC	Torreón, MX
TRI	Tri-City Airport, TN
TTN	Trenton, NJ
TTQ	Tortuguero, CR
TUL	Tulsa, OK
TUP	Tupelo, MS
TUS	Tucson, AZ
TVC	Traverse City, MI
TVF	Thief River Falls, MN
TVL	Lake Tahoe, CA
TWA	Twin Hills, AK
TWF	Twin Falls, ID
TXK	Texarkana, AR
TXL	Berlin-Tegel, DEU
TYR	Tyler, TX
TYS	Knoxville, TN
TZA	Belize City-Municipal, BZ
TZN	South Andros, BS

U

UAK	Narsarsuaq, GL
UCA	Utica, NY
UGB	Ugashik Bay, AK
UGI	Uganik, AK
UII	Utila, HN
UIN	Quincy, IL
UIO	Quito, EC
UKN	Unalakleet, AK
UMD	Uummannaq, GL
UNI	Union Island, VC
UNK	Unalakleet, AK
UPN	Uruapan, MX
UTO	Utopia Creek, AK
UTU	Ustuop, PAN
UUS	Yuzhno-Sakhalinsk, RU
UVF	St Lucia-Hewanorra, LC

V

VAK	Chevak, AK
VCE	Venice, IT
VCP	São Paulo-Viracopas, BR
VCT	Victoria, TX
VDZ	Valdez, AK
VEE	Venetie, AK
VEL	Vernal, UT
VER	Veracruz, MX

VIE	Vienna, AT
VIS	Visalia, CA
VIT	Vitoria, ES
VKO	Moscow-Vnukovo, RU
VLD	Valdosta, GA
VLN	Valencia, VE
VPS	Ft Walton Beach, FL
VQS	Vieques, PR
VRA	Varadero, CU
VSA	Villahermosa, MX
VTU	Victoria de las Tunas, CU
VVI	Santa Cruz-Viru Viru, BO
VVO	Vladivostok, RU

W

WAW	Warsaw, PL
WBQ	Beaver, AK
WDG	Enid, AK
WKR	Walker's Cay, BS
WMH	Mountain Home, AR
WNA	Napakiak, AK
WNN	Wunnummin Lake, ON
WRG	Wrangell, AK
WRL	Worland, WY
WSP	Wespam, NI
WTL	Tuntutuliak, AK
WWT	Newtok, AK
WYS	West Yellowstone, MT

X

XBE	Bearskin Lake, ON
XGR	Kangiqsulujjuaq, QC
XKS	Kasabonika, ON
XLB	Lac Brochet, MB
XNA	Northwest Arkansas Regional, AR
XPK	Pukatawagan, MB
XQP	Quepos, CR
XSC	South Caicos, TC
XSI	South Indian Lake, MB
XTL	Tadoule Lake, MB

Y

YAA	Anahim Lake, BC
YAB	Arctic Bay, NU
YAC	Cat Lake, ON
YAG	Fort Frances, ON
YAJ	Lyall Harbour, BC
YAK	Yakutat, AK
YAM	Sault Sainte Marie, ON
YAP	Yap, FSM
YAQ	Maple Bay, BC

YAT	Attawapiskat, ON
YAV	Miner's Bay, BC
YAX	Wapekeka/Angling Lake, ON
YAY	St Anthony, NF
YAZ	Tolfino/Ucluelet, BC
YBB	Kugaaruk/Pelly Bay, NU
YBC	Baie Comeau, QC
YBE	Uranium City, SK
YBG	Bagotville, QC
YBI	Black Tickle, NF
YBK	Baker Lake, NU
YBL	Campbell River, BC
YBQ	Telegraph Harbour, BC
YBR	Brandon, MB
YBS	Opapamiska Lake/Musselwhite, ON
YBT	Brochet, MB
YBV	Berens River, MB
YBW	Bedwell Harbor, BC
YBX	Blanc Sablon, QC
YCB	Cambridge Bay, NU
YCD	Nanaimo, BC
YCG	Castlegar, BC
YCH	Chatham, NB
YCK	Colville Lake, NT
YCL	Charlo, NB
YCN	Cochrane, ON
YCO	Kugluktuk/Coppermine, NU
YCQ	Chetwynd, BC
YCR	Cross Lake, MB
YCS	Chesterfield Inlet, NU
YCY	Clyde River, NU
YDA	Dawson City, YT
YDF	Deer Lake, NF
YDI	Davis Inlet, NF
YDL	Dease Lake, BC
YDN	Dauphin, MB
YDO	Dolbeau, QC
YDP	Nain, NF
YDQ	Dawson Creek, BC
YEG	Edmonton Intl, AB
YEK	Arviat (Eskimo Point), NU
YEL	Elliot Lake, ON
YER	Fort Severn, ON
YEV	Inuvik, NT
YFA	Fort Albany, ON
YFB	Iqaluit, NU
YFC	Fredericton, NB
YFH	Fort Hope, ON
YFJ	Snare Lake/Wekweti, NT
YFO	Flin Flon, MB
YFR	Fort Resolution, NT
YFS	Fort Simpson, NT

YFX	Fox Harbour, NF
YGB	Gillies Bay, BC
YGG	Ganges Harbour, BC
YGH	Fort Good Hope, NT
YGK	Kingston, ON
YGL	La Grande, QC
YGN	Greenway Sound, BC
YGO	Gods Narrows, MB
YGP	Gaspe, QC
YGQ	Geraldton, ON
YGR	Îles-de-la-Madeleine, QC
YGT	Igloolik, NU
YGV	Havre Saint Pierre, QC
YGW	Whapmagoostui/ Kuujjuaraapik, QC
YGX	Gillam, MB
YGZ	Grise Fiord, NU
YHA	Port Hope Simpson, NF
YHC	Hakai Pass, BC
YHD	Dryden, ON
YHF	Hearst, ON
YHG	Charlottetown, NF
YHI	Holman Island, NT
YHK	Gjoa Haven, NU
YHM	Hamilton, ON
YHO	Hopedale, NF
YHP	Poplar Hill, ON
YHR	Chevery, QC
YHY	Hay River, NT
YHZ	Halifax, NS
YIB	Atikokan, ON
YIF	Pakuashipi, QC
YIK	Ivujivik, QC
YIO	Pond Inlet, NU
YIP	Detroit-Willow Run, MI
YIV	Island Lake/Garden Hill, MB
YJT	Stephenville, NF
YKA	Kamloops, BC
YKG	Kangirsuk, QC
YKK	Kikatla, BC
YKM	Yakima, WA
YKN	Yankton, SD
YKQ	Waskaganish, QC
YKU	Chisasibi, QC
YKZ	Toronto-Buttonville, ON
YLC	Kimmirut/Lake Harbour, NU
YLD	Chapleau, ON
YLE	Wha Ti/Lac la Martre, NT
YLH	Lansdowne House, ON
YLL	Lloydminster, AB
YLR	Leaf Rapids, MB
YLS	Lebel-sur-Quevillon, QC
YLW	Kelowna, BC

YLY	Langley, BC
YMG	Manitouwadge, ON
YMH	Mary's Harbour, NF
YML	Murray Bay, QC
YMM	Fort McMurray, AB
YMN	Makkovik, NF
YMO	Moosonee, ON
YMT	Chibougamau, QC
YMX	Montréal-Mirabel, QC
YNA	Natashquan, QC
YNC	Wemindji, QC
YND	Gatineau/Hull, QC
YNE	Norway House, MB
YNG	Youngstown, OH
YNL	Points North Landing, SK
YNO	North Spirit Lake, ON
YNS	Nemaska, QC
YOC	Old Crow, YT
YOD	Cold Lake, AB
YOG	Ogoki Post, ON
YOH	Oxford House, MB
YOJ	High Level, AB
YOP	Rainbow Lake, AB
YOW	Ottawa, ON
YPA	Prince Albert, SK
YPB	Port Alberni, BC
YPC	Paulatuk, NT
YPD	Parry Sound, ON
YPE	Peace River, AB
YPH	Inukjuaq, QC
YPI	Port Simpson, BC
YPJ	Aupaluk, QC
YPL	Pickle Lake, ON
YPM	Pikangikum, QC
YPN	Port Menier, QC
YPO	Peawanuck, ON
YPQ	Peterborough, ON
YPR	Prince Rupert-Digby Is, BC
YPW	Powell River, BC
YPX	Puvirnituq, QC
YPY	Fort Chipewyan, AB
YQC	Québec City, QC
YQC	Quaqtaq, QC
YQD	The Pas, MB
YQG	Windsor, ON
YQH	Watson Lake, YT
YQI	Yarmouth, NS
YQK	Kenora, ON
YQL	Lethbridge, AB
YQM	Moncton, NB
YQN	Nakina, ON
YQQ	Comox, BC
YQR	Regina, SK
YQT	Thunder Bay, ON

YQU	Grande Prairie, AB
YQX	Gander, NF
YQY	Sydney, NS
YQZ	Quesnel, BC
YRA	Gameti/Rae Lakes, NT
YRB	Resolute, NU
YRD	Dean River, BC
YRF	Cartwright, NF
YRG	Rigolet, NF
YRJ	Roberval, QC
YRL	Red Lake, ON
YRN	Rivers Inlet, BC
YRS	Red Sucker Lake, MB
YRT	Rankin Inlet, NU
YSB	Sudbury, ON
YSF	Stony Rapids, SK
YSG	Lutsel'ke (Snowdrift), NT
YSJ	Saint John, NB
YSK	Sanikiluaq, NU
YSL	St Leonard, NB
YSM	Fort Smith, NT
YSN	Salmon Arm, BC
YSO	Postville, NF
YSP	Marathon, ON
YSR	Nanisivik, NU
YST	Ste Therese Point, MB
YSY	Sachs Harbour, NT
YTA	Pembroke, ON
YTB	Hartley Bay, BC
YTE	Cape Dorset, NU
YTF	Alma, QC
YTG	Sullivan Bay, BC
YTH	Thompson, MB
YTL	Big Trout Lake, ON
YTQ	Tasiujaq, QC
YTS	Timmins, ON
YTZ	Toronto Island, ON
YUB	Tuktoyaktuk, NT
YUD	Umiujaq, QC
YUL	Montréal-Dorval, QC
YUM	Yuma, AZ
YUT	Repulse Bay, NU
YUX	Hall Beach, NU
YUY	Rouyn-Noranda, QC
YUZ	Deer Lake, ON
YVB	Bonaventure, QC
YVC	La Ronge, SK
YVM	Qikiqtarjuaq/Broughton Island, NU
YVO	Val d'Or, QC
YVP	Kuujjuaq, QC
YVQ	Norman Wells, NT
YVR	Vancouver, BC
YVZ	Deer Lake, ON
YWB	Kangiqsujuaq, QC

YWG	Winnipeg, MB
YWH	Victoria-Inner Harbour, Vancouver Is, BC
YWJ	Fort Franklin, NT
YWJ	Deline, NT
YWK	Wabush, NF
YWL	Williams Lake, BC
YWP	Webequie, ON
YWQ	Chute-des-Passes, QC
YWS	Whistler, BC
YXC	Cranbrook, BC
YXD	Edmonton-Municipal, AB
YXE	Saskatoon, SK
YXH	Medicine Hat, AB
YXJ	Fort St John, BC
YXK	Rimouski, QC
YXL	Sioux Lookout, ON
YXN	Whale Cove, NU
YXP	Pangnirtung, NU
YXR	Earlton, ON
YXS	Prince George, BC
YXT	Terrace, BC
YXU	London, ON
YXX	Abbotsford, BC
YXY	Whitehorse, YT
YXZ	Wawa, ON
YYB	North Bay, ON
YYC	Calgary, AB
YYD	Smithers, BC
YYE	Fort Nelson, BC
YYF	Penticton, BC
YYG	Charlottetown, PEI
YYH	Taloyoak, NU
YYJ	Victoria, BC
YYL	Lynn Lake, MB
YYQ	Churchill, MB
YYR	Goose Bay, NF
YYT	St John's, NF
YYU	Kapuskasing, ON
YYY	Mont Joli, QC
YYZ	Toronto-Pearson International, ON
YZE	Gore Bay, ON
YZF	Yellowknife, NT
YZG	Salluit, QC
YZP	Sandspit, BC
YZR	Sarnia, ON
YZS	Coral Harbour, NU
YZT	Port Hardy, BC
YZV	Sept Îles, QC
YZY	Mackenzie, BC

Z

| ZAC | York Landing, MB |
| ZBF | Bathurst, NB |

ZCL	Zacatecas, MX
ZEL	Bella Bella, BC
ZEM	Eastmain, QC
ZFD	Fond du Lac, SK
ZFN	Tulita/Fort Norman, NT
ZGI	Gods River, MB
ZGS	Gethsemani, QC
ZIH	Ixtapa/Zihuatanejo, MX
ZJG	Jenpeg, MB
ZJN	Swan River, MB
ZKE	Kaschechewan, ON
ZKG	Kegaska, QC
ZLO	Manzanillo, MX
ZLT	La Tabatière, QC
ZMT	Masset, BC
ZNA	Nanaimo-Harbour, Vancouver Is, BC
ZPB	Sachigo Lake, ON
ZQS	Queen Charlotte Island, BC
ZRH	Zürich, CH
ZRJ	Round Lake, ON
ZSA	San Salvador, BS
ZSJ	Sandy Lake, ON
ZSW	Prince Rupert-Seal Cove, BC
ZTB	Tete-à-La Baleine, QC
ZTM	Shamattawa, MB
ZUM	Churchill Falls, NF
ZWL	Wollaston Lake, SK

US state/ Canadian province/country digraph decode

AB	Alberta, Canada
AE	United Arab Emirates
AG	Antigua and Barbuda
AI	Anguilla
AK	Alaska, USA
AL	Alabama, USA
AN	Netherlands Antilles
AR	Arkansas, USA
ARG	Argentina
AS	American Samoa
AT	Austria
AU	Australia
AW	Aruba
AZ	Arizona, USA
BB	Barbados
BC	British Columbia, Canada
BCS	Baja California Sur, México
BE	Belgium
BM	Bermuda
BO	Bolivia
BR	Brazil

BS	Bahamas
BZ	Belize
CA	California, USA
CL	Chile
CN	China
CO	Colorado, USA
COL	Colombia
CR	Costa Rica
CT	Connecticut, USA
CU	Cuba
CYM	Cayman Islands
CZ	Czech Republic
DC	District of Columbia, USA
DE	Delaware, USA
DEU	Germany
DF	Distrito Federal, México
DK	Denmark
DM	Dominica
DO	Dominican Republic
EC	Ecuador
EG	Egypt
ES	Spain
FI	Finland
FL	Florida, USA
FR	France
FSM	Federated States of Micronesia
GA	Georgia, USA
GD	Grenada
GF	French Guiana
GL	Greenland
GP	Guadeloupe
GR	Greece
GT	Guatemala
GU	Guam
GY	Guyana
HI	Hawai'i, USA
HK	Hong Kong
HN	Honduras
HT	Haiti
HU	Hungary
IA	Iowa, USA
ID	Idaho, USA
IE	Ireland
IL	Illinois, USA
IN	Indiana, USA
IND	India
IDN	Indonesia
IS	Iceland

ISR	Israel
IT	Italy
JM	Jamaica
JP	Japan
KN	St Kitts & Nevis
KR	Republic of Korea
KS	Kansas, USA
LA	Louisiana, USA
LC	St Lucia
MA	Massachusetts, USA
MB	Manitoba, Canada
MD	Maryland, USA
ME	Maine, USA
MH	Marshall Islands
MI	Michigan, USA
MN	Minnesota, USA
MO	Missouri, USA
MP	Northern Mariana Islands
MQ	Martinique
MS	Mississippi, USA
MSR	Montserrat
MT	Montana, USA
MX	México
MY	Malaysia
NB	New Brunswick, Canada
NC	North Carolina, USA
ND	North Dakota, USA
NE	Nebraska, USA
NF	Newfoundland, Canada
NH	New Hampshire, USA
NI	Nicaragua
NJ	New Jersey, USA
NL	Nuevo León, México
NLD	Netherlands
NM	New Mexico, USA
NO	Norway
NS	Nova Scotia, Canada
NT	Northwest Territories, Canada
NU	Nunavut, Canada
NV	Nevada, USA
NY	New York, USA
NZ	New Zealand
OH	Ohio, USA
OK	Oklahoma, USA
ON	Ontario, Canada
OR	Oregon, USA
PA	Pennsylvania, USA
PAN	Panamá

PE	Perú
PEI	Prince Edward Island, Canada
PF	French Polynesia
PH	Philippines
PL	Poland
PM	St Pierre et Miquelon
PR	Puerto Rico
PT	Portugal
PW	Palau
PY	Paraguay
RU	Russia
QC	Québec, Canada
QR	Quintana Roo, México
RI	Rhode Island, USA
SA	Saudi Arabia
SC	South Carolina, USA
SD	South Dakota, USA
SE	Sweden
SG	Singapore
SK	Saskatchewan, Canada
SR	Suriname
SV	El Salvador
TC	Turks & Caicos Islands
TH	Thailand
TN	Tennessee, USA
TR	Turkey
TT	Trinidad & Tobago
TW	Taiwan
TX	Texas, USA
UK	United Kingdom
UT	Utah, USA
UY	Uruguay
VA	Virginia, USA
VC	St Vincent & The Grenadines
VE	Venezuela
VG	British Virgin Islands
VI	US Virgin Islands
VT	Vermont, USA
WA	Washington, USA
WI	Wisconsin, USA
WV	West Virginia, USA
WY	Wyoming, USA
YT	Yukon Territory, Canada
ZA	South Africa

NOTES

INDEX TO AIRLINES

US = USA, C = Canada, G = Greenland, SP = St Pierre, MX = México, CB = Caribbean, CA = Central America

US = USA, C = Canada, G = Greenland, SP = St Pierre, MX = México, CB = Caribbean, CA = Central America

US = USA, C = Canada, G = Greenland, SP = St Pierre, MX = México, CB = Caribbean, CA = Central America

US = USA, C = Canada, G = Greenland, SP = St Pierre, MX = México, CB = Caribbean, CA = Central America

US = USA, C = Canada, G = Greenland, SP = St Pierre, MX = México, CB = Caribbean, CA = Central America

IATA (2-letter/number) and ICAO (3-letter) Codes

A

AA	AMERICAN AIRLINES
AAH	ALOHA AIRLINES
AAL	AMERICAN AIRLINES
AAY	ALLEGIANT AIR
AB	SUPERIOR AVIATION
ABK	ALBERTA CITYLINK
ABX	ABX AIR
AC	AIR CANADA
ACA	AIR CANADA
AER	ALASKA CENTRAL EXPRESS
AG	PROVINCIAL AIRLINES
AIE	AIR INUIT
AIP	ALPINE AIR
AJI	AMERISTAR AIR CARGO
AJM	AIR JAMAICA
AJT	AMERIJET INTERNATIONAL
AKK	AKLAK AIR
AKN	ALKAN AIR
AL	SKYWAY AIRLINES
ALO	ALLEGHENY AIRLINES
ALZ	ALTA FLIGHTS
AM	AEROMEXICO
AMF	AMERIFLIGHT
AMT	AMERICAN TRANS AIR
AMW	AIR MIDWEST
AMX	AEROMEXICO
ANT	AIR NORTH
APC	AIRPAC AIRLINES
APP	AEROPERLAS
APY	APA INTERNATIONAL AIR
AQ	ALOHA AIRLINES
AQT	AVIOQUINTANA
ARB	AVIA AIR
ARN	AIR CANADA REGIONAL
AS	ALASKA AIRLINES
ASA	ALASKA AIRLINES
ASH	MESA AIRLINES
ASJ	AIR SATELLITE
ATN	AIR TRANSPORT INTERNATIONAL (ATI)
AWE	AMERICA WEST AIRLINES
AWI	AIR WISCONSIN AIRLINES
AWV	AIRWAVE TRANSPORT
A5	TIKAL JETS AIRLINES

B

BAJ	BAKER AVIATION
BB	SEABORNE AIRLINES
BFC	BASLER AIRLINES
BFL	BUFFALO AIRWAYS
BH	HAWKAIR AVIATION SERVICES
BHR	BIGHORN AIRWAYS
BHS	BAHAMASAIR
BLR	ATLANTIC COAST AIRLINES
BLS	BEARSKIN AIRLINES
BMJ	BEMIDJI AVIATION SERVICES
BNC	SUNDANCE AIR
BQ	AEROMAR AIRLINES
BRG	BERING AIR
BSK	MIAMI AIR INTERNATIONAL
BSY	BIG SKY AIRLINES
BTA	EXPRESSJET AIRLINES
BVN	BARON AVIATION SERVICES
BW	BWIA WEST INDIES AIRWAYS
BWA	BWIA WEST INDIES AIRWAYS
BYA	BERRY AVIATION
BZ	KEYSTONE AIR SERVICE
B6	JETBLUE AIRWAYS
B9	CARIBAIR

C

CAA	ATLANTIC SOUTHEAST AIRLINES (ASA)
CAM	VILLAGE AVIATION
CAV	CALM AIR
CAY	CAYMAN AIRWAYS
CBC	CARIBAIR
CBE	AEROCARIBE
CBT	CATALINA FLYING BOATS
CCI	CAPITAL CARGO INTERNATIONAL AIRLINES
CCP	CHAMPION AIR
CCY	CHERRY-AIR
CDL	CCAIR
CEA	CORPORATE AIRLINES
CFS	EMPIRE AIRLINES
CH	BEMIDJI AVIATION SERVICES
CHP	AVIACSA
CHQ	CHAUTAUQUA AIRLINES

CIC	ICC AIR CARGO
CIR	ARCTIC CIRCLE AIR SERVICE
CJC	COLGAN AIR
CJY	BALTIMORE AIR TRANSPORT
CKS	KALITTA AIR
CM	COPA AIRLINES
CME	PRINCE EDWARD AIR
CMI	CONTINENTAL MICRONESIA
CMP	COPA AIRLINES
CMY	CAPE SMYTHE AIR SERVICE
CNI	AEROTAXI
CNK	SUNWEST HOME AVIATION
CNX	ALL CANADA EXPRESS
CO	CONTINENTAL AIRLINES
COA	CONTINENTAL AIRLINES
COM	COMAIR
CPB	CORPORATE EXPRESS
CPT	CORPORATE AIR
CRN	AEROCARIBBEAN
CRQ	AIR CREEBEC
CS	CONTINENTAL MICRONESIA
CSG	AERO COSTA SOL
CSQ	IBC AIRWAYS
CTT	CUSTOM AIR TRANSPORT
CU	CUBANA
CUB	CUBANA
CUO	AERO CUAHONTE
CVU	GRAND CANYON AIRLINES
CWC	CENTURION AIR CARGO
CXP	CASINO EXPRESS AIRLINES
CXT	COASTAL AIR TRANSPORT
C5	COMMUTAIR
C8	CHICAGO EXPRESS AIRLINES

D

DAE	DHL AERO EXPRESO
DAL	DELTA AIR LINES
DCE	DUTCH CARIBBEAN EXPRESS
DCV	DISCOVER AIR
DEL	CARIB AVIATION

DG	CUSTOM AIR TRANSPORT	
DH	ATLANTIC COAST AIRLINES	
DHL	DHL AIRWAYS	
DKT	BUSINESS AVIATION COURIER	
DL	DELTA AIR LINES	
DQ	COASTAL AIR TRANSPORT	
D5	DHL AERO EXPRESO	

E

ED	CCAIR
EGF	EXECUTIVE AIRLINES
EIA	EVERGREEN INTERNATIONAL AIRLINES
EJ	NEW ENGLAND AIRLINES
EM	EMPIRE AIRLINES
EO	EXPRESS ONE INTERNATIONAL
ER	DHL AIRWAYS
ERH	ERA AVIATION
EV	ATLANTIC SOUTHEAST AIRLINES (ASA)
EX	AIR SANTO DOMINGO
EYE	F S AIR SERVICE
EZ	EVERGREEN INTERNATIONAL AIRLINES
E2	RIO GRANDE AIR

F

FAB	FIRST AIR
FAO	FALCON AIR EXPRESS
FB	FINE AIR
FBF	FINE AIR
FDX	FEDEX
FEO	AEROFERINCO
FFT	FRONTIER AIRLINES
FK	KEEWATIN AIR
FL	AIRTRAN AIRWAYS
FLG	EXPRESS AIRLINES I
FRE	FREEDOM AIR
FRG	FREIGHT RUNNERS EXPRESS
FSC	FOUR STAR AIR CARGO
FTA	FRONTIER FLYING SERVICE
FWI	AIR CARAÏBES
FWL	FLORIDA WEST INTERNATIONAL AIRWAYS
FX	FEDEX EXPRESS

FXG	AIR CARGO EXPRESS (ACE)
F2	FALCON AIR EXPRESS
F9	FRONTIER AIRLINES

G

GAE	GRAND AIRE EXPRESS
GB	ABX AIR
GCO	GEMINI AIR CARGO
GD	AIR ALPHA GREENLAND
GFI	CARIBBEAN STAR AIRLINES
GFT	GULFSTREAM INTERNATIONAL AIRLINES
GGN	AIR GEORGIAN
GJB	TRANS-AIR-LINK
GL	GRØNLANDSFLY (GREENLANDAIR)
GLA	GREAT LAKES AIRLINES
GLR	CENTRAL MOUNTAIN AIR
GME	AGUILAS MAYAS INTERNACIONAL
GMT	MAGNICHARTERS
GQ	BIG SKY AIRLINES
GR	GEMINI AIR CARGO
GRL	GRØNLANDSFLY (GREENLANDAIR)
GRN	RIO GRANDE AIR
GRO	ALLEGRO AIRLINES
GS	GRANT AVIATION
GTI	ATLAS AIR
GTV	AEROGAVIOTA
GU	AVIATECA
GUG	AVIATECA
GWY	USA 3000 AIRLINES
G4	ALLEGIANT AIR
G5	ISLAND AIR

H

HA	HAWAIIAN AIRLINES
HAG	HAGELAND AVIATION SERVICES
HAL	HAWAIIAN AIRLINES
HI	PAPILLON GRAND CANYON HELICOPTERS
HK	FOUR STAR AIR CARGO
HKA	SUPERIOR AVIATION
HKN	JIM HANKINS AIR SERVICE
HMA	AIR TAHOMA
HP	AMERICA WEST AIRLINES
HU	NORTHERN AIR CARGO
HW	NORTH WRIGHT AIRWAYS

HX	TRANS NORTH AVIATION
H3	HARBOUR AIR SEAPLANES
H6	HAGELAND AVIATION SERVICES
H9	AIR D'AYITI

I

IAR	ILIAMNA AIR TAXI
IBU	INDIGO CORPORATE JET AIRLINE
II	IBC AIRWAYS
IRO	CSA AIR
IS	ISLAND AIRLINES
ISA	ISLAND AIRLINES
ISV	ISLEÑA AIRLINES
IWY	INTERISLAND AIRWAYS
I9	INDIGO CORPORATE JET AIRLINE

J

JB	HELIJET INTERNATIONAL
JBA	HELIJET INTERNATIONAL
JBU	JETBLUE AIRWAYS
JF	LAB FLYING SERVICE
JI	MIDWAY AIRLINES
JIA	PSA AIRLINES
JM	AIR JAMAICA
JMX	AIR JAMAICA EXPRESS
JOS	DHL DE GUATEMALA
JQ	AIR JAMAICA EXPRESS
JR	AERO CALIFORNIA
JUS	USA JET AIRLINES
JV	BEARSKIN AIRLINES
JX	SOUTHEAST AIRLINES
JY	INTERISLAND AIRWAYS
J3	NORTHWESTERN AIR
J4	BUFFALO AIRWAYS
J6	LARRY'S FLYING SERVICE

K

KAP	CAPE AIR
KBA	KENN BOREK AIR
KDC	KD AIR
KEE	KEYSTONE AIR SERVICE
KFA	KELOWNA FLIGHT-CRAFT AIR CHARTER
KFS	KITTY HAWK CHARTERS
KHA	KITTY HAWK AIRCARGO
KNX	KNIGHTHAWK AIR EXPRESS

KO	ALASKA CENTRAL EXPRESS
KR	KITTY HAWK AIRCARGO
KS	PENINSULA AIRWAYS
KX	CAYMAN AIRWAYS
K3	TAQUAN AIR
K5	WINGS OF ALASKA
K7	CARIB AVIATION
K8	DUTCH CARIBBEAN EXPRESS
K9	SKYWARD AVIATION

L

LAB	LAB FLYING SERVICE
LAL	AIR LABRADOR
LBH	L B LTD
LHN	EXPRESS ONE INTERNATIONAL
LI	LIAT
LIA	LIAT
LL	ALLEGRO AIRLINES
LNT	AEROLINEAS INTERNACIONALES
LOF	TRANS STATES AIRLINES
LR	LACSA
LRA	LITTLE RED AIR SERVICE
LRC	LACSA
LRS	SANSA
LS	ILIAMNA AIR TAXI
LW	PACIFIC WINGS
LXF	LYNX AIR INTERNATIONAL
LYC	LYNDEN AIR CARGO
LYM	KEY LIME AIR
L2	LYNDEN AIR CARGO
L3	DHL DE GUATEMALA

M

MAA	MASAIR CARGO
MAL	MORNINGSTAR AIR EXPRESS
MAW	MUSTIQUE AIRWAYS
MDC	MID-ATLANTIC FREIGHT
MDW	MIDWAY AIRLINES
MEI	MERLIN AIRWAYS
MEP	MIDWEST EXPRESS AIRLINES
MER	METHOW AVIATION
MES	MESABA AIRLINES
MG	CHAMPION AIR
MGE	ASIA PACIFIC AIRLINES
MLA	40-MILE AIR
MO	CALM AIR
MPX	AEROMEXPRESS

MQ	AMERICAN EAGLE AIRLINES
MRA	MARTINAIRE
MTN	MOUNTAIN AIR CARGO
MUA	MURRAY AVIATION
MUI	TRANS AIR
MW	MAYA ISLAND AIR
MX	MEXICANA
MXA	MEXICANA
MY	MASAIR CARGO
MYD	MAYA ISLAND AIR
M5	KENMORE AIR HARBOR
M6	AMERIJET INTERNATIONAL
M7	TROPICAL AIRWAYS

N

NA	EXECUTIVE AIRLINES
NAC	NORTHERN AIR CARGO
NAL	NORTHWAY AVIATION
NAO	NORTH AMERICAN AIRLINES
NCB	NORTH CARIBOO AIR
NEA	NEW ENGLAND AIRLINES
NJ	VANGUARD AIRLINES
NK	SPIRIT AIRLINES
NKS	SPIRIT AIRLINES
NMI	PACIFIC WINGS
NRV	NORTH VANCOUVER AIRLINES
NTA	NT AIR
NTM	NORTH AMERICAN AIRLINES
NW	NORTHWEST AIRLINES
NWA	NORTHWEST AIRLINES
NWL	NORTH WRIGHT AIRWAYS
N2	AEROLINEAS INTERNACIONALES
N7	NATIONAL AIRLINES

O

OAE	OMNI AIR INTERNATIONAL
OH	COMAIR
OO	SKYWEST AIRLINES
OP	CHALK'S OCEAN AIRWAYS
ORA	EXECUTIVE AIRLINES
OWL	MIAMI VALLEY AVIATION
OZR	GREAT PLAINS AIRLINES

P

| PAA | PAN AMERICAN AIRWAYS |

PAC	POLAR AIR CARGO
PAG	PERIMETER AIRLINES
PAL	PROVINCIAL AIRLINES
PCM	WEST AIR
PCO	PACIFIC COASTAL AIRLINES
PD	PEM-AIR
PDT	PIEDMONT AIRLINES
PEM	PEM-AIR
PEN	PENINSULA AIRWAYS
PI	PIEDMONT AIRLINES
PJ	AIR SAINT-PIERRE
PKW	SIERRA WEST AIRLINES
PLR	NORTHWESTERN AIR
PLZ	PLANET AIRWAYS
PM	TROPIC AIR
PN	PAN AMERICAN AIRWAYS
PNV	PANAVIA PANAMA
PO	POLAR AIR CARGO
PRI	ISLAND AIR
PRO	PROPAIR
PSA	PACIFIC ISLAND AVIATION
PSC	PASCAN AVIATION
PSV	SAP
PT	CAPITAL CARGO INTERNATIONAL AIRLINES
PV	ST BARTH COMMUTER
PXS	BOSTON-MAINE AIRWAYS
P4	AEROLINEAS SOSA
P6	TRANS AIR

Q

QA	AEROCARIBE
QC	AVIATION QUÉBEC LABRADOR
QK	AIR CANADA REGIONAL
QLA	AVIATION QUÉBEC LABRADOR
QO	AEROMEXPRESS
QW	TURKS & CAICOS AIRWAYS
QX	HORIZON AIR
QXE	HORIZON AIR
Q4	MUSTIQUE AIRWAYS
Q5	40-MILE AIR

R

| RAX | ROYAL AIR FREIGHT |
| RCT | ARCTIC TRANSPORTATION SERVICES |

RDS	RHOADES INTERNATIONAL
RF	FLORIDA WEST INTERNATIONAL AIRWAYS
RLR	AIRNOW
RLT	RELIANT AIRLINES
RNR	AIR CARGO MASTERS
ROK	NATIONAL AIRLINES
ROM	AEROMAR AIRLINES
RP	CHAUTAUQUA AIRLINES
RSI	AIR SUNSHINE
RU	SKYKING AIRLINES
RWG	C&M AIRWAYS
RYN	RYAN INTERNATIONAL AIRLINES
RZ	SANSA
R9	VILLAGE AVIATION

S

SBR	SABER CARGO AIRLINES
SBU	ST BARTH COMMUTER
SBX	NORTH STAR AIR CARGO
SCX	SUN COUNTRY AIRLINES
SDO	AIR SANTO DOMINGO
SDP	SUDPACIFICO
SDY	ISLAND EXPRESS
SE	SAMOA AIR
SER	AERO CALIFORNIA
SFC	SHUSWAP AIR
SGK	SKYWARD AVIATION
SGV	AEROSEGOVIA
SGY	SKAGWAY AIR SERVICE
SI	SIERRA PACIFIC AIRLINES
SKI	SKYKING AIRLINES
SKW	SKYWEST AIRLINES
SKZ	SKYWAY ENTERPRISES
SLI	AEROLITORAL
SM	SUNWORLD INTERNATIONAL AIRLINES
SNC	AIR CARGO CARRIERS
SNK	SOUTHEAST AIRLINES
SOO	SOUTHERN AIR
SPA	SIERRA PACIFIC AIRLINES
SPD	AIRSPEED AVIATION
SPK	NORTH SOUTH AIRWAYS
SPM	AIR SAINT-PIERRE
SSV	SKYSERVICE AIRLINES
STT	AIR ST THOMAS
SUB	SUBURBAN AIR FREIGHT

SVD	SVG AIR
SWA	SOUTHWEST AIRLINES
SWI	SUNWORLD INTERNATIONAL AIRLINES
SY	SUN COUNTRY AIRLINES
SYX	SKYWAY AIRLINES
S5	SHUTTLE AMERICA

T

TA	TACA
TAI	TACA
TAO	AEROMAR AIRLINES
TCF	SHUTTLE AMERICA
TCI	TURKS & CAICOS AIRWAYS
TDX	TRADEWINDS AIRLINES
TEL	TELFORD AVIATION
TFA	TRANS FLORIDA AIRLINES
THU	THUNDER AIRLINES
TI	TOLAIR SERVICES
TKC	TIKAL JETS AIRLINES
TMM	TMC AIRLINES
TNR	TANANA AIR SERVICE
TOL	TOLAIR SERVICES
TOS	TROPIC AIR
TQN	TAQUAN AIR
TRD	TRANS ISLAND AIR 2000
TRS	AIRTRAN AIRWAYS
TRZ	TRANSMERIDIAN AIRLINES
TS	AIR TRANSAT
TSC	AIR TRANSAT
TSP	INTER
TSU	CONTRACT AIR CARGO
TX	AIR CARAÏBES
TXX	AUSTIN EXPRESS
TZ	AMERICAN TRANS AIR
T9	TRANSMERIDIAN AIRLINES

U

UA	UNITED AIRLINES
UAL	UNITED AIRLINES
UCA	COMMUTAIR
UI	ALASKA SEAPLANE SERVICE
UJ	MONTAIR AVIATION
ULD	LAN HONDURAS
UNF	UNION FLIGHTS
UP	BAHAMASAIR
UPS	UNITED PARCEL SERVICE

US	US AIRWAYS
USA	US AIRWAYS
UW	PERIMETER AIRLINES
UYA	YUTE AIR ALASKA
U3	TRAVELAIR
U7	USA JET AIRLINES

V

VAL	VOYAGEUR AIRWAYS
VES	VIEQUES AIR LINK
VF	NEVIS EXPRESS
VGA	AIR VEGAS
VGD	VANGUARD AIRLINES
VI	VIEQUES AIR LINK
VL	NORTH VANCOUVER AIRLINES
VNA	WARBELOW'S AIR VENTURES
VW	AEROMAR AIRLINES

W

WAE	WESTERN AIR EXPRESS
WAK	WINGS OF ALASKA
WC	ISLEÑA AIRLINES
WCY	VIKING EXPRESS
WDY	CHICAGO EXPRESS AIRLINES
WE	CENTURION AIR CARGO
WES	WESTEX AIRLINES
WEW	WEST WIND AVIATION
WG	WASAYA AIRWAYS
WI	TRADEWINDS AIRLINES
WIA	WINAIR
WIG	WIGGINS AIRWAYS
WIL	WEST ISLE AIR
WJ	AIR LABRADOR
WJA	WESTJET AIRLINES
WL	AEROPERLAS
WM	WINAIR
WN	SOUTHWEST AIRLINES
WNT	WINNPORT AIR CARGO
WO	WORLD AIRWAYS
WOA	WORLD AIRWAYS
WP	ISLAND AIR
WS	WESTJET AIRLINES
WSG	WASAYA AIRWAYS
W4	M&N AVIATION
W6	WEST ISLE AIR
W8	WINNPORT AIR CARGO

X

| XC | KD AIR |
| XG | NORTH AMERICAN AIRLINES |

XJ	MESABA AIRLINES	2G	NORTHWEST SEA-PLANES	7F	FIRST AIR
XNA	EXPRESS.NET AIRLINES			7G	BELLAIR
XP	CASINO EXPRESS AIRLINES	2Q	AIR CARGO CARRIERS	7H	ERA AVIATION
		2S	ISLAND EXPRESS	7J	SKAGWAY AIR SERVICE
X9	OMNI AIR INTERNATIONAL	3C	CORPORATE AIRLINES	7L	AEROCARIBBEAN
		3F	PACIFIC AIRWAYS	7P	APA INTERNATIONAL AIR
		3H	AIR INUIT	7S	ARCTIC TRANSPORTATION SERVICES
Y		3K	TATONDUK FLYING SERVICE		
YI	AIR SUNSHINE	3K	AIR CARGO EXPRESS (ACE)	7V	AUSTIN EXPRESS
YL	EXECUTIVE AIRLINES			7Z	L B LTD
YN	AIR CREEBEC	3M	GULFSTREAM INTERNATIONAL AIRLINES	8B	CARIBBEAN STAR AIRLINES
YR	SCENIC AIRLINES			8C	AIR TRANSPORT INTERNATIONAL (ATI)
YRR	SCENIC AIRLINES	3R	AVIA AIR		
YV	MESA AIRLINES	4A	F S AIR SERVICE	8E	BERING AIR
YX	MIDWEST EXPRESS AIRLINES	4B	OLSON AIR SERVICE	8G	GULF AND CARIBBEAN AIR
		4E	TANANA AIR SERVICE		
		4K	KENN BOREK AIR	8O	WEST COAST AIR
Z		4N	AIR NORTH	8P	PACIFIC COASTAL AIRLINES
		4V	VOYAGEUR AIRWAYS		
ZAN	ZANTOP INTERNATIONAL AIRLINES	4W	WARBELOW'S AIR VENTURES	8Q	BAKER AVIATION
				8T	AIR TINDI
ZE	AZTECA AIRLINES	4Y	YUTE AIR ALASKA	8V	WRIGHT AIR SERVICE
ZK	GREAT LAKES AIRLINES	5A	ALPINE AIR	9E	EXPRESS AIRLINES I
ZO	GREAT PLAINS AIRLINES	5C	AIR TAHOMA	9J	PACIFIC ISLAND AVIATION
ZP	AIR ST THOMAS	5D	AEROLITORAL		
ZV	AIR MIDWEST	5F	ARCTIC CIRCLE AIR SERVICE	9K	CAPE AIR
ZW	AIR WISCONSIN AIRLINES			9L	COLGAN AIR
		5S	SAP	9M	CENTRAL MOUNTAIN AIR
Z3	PROMECH AIR	5T	CANADIAN NORTH		
		5X	UNITED PARCEL SERVICE	9N	TRANS STATES AIRLINES
NUMERICAL		5Y	ATLAS AIR	9S	SOUTHERN AIR
		6A	AVIACSA	9T	TRANSWEST AIR
1I	RYAN INTERNATIONAL AIRLINES	6C	CAPE SMYTHE AIR SERVICE		
2E	SMOKEY BAY AIR	6L	AKLAK AIR		
2F	FRONTIER FLYING SERVICE	6V	AIR VEGAS		

NOTES

INDEX TO RADIO CALL-SIGNS

INDEX TO AIRCRAFT TYPES ILLUSTRATED

US = USA, C = Canada, G = Greenland, SP = St Pierre, MX = México, CB = Caribbean, CA = Central America

US = USA, C = Canada, G = Greenland, SP = St Pierre, MX = México, CB = Caribbean, CA = Central America

Notes

Notes